CHRYSTIA

CHRYSTIA

From PEACE RIVER *to* PARLIAMENT HILL

CATHERINE TSALIKIS

ANANSI

Published in Canada in 2025 and the USA in 2025 by House of Anansi Press Inc.
houseofanansi.com

29 28 27 26 25   1 2 3 4 5

Library and Archives Canada Cataloguing in Publication

Title: Chrystia : from Peace River to Parliament Hill / Catherine Tsalikis.
Names: Tsalikis, Catherine, author.
Description: Includes bibliographical references and index.
Identifiers: Canadiana (print) 20240485246 | Canadiana (ebook) 20240488334 |
 ISBN 9781487011215 (hardcover) | ISBN 9781487011222 (EPUB)
Subjects: LCSH: Freeland, Chrystia, 1968- | LCSH: Women politicians—Canada—
 Biography. | LCSH: Women journalists—Canada—Biography. | LCSH:
 Politicians—Canada—Biography. | LCSH: Journalists—Canada—Biography. |
 CSH: Women cabinet ministers—Canada—Biography. | CSH: Cabinet ministers—
 Canada—Biography. | CSH: Canada—Politics and government—2015- |
 LCGFT: Biographies.
Classification: LCC FC656.F74 T73 2025 | DDC 971.07/4092—dc23

Book and jacket design: Alysia Shewchuk
Jacket photograph: Todd Korol

Every reasonable effort has been made to trace ownership of copyright materials.
The publisher will gladly rectify any inadvertent errors or omissions in credits in
future editions.

*House of Anansi Press is grateful for the privilege to work on and create from the Traditional
Territory of many Nations, including the Anishinabeg, the Wendat, and the Haudenosaunee,
as well as the Treaty Lands of the Mississaugas of the Credit.*

Canada Council   Conseil des Arts
for the Arts   du Canada

ONTARIO ARTS COUNCIL
CONSEIL DES ARTS DE L'ONTARIO
an Ontario government agency
un organisme du gouvernement de l'Ontario

With the participation of the Government of Canada
Avec la participation du gouvernement du Canada | Canadä

*We acknowledge for their financial support of our publishing program the Canada Council
for the Arts, the Ontario Arts Council, and the Government of Canada.*

Printed and bound in Canada

MIX
Paper | Supporting
responsible forestry
FSC   FSC® C016245
www.fsc.org

For APS

Contents

A Changed World

IN THE EARLY HOURS of February 24, 2022, war descended on Europe. On the orders of President Vladimir Putin, Russia launched a large-scale military invasion of neighbouring Ukraine—an independent, democratic country—igniting the largest, bloodiest conflict on the continent in nearly eighty years.

For months, as an estimated 150,000 Russian troops had massed on Ukraine's borders, Western politicians, security officials, and foreign policy experts struggled to divine Putin's true intentions. Was the military buildup an aggressive display of sabre-rattling or a precursor to something more dangerous? As missiles began to rain down on cities throughout Ukraine, including the capital of Kyiv, they had their answer.

In a televised pre-dawn address, Putin said the invasion would seek to "demilitarise and denazify Ukraine" while also rolling back what he considered to be encroaching and hostile Western influence in the region. To those who would oppose him, he cautioned that Russia—a nuclear power—"will respond immediately, and the consequences will be such as you have never seen in your entire history."

That afternoon, Canadian prime minister Justin Trudeau made his way to a wood podium etched with a maple leaf in the Sir John A. Macdonald Building on Wellington Street, across from Ottawa's Parliament Hill. Speaking to the nation, he warned that Putin's actions posed the greatest threat to stability in Europe since the Second World War.

As Trudeau spoke, his deputy prime minister, Chrystia Freeland, waited behind him, alongside Foreign Minister Mélanie Joly and Defence Minister Anita Anand. While Joly and Anand stood mostly motionless, gazes fixed ahead, Chrystia found it impossible to remain still. Behind her pandemic-era surgical mask, she inhaled deeply and exhaled sharply, shoulders rising and falling visibly with each breath. Her eyes darted around the room and she nodded vigorously at Trudeau's remarks. Every so often, she lifted a hand to adjust the double strand of pearls that she had received as a gift on her wedding day.

Her paternal grandfather, Wilbur, the son of American pioneers who had settled in the Canadian north, had originally given the necklace to her grandmother, Helen, a Scot. The two met in Glasgow during the Second World War, near Helen's hometown. As a young man in his twenties, Wilbur had left his beloved Peace River in northern Alberta to serve in the Royal Canadian Air Force, one of a generation of Canadians who fought and died overseas with the goal of ensuring a lasting peace in Europe.

When Trudeau was done speaking, it was Chrystia's turn. Stepping to the podium, her restlessness vanished entirely. Composed and unusually grave, with her face tightly drawn, she aimed her remarks directly at Russia's president.

"Today, we woke up to a changed world," she began. "Russia has launched a brutal and unprovoked attack on Ukraine, a country of more than forty million people who have sought nothing but peace and freedom. The horrific human costs of this cruel invasion are the direct and personal responsibility of Vladimir Putin, who has chosen to invade a sovereign democracy and challenge the rules-based international order. History will judge President Putin as harshly as the world condemns him today. Today, he cements his place in the ranks of the reviled European dictators who caused such carnage in the twentieth century."

The response by Canada and its allies, she continued, "will be swift, and it will bite." She implored Canada's Ukrainian community to remain strong and to remember: "Shche ne vmerla Ukrainy"—"Ukraine has not yet died." It was the defiant first line of the Ukrainian national anthem, banned in the 1920s when the country became a part of the Soviet Union.

As a university exchange student in the late 1980s, Chrystia—initially regarded with curiosity and some trepidation by her Ukrainian classmates—was approached one afternoon by a young man, who asked in hushed tones if she knew the anthem's words. "The verses were illegal, and my handwritten rendering was passed around in a sort of junior samizdat," she would later recall, referring to forbidden material that was shared clandestinely in the late Soviet era.

More than anyone in the Canadian government, Chrystia was intimately familiar with Ukraine's hard-fought battle for freedom. In 1939, as Soviet troops advanced at the outbreak of the Second World War, her maternal grandparents had fled western Ukraine, eventually settling in Edmonton. Chrystia would spend her formative childhood years as a part of the city's close-knit Ukrainian community, whose émigré elders believed fervently that one day their homeland would be liberated. Born Christina Alexandra Freeland, she decided as a teenager to go by Chrystia, as an homage to her Ukrainian heritage.

In 1991, as the once-mighty Soviet Empire crumbled, Chrystia returned to Kyiv as a young reporter and soon realized her grandparents' faith had not been misplaced. In a December 1 referendum, Ukrainians voted overwhelmingly for independence, and she found herself witnessing the birth of a new, democratic nation. Three decades later, its future hung in the balance.

There was perhaps no other Western politician who understood so acutely and instinctually the stakes for Ukraine, and for the entire liberal order that Wilbur and his generation had been so determined to uphold. For years, Chrystia had argued that Western democracies were facing an existential challenge from authoritarian countries—and that Canada had the ability to make a real difference in the battle between these competing systems. Putin's brazen aggression offered an opportunity—though certainly not wanted, nor the first of its kind for this now seasoned politician—to turn words into action.

At home, she convinced her cabinet colleagues—many of them initially reluctant—to send arms and ammunition to bolster the Ukrainian war effort. "It's hard to overstate how central and critical Chrystia Freeland has been to this government's response to Russia's invasion of Ukraine, and how much the prime minister has relied on her advice. It is her relationships, it's her knowledge, and it's also her commitment to and belief in what is just and what is right," says Brian Clow, Trudeau's deputy chief of staff. "The amount of money and support we have given is huge—I mean, we're talking billions and billions of dollars."

Abroad, she persuaded her counterparts to impose harsh sanctions on Russia's central bank, in hopes of crippling its economy. Canadian senator Peter Boehm credits the professional and personal relationships Chrystia built throughout her time in government for tipping the scales with international leaders such as German chancellor Olaf

Scholz: "She convinced him. He is a very cautious man, but when he decides to jump, he jumps."

Denys Shmyhal, Ukraine's prime minister, says that when he thinks about Western politicians with whom he has been in touch frequently during the war, Chrystia's name is among the first that come to his mind. In meetings with allies, he points to Canada as an example of how to move "fast and effectively" on the sanctions front, and says Chrystia has been "absolutely crucial" in galvanizing the international community's support for Ukraine.

On a Saturday morning in May 2022, Trudeau, Chrystia, Joly, and a small delegation including Clow and the prime minister's chief of staff, Katie Telford, boarded a Royal Canadian Air Force aircraft in Ottawa for an eight-hour flight to Rzeszów, in southeastern Poland. After a fifty-minute drive to the town of Przemyśl, not far from the Ukrainian border, they embarked on the dangerous overnight journey to Kyiv by train. Like other foreign leaders, including the United States' Joe Biden, the United Kingdom's Boris Johnson, and France's Emmanuel Macron, Trudeau was installed in one of the luxury wood-panelled train carriages used to transport VIPs to the capital during the war.

After meeting with the prime minister, Chrystia and the others retired to their sleeper car for the remainder of the sixteen-hour trip. (In contrast to Trudeau's car, theirs was rather more utilitarian in design—bunks were clean but sparse, each occupant's name written in marker on red electrical tape stuck to the door.) Desperate for some wine to take the edge off, they were disappointed to learn that there was no alcohol on board—or so they thought. After chatting with the attendants who staffed the train—in Ukrainian, because they spoke no English—Chrystia discovered that one was in possession of half a bottle of bourbon that she was happy to share.

It's a glib anecdote, perhaps, but it serves as a vivid demonstration of something that has become obvious to both colleagues and political observers over nearly a decade: in the Trudeau government, some things just would not happen without Chrystia Freeland.

IN POLITICS, AS IN her previous career in journalism, Chrystia's star has risen at a remarkable rate. Since the Liberals' historic win in 2015, she has held a succession of cabinet posts: international trade, foreign affairs, intergovernmental affairs, and finance. She has been the government's point person on major trade negotiations, has proven herself willing to harness Canada's power to fight tyranny head on, and has been responsible for guiding Canadians through the unprecedented economic disaster caused by the COVID-19 pandemic.

In politics, she has successfully employed the traits that served her so well in journalism: a seemingly endless supply of energy, a quirky charm, a capacity for coalition building, her dogged determination, a propensity for loyalty. Friends and colleagues describe her as principled but pragmatic, willing to consult widely and hear out the other side before landing on a decision. As a politician, she subscribes to the theory of positive intent, assuming until proven otherwise that the actions of her counterparts stem from a place of goodwill. As a cabinet minister, she has maintained an air of informality, insisting that everyone, from political staffers to members of the Senate, call her, simply, Chrystia. She has a mischievous sense of humour and doesn't take herself too seriously, jogging or cycling to events in her running shoes and leggings. At her home in Toronto's Summerhill neighbourhood, she hosts government officials, foreign dignitaries, and big-name intellectuals for meals that she cooks herself, her kids practising their musical instruments and chatting in Ukrainian in the background.

Chrystia has undoubtedly become the cabinet minister Trudeau relies on most. As his number two, she has been called the "minister of everything," and few would be surprised if she were to eventually become the leader of the Liberal party—or a prime minister of Canada.

So, who is Chrystia, really, and how did she become the most powerful woman in Canadian politics? What makes her tick and what kind of leader might she be?

What follows is a biographical account of Chrystia's life, from Peace River to Parliament Hill. While it is by no means definitive, it is written in hopes of furthering readers' understanding of Canada's deputy prime minister—a figure who, for almost ten years, has been instrumental in shaping policies that directly affect all Canadians and who will likely continue to do so for years to come.

PART ONE

BECOMING CHRYSTIA

ONE

Promised Lands

IN 1876, TO CELEBRATE one hundred years of American independence, the city of Philadelphia hosted the Centennial Exposition—the first World's Fair to be held in the United States. From May to November, nearly ten million visitors wandered through Philadelphia's sprawling Fairmount Park, marvelling at the latest industrial, technological, and gastronomic innovations from around the world. Bananas, Hires root beer, and Heinz ketchup all made their debut. In June, Alexander Graham Bell astounded the fair's judges with the first public demonstration of his latest invention, the telephone.

The ornate Agricultural Hall was one of the largest buildings on the fairgrounds. Inside, a thousand stalls showcased vegetables, seeds, tobacco, tea, and coffee. Among the products on display, as a contemporaneous writer, J. H. Ward, would report, none claimed higher importance "than the great life-sustaining article of wheat."

Representatives from as far as Russia, Tibet, Egypt, and Australia, as well as from a dozen American states, exhibited bushels of their finest grains, arguing passionately that their specimens were superior to all others. Participants were stunned when the judges, in a major upset, unanimously agreed to award the first-prize medal to "an obscure farmer named McLeod" for wheat raised at Fort Chipewyan, on the shores of Lake Athabasca in northern Alberta. Honourable mention went to samples from the "vast and still more distant" Peace River country.

"To say that leading agriculturalists, statesmen and representatives of the great nations of the earth were astonished," wrote Ward, "would only half tell the story. Much more, they would have been scarcely more astonished if they had been informed of a new wheat-growing continent in the midst of the Pacific Ocean."

AT THE TIME, most Canadians would themselves have been similarly amazed. Peace River country—five hundred kilometres northwest from the city of Edmonton, which would eventually become the capital of Alberta—was thought to be an isolated, barren land of ice and snow, beyond the reach of all but the hardiest and most determined adventurers.

Indigenous peoples—first the Dane-zaa (Beaver) and then the Knisteneaux (Cree)—had called northwestern Alberta home for thousands of years. Alexander Mackenzie, the Scottish explorer, was the first European to traverse the region. In 1792, Mackenzie was stationed at a North West Company fur-trading post in Fort Chipewyan. Tasked with finding a land route to the Pacific Ocean, Mackenzie and his crew paddled up the Peace River, following the water for nearly two thousand kilometres before reaching the coast of British Columbia the following summer. From his Indigenous interpreter, Mackenzie learned that the river got its name from Peace Point, near Lake Athabasca, where the Dane-zaa and Knisteneaux had settled a bitter dispute over hunting territory.

A century later, at the time of the World's Fair, the area remained mostly untouched. On July 1, 1867, the Fathers of Confederation had established the Dominion of Canada, made up of four provinces: Quebec, Ontario, Nova Scotia, and New Brunswick. The Canadian government was keen to expand westward, but was hesitant about Peace River country's prospects for homesteading, given its remote location and lack of railway access.

Nevertheless, after two days of negotiation in the summer of 1899, the government signed Treaty 8 with the region's Indigenous peoples, which cleared the way for the settlement of 840,000 square kilometres of land—nearly the size of France and Germany combined.

By the beginning of the twentieth century, newspapers were filled with reports by surveyors, geologists, and scientists extolling the natural wonders awaiting anyone who dared to venture north. It turned out that, far from a forbidding, frozen wasteland, Peace River country was actually, as one headline proclaimed, a "twenty million acre hothouse of fertility." As the handful of homesteaders who made it to the very first newly surveyed land plots would discover, its rich soil, abundant precipitation, and long summer days filled with sunshine made for ideal conditions in which to grow crops and raise cattle. Wild game, fish, and berries were plentiful, as was timber to build shelter. For ten dollars, a homesteader could claim a 160-acre plot of land—though they did have to clear and cultivate most of that land themselves.

"The Peace River country is on every man's tongue in the West," wrote a visitor from Ontario in *Maclean's* magazine. "No longer is it the dread, rather mysterious and almost unattainable land of Arctic rigors and natural obstacles. It has become instead a country of commercial and agricultural possibilities, and as such is now the objective point of the pioneer."

By 1913, Edmonton, which had grown from a small frontier town of three thousand in 1901 into a booming metropolis with a population of over fifty-three thousand, was facing a severe economic downturn. The construction of the Canadian Pacific Railway and Canadian Northern Railway lines had allowed for an influx of people from Canada's eastern provinces, the United States, and Europe, but with opportunities for prosperity waning, thousands of settlers set their sights farther north.

Among these were John and Olive Freeland—Chrystia Freeland's paternal great-grandparents. Their daughter Beulah later chronicled their journey in her book *The Long Trail: The Story of a Pioneer Family*.

As a young man in Illinois, John Freeland, who went by Wilbur, his middle name, craved adventure. Shortly after he turned eighteen, he stole aboard a freighter bound for England, hiding under a tarp in a lifeboat. He eventually made his way to South Africa, where he worked in a diamond mine; during the Boer War, he enlisted as a scout for Queen Victoria.

Fourteen years later, Wilbur returned to the United States, where, at his homecoming party, he met Olive Houck. She was twelve years his junior, with a heart-shaped face, a perfect widow's peak, and a whole lot of pluck. It was love at first blush.

They were married in Omaha, where Wilbur had bought a movie theatre. In 1911, they moved to Edmonton, where they ran a small hotel in the Strathcona District. Given Wilbur's track record of wanderlust, wrote Beulah, "Mother wasn't particularly surprised when Dad came home one day and announced that they, too, were heading north."

On a chilly February morning in 1913, Wilbur, Olive—four months pregnant with Beulah—and their eighteen-month-old son, Carlton, set out on a horse-drawn sleigh, with only canvas and blankets to protect them from the harsh winter elements as they made the arduous journey north on the Athabasca Trail. (Travel by rail or commercial boat was possible but expensive, so most pioneers chose to travel during the winter months when the lakes and rivers along the trail were frozen.)

Their initial destination was the pioneer settlement of Grouard, where Wilbur had purchased a second hotel, sight unseen. They managed the property for a couple of years, but when it became clear that the expanding railway network would bypass Grouard, greatly curtailing the town's potential for growth, the couple decided to continue on to what was then known as Peace River Crossing.

In the summer of 1915, after a 150-kilometre trek through dense bush in a covered wagon, the Freelands came to a cliff overlooking the mighty Peace River, set in a valley below. Wilbur held two-year-old Beulah on his shoulders, and the family took in the majestic view. Emerald-green hills sloped gently toward the water, where the beginnings of a new town were being built on either side.

"Mother gazed down into the beautiful valley below and knew that it had all been worth it," wrote Beulah. "They had reached their promised land."

Nevertheless, there were hardships ahead. At first, the Freelands lived in a canvas tent. As the winter and its freezing temperatures approached, they moved to an uninsulated wooden shack, where John Wilbur Jr.—Chrystia's grandfather—was born on January 27, 1916. On their first property, Wilbur and Olive used an axe and hatchet to clear their land, and, with the help of friends, built themselves a log cabin.

Eventually, they settled on a farm on the scenic Shaftesbury Trail, just a few kilometres out of town. Nestled at the foot of Misery Mountain, it had a breathtaking view of the confluence of the Peace and Smoky Rivers. In spite of the name, the Freeland children would spend many happy hours riding horseback over the mountain in the summer; in the fall, they would scour its slopes for saskatoon berries.

Wilbur, who had for so long found it difficult to be satisfied while staying in one place, was finally content. "Never was there a happier man than my father as he strode over his fields and watched his cattle lift their heads in trusting curiosity as he came to bring them in," wrote Beulah. "The land was his, and in all his life he had never known such a feeling of accomplishment." It was impossible to persuade Wilbur to leave the farm until 1934, when he travelled south to watch Wilbur Jr., by then eighteen, ride in the Calgary Stampede.

When the Second World War broke out in Europe, Wilbur Jr., along with his older brother Carlton and their younger brother Warren, enlisted. On the hills of Misery Mountain, where he and his siblings had played as children, he trained in preparation for serving with the Royal Canadian Air Force's Air-Sea Rescue. While he and Carlton would survive the war, Warren, shot down over France, didn't make it home.

While in Glasgow during these tumultuous years, Wilbur Jr. met Helen Caulfield, a spirited Scot with an exceptional work ethic and a green thumb. Not long after they were married, Chrystia's father, Donald, was born.

After the war, the young family returned to Peace River, where they would farm their own land as Wilbur Jr.'s parents had. Wilbur Jr. moved to Edmonton briefly to pursue his law degree at the University of Alberta, but after graduating in 1953, he returned home and opened his own practice. Helen started a market vegetable garden, where many of the town's young men worked, and she later managed Wilbur's office. Years later, Don, too, would find himself in law school at the University of Alberta. And like his father, he wouldn't be away from Peace River for very long.

. . .

LOVE OF BOTH THE land and the law flows strong in the Freeland veins. But the connection to Peace River is just half of Chrystia Freeland's fundamental makeup. The other half is also connected to the land and deeply rooted in history—but of a very different place.

It is impossible to understand Chrystia without at least a cursory understanding of the history of Ukraine. Both Ukrainians and Russians trace their roots to the medieval Kyivan Rus, a loose federation of Eastern Slavic tribes believed to have been founded by Scandinavian Vikings in the ninth century. The city of Kyiv, with its strategic location along the banks of the Dnipro River, became its political and cultural capital. The magnificent Saint Sophia Cathedral was built during the height of the Kyivan Rus's power, under the reign of Yaroslav the Wise, whose father had converted the state to Christianity. It still stands, in restored form, in the centre of Kyiv today.

In the mid-1200s, the Mongols invaded the Kyivan Rus, which according to many historians effectively splintered the federation and led to major divisions within the East Slavs, producing three distinct peoples: modern-day Ukrainians, Russians, and Belarusians. (Since the early 2000s, the Kremlin under Vladimir Putin has disputed this narrative, arguing instead that Ukrainians and Belarusians are "sub-nations" of a single, all-Russian nation, and thus part of Russia's "natural" sphere of influence.) Over the next few centuries, control of the area would shift between warring neighbours. By the end of the 1700s, most of the territory that makes up present-day Ukraine had been incorporated into the Russian Empire under Catherine the Great. The western Ukrainian region of Galicia, however, became part of the Austro-Hungarian Empire, ruled by the Habsburg dynasty.

In March 1917, after mass protests in Saint Petersburg, Emperor Nicholas II was forced to abdicate his throne, and the monarchy that had ruled Russia for centuries was abolished. A provisional government was put in place but was overthrown a few months later by leftist revolutionaries led by Bolshevik party leader Vladimir Lenin. Following a bloody civil war between the Red Army and anti-Bolshevik forces, the Soviet Union was established in 1922. It was the world's first communist state, and Ukraine was one of its four original republics.

Western Ukraine, for its part, remained outside the Soviet Union. But with the collapse of Austria-Hungary at the end of the First World War, control of Galicia passed to the newly created Republic of Poland. An independent Western Ukrainian National Republic was declared in November 1918, with the city of Lviv as its capital, but it was short-lived.

Lviv, western Ukraine's largest city, had for decades been the centre of Ukrainian political activism. In the early twentieth century, Poles, Ukrainians, and Jews made up a majority of the city's population, co-existing even while they competed for economic influence. But during the interwar period, under Polish control, Ukrainians were treated as second-class citizens; their civil rights were limited and they were excluded from public life, including from many universities.

Mykhailo Khomiak (or Michael Chomiak), Chrystia's maternal grandfather, was born in 1905 to a Ukrainian-Catholic peasant family in a village outside Lviv. In his twenties, he was in the minority of Ukrainians who were permitted to attend Lviv University. He studied law and graduated with a master's degree in 1931.

Though he enjoyed it, Michael's legal career lasted only a couple of years. He soon caught the eye of the editor-in-chief of *Dilo*, a daily newspaper that played a hugely significant role in shaping the public thinking of western Ukrainians. In its pages, the region's most notable public figures debated how to best achieve the ultimate goal of Ukrainian nationalists: an independent, democratic state of their own. Throughout the 1930s, *Dilo* also reported on the terror facing Ukrainians inside the Soviet Union, as dictator Joseph Stalin arrested, imprisoned, or executed political and cultural leaders, took control of Ukraine's rich agricultural resources, and starved millions during the Holodomor, a man-made famine.

In 1934, after being offered a position at the paper, Michael became a full-time journalist. According to people who knew him, though he moved in Ukrainian-Catholic intelligentsia circles, Michael himself wasn't terribly intellectual. "Sophistication was not his strength, so he often approached things through ethnic lenses: 'This is good for Ukrainians and Ukrainian causes, or it's not as good,'" says historian Ernest Gyidel, who has studied the material in Michael's records at the Provincial Archives of Alberta.

By the end of the 1930s, it was becoming clear that the tenuous postwar peace in Lviv—and in Europe—was not to last. Storm clouds had been gathering across the continent for months: German chancellor Adolf Hitler, whose right-wing, extremist Nazi party had come to power in 1933, had annexed Austria and Czechoslovakia, and it looked like Poland would be next. Farther east, Hitler had designs on Russia, whose territory he considered crucial to his objective of acquiring the *Lebensraum*—living space—he desired for the German people.

Before invading Poland, however, Hitler needed to ensure he wouldn't be fighting a war on two fronts. In August 1939, despite their opposing ideologies, Germany and the Soviet Union unexpectedly signed a non-aggression treaty, promising not to attack each other. (Stalin, for his part, viewed the pact as a way to delay conflict with Germany while the Soviet Union built up its military.) Secretly, Hitler and Stalin also agreed to divide Poland between themselves, as part of a larger plan to establish German and Soviet spheres of influence in eastern Europe.

At dawn on September 1, Germany launched its invasion of Poland, with 1.5 million Nazi troops storming the border by land, by sea, and by air. Two weeks later, the Red Army crossed into Poland from the east, its sights set on Lviv.

As the Second World War began, western Ukrainian intellectuals and political activists in Lviv had a choice to make: stay and risk arrest by Soviet forces, or escape to German-occupied areas of Poland. Michael, all too aware of the political repression suffered by Ukrainians under the Soviet authorities during the interwar years, decided to take his chances with the Germans, who were at the time perceived as friendlier to the goal of an independent Ukraine. Along with thousands of Ukrainians, he fled to Kraków, the capital of the General Government set up by the Germans in Poland. Like Lviv, Kraków was a diverse city that had long seen friction between its Polish, Ukrainian, and Jewish populations. Under its "divide and rule" strategy, the General Government was keen to exploit pre-existing ethnic tensions, favouring the Ukrainians—temporarily, at least.

As part of the limited freedoms bestowed on Ukrainians in Kraków, the Ukrainian Central Committee was allowed to conduct cultural and educational activities meant to promote Ukrainian national interests. It was led by Volodymyr Kubijovyč, an openly antisemitic nationalist from Galicia. He had close ties to both a faction of the far-right Organization of Ukrainian Nationalists and the Nazis, and helped to establish the Waffen-SS Galizien, a German military unit made up of Ukrainian volunteers that would be responsible for the massacre of hundreds of Polish citizens in 1944.

In January 1940, Kubijovyč began publishing a new pro-Ukrainian newspaper called *Krakivski Visti* (Kraków News). The German press chief in Kraków, Emil Gassner, not only gave his backing but allowed the Ukrainian Central Committee to take over a Jewish printing press that had been forced to close by the Nazis. Within weeks, the paper's first editor-in-chief was fired for failing to run an article past the General Government's censors before printing it, and Kubijovyč invited Michael to replace him.

Gyidel, who did his doctoral thesis on the newspaper, says *Krakivski Visti* "had two faces, like Janus." Considered by most historians to be deeply antisemitic, it followed the ideology of the General Government, on which it was substantially dependent for support, and its pages were filled with Nazi propaganda attacking Jews, Poles, and Soviets. But it also contained a layer of Ukrainian nationalism, which would have appealed to Michael.

According to a letter he wrote years later, Michael accepted the position of editor-in-chief reluctantly. But as a result of his station, he would be relatively insulated from the harsh totalitarian rule imposed by the German authorities, as they systematically exterminated the city's Jewish population and attempted to extinguish Polish culture, forcibly closing schools, libraries, and museums.

"He was in a position of power, which he used for his benefit and the benefit of his own family," says Gyidel. "He was well paid and enjoyed privileges which for most people under Nazi occupation were simply unreachable. He enjoyed a degree of personal security. It was not uncommon for Germans to force or trick people into agricultural labour—'Germany needs seasonal workers, go work the fields.' He was untouchable in that regard."

Shortly after arriving in Kraków, Michael met Alexandra Loban, a writer of children's literature. A decade younger than Michael, Alexandra was born to Ukrainian Orthodox parents from the region of Volhynia, north of Lviv. A family of clerics, the Lobans had lived comfortably, but lost everything in the 1917 Russian Revolution. Alexandra's mother died in childbirth shortly thereafter, when Alexandra was just three years old. For a time, she and her grandmother worked as beggars; one of her sisters was sent to be a housekeeper, another worked as a milkmaid.

"My mother's schooling was interrupted often, but she was very intelligent," says Alexandra and Michael's daughter Chrystia Chomiak, now in her seventies and living in Edmonton. "She was a voracious reader—she read in Russia, Ukrainian, and Polish. It was always very painful for her that her education was in bits."

Alexandra, too, had escaped the Red Army by fleeing to Kraków; she found employment with the publishing house that Kubijovyč had started, where she and Michael met and fell in love. While Alexandra considered converting to Catholicism, she ultimately decided to stick with her own Orthodox faith.

"They went first to the Catholic church and got married there. And then they walked over to the Orthodox church and got married there," says Chrystia. "That was wartime—I don't think you're supposed to do that. But that's what my parents did, because my mother was a very strong woman."

BY 1944, HITLER AND Stalin's non-aggression pact was in tatters, following Germany's surprise invasion of the Soviet Union, which had ended in failure. The Red Army was once again on the move in Poland and Nazi forces were retreating. In October, the *Krakivski Visti* staff was transferred to Vienna, where publication of the newspaper resumed briefly until April 1945, when the Austrian capital, too, was captured by Soviets troops. By May, the Red Army had conquered Berlin and Hitler was dead.

From Vienna, the Chomiaks tried to get as far west as they could. Alexandra was responsible for their two young daughters, Oksana and Marusia. Michael, conscious of the importance of *Krakivski Visti* to the history of the Ukrainian independence movement, carried with him the entire newspaper archive. Thanks to information gleaned from Michael's connections, the family was able to move into the American zone of occupation in southwestern Germany.

As the war came to an end, more than a million eastern Europeans found themselves stranded in the country. "Their ranks included, among others, Jewish concentration camp survivors; Polish forced laborers; and Ukrainian, Lithuanian, Latvian and Estonian Nazi collaborators," wrote Adina Hoffman in a *New York Times* review of David Nasaw's 2020 book *The Last Million*. They "shared little besides having just lived through one of the most traumatic periods in modern history and finding themselves homeless in its wake." Many who had been forced to work for the Germans during the war feared punishment by Stalin and refused to return home.

In Lviv, now a part of the Soviet Union, nothing was left for the Chomiaks. They found refuge in a displaced persons camp in Bad Wörishofen, a Bavarian resort town known for its health spas. Lithuanians made up the majority of the camp's residents, but a few hundred Ukrainians were housed in the town's hotels. Alexandra gave birth to Chrystia Freeland's mother, Halyna, in a Bad Wörishofen hospital on September 2, 1946; Chrystia Chomiak followed a year and a half later.

The Chomiaks were eventually granted Canadian visas, sponsored by a sister of Michael's who had immigrated to Alberta in the 1920s. In the fall of 1948, they joined tens of thousands of Ukrainians making the journey to Canada, Alexandra shepherding her four children along while battling an infection, and Michael lugging the *Krakivski Visti* archives across the Atlantic Ocean.

In 2017, reports of Michael's work with *Krakivski Visti* would put his granddaughter Chrystia Freeland, then Canada's foreign minister, in a difficult position.

"Did he regret [his involvement]? I don't know," says Chrystia Chomiak of her father, who lived in Alberta until his death in 1984, after which his papers and his copies of *Krakivski Visti* were donated to the province's archives. "He always wanted to write his memoirs, and he was never able to. So he wasn't able to come to terms with his wartime activity."

According to Gyidel, for Michael, it was simply a question of survival. "Many people who later in the war became entangled in antisemitic or xenophobic activity did not start that way; they had no intention of being involved in that way. For many people in eastern Europe during World War II, under Nazi occupation, there were simply no good options available," he says.

"That does not absolve these people from responsibility," he continues. "But imagine yourself in a world where your choice is between terrible and horrible: starving to death in a Nazi camp for prisoners of war or becoming a guard in a Nazi concentration camp. Chomiak's situation was obviously not that extreme, but still it was a choice between having a job and personal security—in very dangerous times—or risking having neither."

Mother, Mentor

L EAVING EUROPE AND ALL its complications behind, the
Chomiaks arrived in Canada in October 1948. They stayed
briefly with Michael's sister in Cherhill, an Alberta hamlet about an
hour's drive from Edmonton. Michael soon got a job digging ditches
for the city, and with the help of Alexandra's sister, whose family had
immigrated to the United States, the Chomiaks were able to cobble
together a down payment for a small bungalow in Jasper Place, just
west of Edmonton. (Jasper Place would be amalgamated into the
provincial capital in 1964.) Most of Edmonton's Ukrainian population lived in the city's northeast, but Alexandra did not want to live
near other Ukrainians. "She said, 'When they come to round us up,
they won't know [where] we are,'" remembers her daughter Chrystia
Chomiak. "There was a lot of trauma from the war that remained."

At home, Michael and Alexandra spoke Ukrainian, Russian, and
Polish interchangeably. After living in eastern European cities with
grand architecture and storied histories, even if during wartime,
Alexandra experienced something of a culture shock in Alberta. At
first, the bungalow had no running water or electricity. It had one

bedroom—and one outhouse—for what had become a family of eight (the two youngest Chomiak children, Natalka and Bohdan, were born in Canada).

Nevertheless, growing up, the Chomiak children never felt poor. Alexandra was a brilliant gardener. "Truly, she communicated with flowers," says Chrystia Chomiak. "That's really how we lived. My mother would garden, and then she would can, and we'd always have this wonderful fresh food. First Nations people would come around with fish—usually white pike—and the Hutterites would come with chickens. And then of course we had a milkman and a bread truck. If we had the funds, we'd buy some cinnamon rolls, baked fresh that morning."

Eventually, the family built a second bedroom and a basement, where Oksana, Marusia, Halyna, and Chrystia all slept. Halyna and Chrystia were very close; they only stopped pretending to be twins when Chrystia, reaching five feet, surpassed her older sister in height. Until they were teenagers, they shared a double bed, whispering late into the night. "She was very intense. We both wanted to save the world. We understood that housing was really important so we would build these imaginary houses in our dreams," says Chrystia, who credits their father, Michael, with teaching his children the value of hard work.

Through connections with other Ukrainians who had come to Canada after the Second World War, Michael was hired by Sherritt Gordon Mines, where he would be employed as a lab assistant until his retirement. In addition to working at his day job, he was actively involved in the Ukrainian émigré community, becoming a cantor at his church and helping to found various local Ukrainian organizations.

"He worked all day and then he'd come home, eat, shave, and then be off to a meeting," says Chrystia. "He was of that generation—10 percent of your income goes to the community. You support, and you work, and you build. My sister was of the same cloth."

Where Halyna and her father diverged, however, was in their view of religion and the church. As children, the Chomiaks attended two different churches, one Ukrainian Orthodox and one Ukrainian Catholic, both located in north Edmonton. Halyna and Chrystia would take public transportation, because the family never owned a car. Before Easter, they were required to go to confession. As they walked to the bus stop, they would attempt to come up with "sins"—such as sometimes not listening to their parents—that would satisfy their priest.

"We were just kids, and we didn't have a lot of sins," says Chrystia. At one point Halyna, not yet a teenager, turned to her sister and simply declared: "This is not real . . . This is wrong." For the rest of her life, Halyna would be an "atheist by intellectual conviction."

And in the Chomiak household, that was acceptable. "There was never a need to be on the same page. We grew up believing that one should have critical discussions on all questions, and that that's the way the world functions," says Chrystia.

IN 1964, AFTER GRADUATING from Jasper Place High School, Halyna began her undergraduate degree at the University of Alberta, where she studied political science and philosophy. She threw herself into the 1960s counterculture that animated life on campus, particularly the women's movement and the New Democratic Youth. "At one point," remembers her sister, "the New Democrats dissolved the New Democratic Youth because we were way too radical for them."

Despite Halyna's strong social conscience, she had a sense of humour about herself and the world around her, and was quick to laugh. Throughout her undergrad years, she was on staff at *The Gateway*, the student newspaper. One Thanksgiving, under the byline "Helene Chomiak," she compiled a tongue-in-cheek list of "the many good things" students should be grateful for.

"Let us give thanks for empty bank accounts, for surely we would spend our money drinking if we had any," she wrote. "Let us give thanks for large lecture rooms and oversized classes, for then the professors are less likely to notice when we are away ... Let us be joyous that Edmonton is having another civic election for this may give us reasons to go across town and carry posters. If we are extremely fortunate, we may even have a fight."

Halyna loved a good party. Often inviting her younger sister Chrystia along, she'd attend gatherings hosted by the New Democratic Youth in an old house on the outskirts of campus that had portraits of German philosopher Karl Marx and Ukrainian national poet Taras Shevchenko on its walls.

Another frequent attendee of these parties was Donald Freeland, of Peace River, Alberta, an upperclassman who was studying physics. Extremely bright, with an in-your-face conversational manner, Don loved to engage members of the New Democratic Youth in discussion, though the Freelands themselves mostly fell further to the right on the political spectrum. "He was progressive," says Chrystia Chomiak, "but he was also a Liberal."

Despite their shared fondness for political gatherings, Halyna and Don's first encounter actually took place elsewhere on campus and involved a case of mistaken identity. In October of Halyna's freshman year, the university's Student House Services recommended that students of the opposite sex be barred from visiting each other in off-campus housing. In an article for *The Gateway*, Halyna mistakenly quoted "Don Freeland" as being supportive of sex segregation (the real interviewee was another student with a similar name).

"In college, he liked the ladies," says Natalka Freeland, Don and Halyna's youngest daughter, of her father. "All of his friends were teasing him that he supposedly said boys shouldn't be allowed in the girls' dorms, because he wanted to be in the girls' dorms every day if he could! So he went down to the newspaper office and said, 'Who's this Helene Chomiak, I ought to give her a piece of my mind.'"

When Don and Halyna, still an undergraduate, moved in together and then announced their plans to wed, they had to contend with the vicious wagging tongues of many in the Ukrainian Canadian community for whom this was considered to be a huge scandal. Halyna's parents also did not approve. Alexandra was concerned about how young her daughter was; Halyna was exceptionally intelligent, and the expectation was not that she would get married at twenty. Michael, for his part, was deeply unhappy with the idea of Halyna marrying someone who was not Ukrainian.

According to Chrystia Chomiak, Don's Scottish mother, Helen, "was equally as freaked out" at the idea of the union. The parents met, Alexandra put out the "finest everything," and everyone—politely, of course—gazed at one another with mutual suspicion.

But Michael needn't have been too worried. Surveying their romantic prospects in the Ukrainian community and finding them lacking, Halyna and her sister Chrystia had promised each other that, no matter who they married, their respective future children would be christened and raised Ukrainian.

The wedding itself, held at Saint George Ukrainian Catholic Church, was organized by Alexandra, who pulled out all the stops to make it a splendid Ukrainian affair. But Don's mother was not to be outdone. "Everything had been catered, the whole schmear. We walk into the reception hall, and Helen Freeland had arranged for a bagpiper," says Chrystia Chomiak, laughing at the memory. "What a wonderful woman. She was just full of life, strong, independent, in-your-face. It was great."

As it turned out, Alexandra's fears that Halyna would be jeopardizing her education and professional future were also unfounded. Like his father, Wilbur, Don had enrolled in the University of Alberta's Faculty of Law, and Halyna was determined to do so as well. As a woman in the 1960s, however, she faced obstacles that didn't exist for Don. During an entrance interview, the university's dean asked Halyna if her marriage was strong enough to survive the strain that might arise from achieving a higher grade than her husband.

When she started law school in the fall of 1967, there were more women in her class than had ever been in a law class in Alberta—thirteen in total. By the end of their freshman year, only seven remained, which Halyna later pegged to unwanted sexual attention and a lack of support for women who wanted to have children.

As she later told *Alberta Women* magazine, law school was a "radicalizing" experience, cementing a lifelong commitment to the women's movement and feminist causes. On campus, she fought to challenge the status quo—and her efforts weren't always welcome. After Canada's Criminal Code was amended to allow the distribution of information on contraceptives, she handed out birth control pamphlets. As a result, Halyna said, "I ... was told I was a dirty disgusting person. I also received obscene telephone calls. We were really harassed." She also lobbied for the university to accept more female law students and for young children to be permitted in class.

For Halyna, the latter was no mere hypothetical. During the summer after her first year of law school, at the age of twenty-two, she delivered a baby girl. Christina Alexandra Freeland was born on August 2, 1968, three weeks premature and weighing five pounds, in the Peace River Municipal Hospital. Two weeks later, Halyna returned to her father-in-law Wilbur's criminal and civil practice, where she and Don had been working. Baby Christina was so small that Halyna could place her in the desk drawer next to her. In September, with their child snug in an apple box, Halyna and Don drove the five hours south to Edmonton, where they would live in an apartment right down the street from the Chomiaks.

Most mornings, Alexandra would look after the infant, but sometimes Halyna would bring her daughter to class. Years later, while giving a lecture at the University of Alberta's law school, Chrystia Freeland (as she had by then become known) would joke that she considered herself to be more at home there than any place on earth.

At twenty-four, Halyna was awarded her law degree—and she also gave birth to a second daughter, Natalka. Despite her intellect, as she considered her future, there were fewer options available to Halyna than to her male classmates. "Those of us who did complete law school had a more difficult time getting articling jobs than did the men," Halyna told *Alberta Women*. "This was particularly evident in Calgary. At that time—1970—a woman could not get a position as an articling student in that city."

As Chrystia Chomiak remembers it, Don had been offered a scholarship to the University of California, and Halyna was keen to move to the United States. But for Don, the pull of Peace River was strong, so the couple decided to temporarily move north and work in Wilbur's practice, where they could cut their teeth as young lawyers. They acquired a plot of land that they would farm themselves, just half a mile from the original Freeland homestead.

Throughout her twenties, Halyna wore her dark hair cut short and was always impeccably dressed. (Don, a head taller, with his shock of orange hair and scruffy beard, looked more like a farmer than a lawyer.) As the first woman to live in Peace River and practise law, she made it a priority to fight against injustice and advocate for the rights of marginalized women.

"It is hard to overstate just how out of sync with the local cultural mores her leftist, feminist views were in the rural Alberta of our childhood: suffice it to say that her nickname, among the crown prosecutors she jousted with, was 'the little communist,'" Chrystia Freeland would later write. In 1975, Halyna successfully persuaded a judge to grant a divorced lesbian woman custody of her infant child—the first time Canadian courts had made such a decision. Out of all of her mother's achievements, this was one of Chrystia's favourites.

The dozen or so lawyers in the area served communities as far north and west as the Northwest Territories and British Columbia borders, so Halyna sometimes had to travel out of town, occasionally bringing her two daughters along. Her work ethic left a lasting impression on Chrystia. "I remember how hard that was for my mother, who was just determined to work as a lawyer even though she had two little children," she said in a 2021 interview with the *Toronto Star*. "I remember her putting us in a bathtub at High Level because there was no air conditioning and it was really, really hot. There was nothing else she could do to cool us down."

Like her father, Halyna was never content to rest on her laurels. In northern Alberta, she managed to create a version of the Ukrainian community she had been a part of in Edmonton, founding the Peace River Ukrainian Society and a Ukrainian dance club (the instructor would take the overnight bus from Edmonton, arriving in Peace River at five in the morning). She also taught Ukrainian classes and, as promised, raised her two girls to be fluent in both English and Ukrainian.

(Don, for his part, was happy to have his children raised in a bilingual household—though perhaps he would have felt differently if the second language was French. In 1977, *Chatelaine* sent writer Myrna Kostash to interview Albertans about their views on the possibility of Quebec separating from the rest of Canada. "Why the French language in Alberta? The people won't have it. It's the language of a country 3,000 miles east of here," Don told Kostash. He also threatened to go and paint over the *Arrêt* on the federally mandated bilingual stop signs in Banff and Jasper nationals parks.)

Intimately familiar with how difficult pursuing a busy career while taking care of young children could be, Halyna encouraged Peace River to open its first town-run daycare. She also made friends, hosting groups of like-minded women at the Freeland home for consciousness-raising meetings, popular with second-wave feminist groups, where they would discuss their personal experiences in a society that was still predominantly designed for men.

But despite all this, Peace River was never meant to be Halyna's permanent home. In 1977, when their daughters were eight and six, Don and Halyna decided to separate, and Halyna moved back to Edmonton with the girls.

Though the plan had been to eventually relocate to California, says her sister Chrystia Chomiak, "it became clear that would never happen. Don's father didn't want him to, and Don didn't want to. [Halyna] didn't want to live in Peace River; she wanted to be in a bigger city. She wanted to have that life." And Halyna wanted her children to have it as well.

THREE

A Peace River Kid

FOR CHRYSTIA FREELAND, northern Alberta was an idyllic place to grow up—to this day, it remains an essential, incontrovertible part of her identity. She has described her childhood in Peace River as "magical." As a girl, she rode horses and eagerly helped Don farm the land, never afraid of getting her hands dirty.

"One of my earliest memories is of sitting on my dad's lap as he drove the breaking ploughs. And the work didn't end there. We had to seed every spring, and fertilize and spray, and harvest every season. And then we had to do it over again," she told *Chatelaine* in 2019.

Even after their parents had divorced, Chrystia and Natalka spent their summers with their father in Peace River. (Don eventually remarried and, with his second wife, Carol, had two more daughters.) Natalka answered phones in Don's office, a "terribly boring" job, but preferable in her mind to toiling in a "hot, sweaty field." Chrystia, meanwhile, would be out driving a combine.

"She was very connected to that piece of things," says Natalka. "I think like our dad and grandfather and great-grandfather, she really did feel a strong connection to our family farm, to the land, to doing that sort of work."

Later in Chrystia's life, when she was making her way as a journalist and as a politician, colleagues would marvel at her ability to multitask, pairing an almost frenetic energy with a determination to get things done. It seems likely that these traits had their roots in Peace River.

"Living with anybody as high-strung as Donnie, you got up and did things," says Adele Boucher, a former Peace River teacher who lived on a farm herself. "It didn't matter when we were kids whether the best movie of the year was in the theatre on Saturday night. If that was the day of the week where the threshing crew was moving from the neighbour's farm to your farm, you threshed. That's your livelihood."

She adds: "Peace River kids—I think that pioneer spirit in the grandparents has led to people who have a lot of gumption, a lot of drive. And they strive. Where we grew up, you get what you work for."

Lucan Way, one of Chrystia's best friends, describes Don as having a "kind of Western, screw convention" sensibility (as evidenced by his thoughts on the use of the French language in Alberta). Despite his profession, he didn't always follow the law to the letter. In 1985, for example, Don was fined $500 following a "slight altercation" with the Royal Canadian Mounted Police after resisting arrest for unpaid parking tickets from the City of Edmonton. There's an "element of going against convention" that Lucan thinks Chrystia got from Don— within the parameters of the strong moral compass instilled in her by Halyna. As a Canadian cabinet minister, Chrystia would become known for taking quick, decisive action when she believed it was the right thing to do—even if that led to adverse consequences for her government.

Education was very important for both Don and Halyna, and by the age of three, Chrystia had—unsurprisingly, given her parents' and grandfathers' profession—expressed interest in becoming a lawyer. Chrystia and Natalka (known to their teachers as Christine and Natalie) attended Springfield Elementary School, set at the bottom of green rolling hills in the eastern part of town, across the river from where the Freelands lived.

Teddy Harpe, who taught Chrystia in second grade, recalls her being very self-possessed, independent, and determined. She would come to class every day with her chestnut hair in either pigtails or curls, always in pretty dresses. But she wasn't prim and proper, and never hesitated to join in during gym class.

"Christine—Chrystia—was extremely bright; I was pressed to challenge her," says Harpe. Already reading at a level several grades beyond her own, Chrystia would bring in novels from home. If they had a few quiet minutes, she would ask to read to her teacher out of her book.

"I think she would have climbed right up on my lap, because she was quite petite. She would snuggle right up beside me. She was very gentle. She never, ever lorded it over the other kids that she was so much brighter than them, or was able to do the work so much better than them or so much quicker. She was never in a hurry, she never got flustered. Her dad scurried everywhere," says Harpe, who has closely followed her former student's career as a politician. "I think when you see her delivering her talks, that's her mom—the very strong, measured, and absolutely-in-control mannerisms."

AFTER MOVING BACK TO Edmonton in 1977, Halyna applied her characteristic vigour and zeal to both her career and community involvement. Even at nine, Chrystia was old enough to understand and internalize the importance of her mother's advocacy, and to appreciate Halyna's determination to give a voice to women who were used to not being heard.

In addition to being a partner in her own law firm, Halyna taught courses at the University of Alberta and opened a bookstore, Common Woman Books, with the goal of supplying feminist literature to the province's women. In the mid-1980s, she was the driving force behind the founding of a Ukrainian, feminist, socialist housing co-op in Old Strathcona called Hromada (community). She tried her hand at politics, too, running under the New Democratic Party banner in the 1988 federal election, and ultimately coming in second to the Progressive Conservative candidate. Friends and colleagues remember her as a trailblazer who always found time to appreciate good food, wine, and company.

Of all her contributions to the legal field in Alberta, Halyna was most proud of the role she played in helping to modernize the province's matrimonial property laws. Until the late 1970s, divorced women in Alberta had no legal entitlement to their matrimonial property if that property was in their spouse's name. In the 1975 Supreme Court of Canada case *Murdoch v. Murdoch*, for example, the court ruled that following her divorce, Irene Murdoch had no right to a share in the ranch on which she had lived and worked with her husband. Despite having laboured alongside him for years, she was left with nothing.

After public outcry across Canada, Alberta's attorney general introduced legislation meant to allow for a more equitable distribution of property following divorce. Halyna, never a one-woman band, set to work with a group of fellow female lawyers. They travelled to over one hundred locations, encouraging people to lobby the provincial government to improve the legislation. On May 16, 1978, Alberta's

Matrimonial Property Act was enacted, guaranteeing women a legal remedy following the breakdown of their marriage.

As a single mother, Halyna's commitment to her work necessarily meant something had to give on the child-care front. "My mom explicitly—like as a deliberate program, not as something that just happened—thought a good way to raise kids is what she called 'benign neglect,' which is that she would just kind of leave us to our own devices," says Natalka. "I think now they'd call it 'free range parenting.' [This was] an extreme version of that."

When Chrystia and Natalka first moved to Edmonton, they were in fourth and second grade, respectively. From then on, they never had babysitters after school, which meant that Chrystia was in charge of Natalka. After safely walking her sister home, Chrystia would present her with an after-school snack menu featuring a selection of exotic delicacies (frog's legs, for instance) and one option that was actually in the kitchen (peanut butter and jelly).

As a child, Chrystia didn't "play a ton" and had "adult temperament and proclivities," says Natalka. It was also important for her to be seen as an adult. Every other weekend, the two sisters would fly to Peace River by themselves. While unaccompanied children could pre-board, Chrystia would never let them do so, for fear of being treated "like kids."

"I was like, 'We are kids!' We were very close, but she was always kind of in the role of taking care of me," says Natalka. "And she took it seriously."

When Chrystia was in fifth grade, she attended a public Ukrainian bilingual elementary school, where she and Natalka were part of an enrichment program. But Chrystia felt the preferential treatment was unfair and, with encouragement from Halyna, organized a student strike, complete with marching and chanting.

"It certainly wouldn't have occurred to me—I liked having the enrichment class. I thought it was cool and fun," says Natalka. "I think that's like her in a couple of ways. She really has and has always had a very strong sense of fairness ... but also she likes to organize. Even if another kid thought everyone should have enrichment, who would have thought to organize a strike in fifth grade?"

IN EDMONTON, LIKE THEIR mother and grandparents, Chrystia and Natalka were very much a part of the city's vibrant Ukrainian community. In addition to bilingual school, the girls attended Ukrainian Saturday school, Ukrainian dance classes, and Plast (a Ukrainian scouting organization). Every Sunday, at Halyna's insistence, Michael Chomiak would pick up Chrystia and Natalka and take his granddaughters to church.

Alexandra had developed a reputation as a generous hostess, throwing Orthodox Christmas parties for family, friends, and neighbours that were famously lively. "I don't know how she managed to do it," says Bohdan Krawchenko, a family friend. Upon reflection, he adds, "she managed to do it because she started two weeks before. We were always invited and we were always a part of the family." As an adult, Chrystia, too, would have an open-door policy when it came to hosting, whether at her flat in Moscow, her apartment in midtown Manhattan, or her semi-detached Victorian in Toronto.

Because Orthodox Christmas, traditionally celebrated by Ukrainians on January 7, typically fell on a weekday, young Chrystia could often be found off in a corner, finishing up her homework. But the discussion and debate going on around her—always animated, usually at high volume—would shape her thinking on geopolitics for decades to come.

After the Second World War, the United States and the Soviet Union had emerged as competing superpowers. In the late 1970s, following a period of détente, their Cold War rivalry was once again heating up. To most Western observers, it looked as if the Soviet Empire—which had grown to include fifteen republics from its original four—had become a permanent fixture of the international system.

But growing up in Edmonton's patriotic Ukrainian diaspora, it was a question of faith that one day, though no one knew quite how or when, Ukraine would gain its independence from Soviet control. "I was taught at the kitchen table that the collapse of the USSR was inevitable," Chrystia would later write. "I was told that the Soviet Union was fragile, and when it did collapse, Ukraine would emerge."

In 1980, at the age of twelve, Chrystia got the chance to experience the Soviet Union as more than just an intellectual exercise. That summer, Moscow hosted the Summer Olympics, but more than sixty nations boycotted the Games as a response to the Soviet Union's 1979 invasion of Afghanistan. Soviet officials were eager to make up for the resulting dearth of tourists, and so Halyna jumped at the opportunity, securing visas for herself, her sister Chrystia Chomiak, and her two daughters to visit their homeland for the first time.

The two young girls were immediately struck by the basic ways the Soviet Empire was fundamentally failing to serve its people. En route to Ukraine, Aeroflot managed to lose their luggage, and they were left with nothing to wear.

"Here, that would not be the world's biggest deal; you'd go to Macy's and you'd buy some clothes," says Natalka, who now lives in Brooklyn. "It really wasn't that doable [there]. It was the same with food stores—you just really couldn't get things." Later, after they had been reunited with their luggage, they wore their regular Canadian clothes and were stopped in the street by people who wanted to know where they had purchased them.

The visit was also the first time Chrystia and Natalka, born and bred in a Western democracy, experienced the visceral fear that comes with living under an oppressive, autocratic regime. As with all foreign visitors, they were followed by agents of the Soviet Union's security service, the KGB. "Late at night, my mom and aunt would go down to the hotel bar and some guy would just happen to come over and be like, 'Hey! Don't you just *hate* the Soviet Union? It sucks!'" says Natalka.

While trying to buy a loaf of bread or fill their rental car with gas, the girls would speak in Ukrainian, though the language was still spoken infrequently in Kyiv, where conversation took place predominantly in Russian. People would pretend not to understand them, thinking it was a trap.

Still, Chrystia Chomiak says, the trip was "wonderful. It was just divine. We had such a great time—the good, bad, and the ugly." They visited some of Ukraine's major cities and experienced a homecoming in Lviv, where they met Michael's relatives for the first time. "We sat, had food—oh my God, so much food."

The girls also saw flickers of what young Chrystia later described as Ukraine's covert tradition of dissent. Their great-aunt Maria, one of Michael's sisters and a nun in the underground Catholic Church, recalled how she had once told a KGB officer who was interrogating her: "You can do anything to me, because I know that if you kill me, tomorrow I will be in heaven, and one day you will be in hell." She showed the girls her nun's habit, which she kept hidden under the floorboards of her apartment.

For the young Canadians, it was a vivid demonstration of how the Soviet Union was neglecting to treat Ukrainians as human beings, and of what could happen when the pendulum swung too far into state control. Later in life, Chrystia would describe her political philosophy as being simply "Canadian," which, according to her sister, translates into a belief that everyone deserves a social safety net, along with whatever leg up the system can provide, within the context of capitalism.

"I think some of that comes from having a Ukrainian Canadian family and actually going to Ukraine and seeing that if you're going to insist on actual communism, it tends to go very wrong," says Natalka.

Though she had been going by the anglicized version of her name since birth, as Chrystia grew into a teenager, she decided she no longer wanted to be known as Christine or Christie—she wanted to be Chrystia Freeland. She discussed the matter with her aunt Chrystia, who had gone through the same experience as a young adult after witnessing how others in the Ukrainian community had faced discrimination and been forced to assimilate.

"As Christina, I was invisible. But as Chrystia, I forced people to butcher my name, and know me as other. Because I was other," says Chrystia Chomiak. "I told her, and she said, 'That works for me. That is who I will be—that's the name I will use.'"

IN 1982, CHRYSTIA WAS accepted into the International Baccalaureate program at Old Scona Academic, a small Edmonton high school known for its academic rigour. According to an interview given by twelve-year-old Natalka to writer Myrna Kostash for a *Chatelaine* article on sisters, Chrystia had always been "self-righteous" about her non-conformity. She was never hip, never on trend: "I wear a bit of makeup or high-heeled shoes, and she looks at me like she's above all that." Having entered high school, however, Chrystia was suddenly sporting "a brand-new chic haircut and wearing her fanciest clothes to school."

Despite her sartorial awakening, Chrystia's main focus remained her studies. "We had a lot of very bright students, [but] I specifically remember her so well because she was one of the brightest students, I believe, that I have ever taught," says Linda Fortin, Chrystia's grade eleven European history teacher.

"The other kids liked her a lot. She showed leadership qualities, that's for sure. And she would have her causes—certainly, women's liberation, women's freedoms were important to her at that time, and Ukrainian nationalism—but she was never pushy. She was a very kind kid and thoughtful of others."

She was also conscious that there was a wider world outside Canada to be explored. One of Halyna's cousins, Larissa Blavatska, who would go on to become an accomplished Canadian diplomat, had recently started a position in the federal government's foreign ministry, then known as the Department of External Affairs. Part of Larissa's job was liaising with United World Colleges (uwc), a global network of schools that prides itself on bringing together a diverse student body and driving social change. She suggested to Halyna that a uwc college might be a good fit for Chrystia, who subsequently applied to and was accepted by uwc Adriatic, near Trieste, in 1984.

And so it was that at the relatively young age of sixteen, Chrystia moved to Italy, where she completed her high school education, earning an International Baccalaureate Diploma. The two years she spent there broadened her horizons, as she immersed herself in local culture, learned Italian, and expanded her network of friends.

uwc students were considered by Ivy League universities to be attractive candidates, and in 1986, Chrystia received an offer of admission from Harvard University. Speaking with Natalka about her decision to accept, Chrystia referenced the old foreign affairs adage that when the United States sneezes, Canada catches a cold. She didn't yet know what she wanted to be—a lawyer? a journalist? an academic? a politician?—but she knew she wanted to be at the epicentre of the room where things happened. And the institution that was most likely to get her there was Harvard.

FOUR

A Canadian at Harvard

I T WAS THE FIRST week of September 1986, and the Harvard University campus was abuzz. America's oldest educational institution—and one of the world's most prestigious—was celebrating its 350th anniversary, and an extravagant bash had been planned to mark the occasion.

Over forty thousand alumni and special guests were in attendance, including a young Prince Charles of Britain, who gave a keynote address in an academic gown threaded with gold. Harvard Yard, the historic twenty-five-acre green space that serves as the heart of the campus, had been decorated with thousands of potted white and crimson chrysanthemums. A "floating birthday party" on the banks of the Charles River featured fireworks, musical performances, laser projections, and a six-hundred-foot inflated arch that hovered in the sky above the water like a rainbow.

Hundreds of reporters had descended on Cambridge, Massachusetts, to document the festivities. In the *Washington Post*, one wrote that it felt as if the "center of the universe had briefly lodged itself" in Harvard Square, the triangular plaza adjacent to the school.

Of course, not everyone was thrilled with the overt display of pomp and pageantry. On the evening of September 5, a group of alumni, students, and local activists demanding that Harvard sell off its investments in companies doing business with South Africa's apartheid government blocked the entrance to Memorial Hall, where a black-tie dinner for several hundred of the school's most generous donors was to be held. The dinner was cancelled and, according to a report in the *Harvard Crimson*, the uncorked wine poured down the drain.

For the incoming freshman class—among them an eighteen-year-old Chrystia Freeland—it was a quintessential introduction to the Ivy League undergraduate experience, equal parts splendour and protest. Apartheid in South Africa would be a hot-button issue on campus for the next few years, along with the Iran-Contra affair, the Gulf War, and—of particular interest to Chrystia, who would be studying Russian history and literature—the beginning of the end of the decades-long Cold War between the United States and the Soviet Union.

Alexandra Chomiak, for her part, wasn't exactly enthused about the field of study Chrystia had chosen. Before Chrystia departed for Harvard, Alexandra advised her granddaughter that the world was unpredictable and that she'd be better off undertaking a more practical degree.

But unbeknownst to Alexandra, the winds of change would soon be sweeping through the communist countries of eastern Europe. By the end of the decade, the Soviet Union would be on the verge of collapse, and Chrystia would have a front-row seat to one of the biggest stories of the twentieth century.

Arriving in Cambridge that fall, however, she had more immediately pressing concerns. Chrystia would be living in Canaday Hall, the newest of the freshman dormitories located in Harvard Yard. In the stairwell on the way up to her room, she met Alison Franklin, a student from San Francisco who had been assigned to the same suite. As they peered into their new dorm, they saw it had a common living space attached to four single rooms. The trouble was, five girls had been assigned to the suite. One of the single rooms, it turned out, contained a bunk bed.

To Chrystia and Alison's dismay, they discovered that their suitemates, instead of waiting to figure out a more equitable way of distributing room assignments, had already claimed the three single beds for themselves and had begun to unpack.

"This is probably one of the reasons we bonded for life," says Franklin. "The situation was unreasonable—we weren't going to start college being bullied by three girls and their tapestries and their dresses in the closet."

Alison seethed, but Chrystia told her not to assume the worst. "She has a very strong injustice nerve, but I don't think it comes from a cynical place, like, 'Everyone's out to get me and I won't let it happen,'" says Franklin. "More that, 'Sometimes people do things that they might not realize are unfair.'" As they huddled in the tiny single room meant for one person, they came up with a plan.

Back in the common room, they announced to their suitemates that they would live together in the fourth bedroom—for half a year. When they all returned to campus in January, after the winter break, Chrystia and Alison would get their own rooms and two others would share the bunk beds.

Spluttering, their suitemates had little choice but to agree. The issue settled, Chrystia and Alison went into their room to unpack. Alison, a foot taller than Chrystia, took the top bunk.

Rooming situation sorted, Chrystia threw herself into life on campus. In Edmonton, she had developed an interest in journalism, writing articles for the city's *Ukrainian News* and entries for the *Encyclopedia of Ukraine*, a multi-volume project on the country's history and people. At Harvard, she took part in a rigorous application process, known as "comping," for *The Crimson*, the university's daily paper.

Robyn Fass, who met Chrystia during freshman orientation, remembers hanging out in Chrystia's common room and observing her during the comp process, which involved writing several articles in a certain amount of time. "I was just sitting around, Alison was sitting around, whoever was there was sitting around," she says. "And Chrystia was sitting around, but she was also actually getting something done, which just blew my mind. She was like boom, boom, boom, just write, just do it."

To Fass, this is indicative of Chrystia's approach to life: she decides what she's going to do, and then she does it. "She doesn't have this stress that many of us experience—'I was going to work on this but then this other thing came up, now what should I do?' She can do both calmly."

As in high school, Chrystia was active in feminist causes, participating in Take Back the Night marches. Her favourite chant was "Whatever I wear, wherever I go, yes means yes and no means no," a jingle, she later wrote, that "was invented to popularize one of the most radical and important ideas of the second-wave feminists—that rape and promiscuity were entirely separate issues."

In addition to *The Crimson*, Chrystia joined the staff of a liberal magazine called *Perspective*, where she wrote opinion and longer think pieces. Along with other *Perspective* writers, she was a member of Stop Withholding Access Today, a student group that worked to open up Harvard's exclusive all-male social clubs, known as "final clubs," to women.

While Chrystia had been, as her sister Natalka described her, a "giant bookworm" in high school, in university she formed close friendships and was "very, very social." Like her mother before her, Chrystia took advantage of the full breadth of the college experience.

"We got drunk all the time—she definitely enjoyed all that life had to offer and [had] the ability to connect with literally everyone," says Lucan Way, who met Chrystia in the smoking section of the freshman dorms and worked with her on *Perspective*. "She was also someone who immersed herself in her surroundings. She was involved in opening up the final clubs, but she also accepted a date in a final club. I remember her telling me this story that they brought multiple bottles of champagne and she got on a pool table ... She was just willing to throw herself in."

In addition to sharing an interest in the Soviet Union, Chrystia and Lucan bonded over growing up as "latchkey kids" largely left to take care of themselves after school. Alison, too, had been raised by a working mom. She says that while it was common for female students at Harvard to be "hard-charging" and vocal about what they hoped to achieve in their professional lives, few were as pointed or sure about wanting a family of their own. Chrystia, however, "always knew she wanted to have kids—she was very unusual in that way."

"She was like, 'I'm going to do it all,'" remembers Way. "Everybody kind of knew at the time that she was destined for greatness. She would joke that she didn't want to be foreign minister of Canada, because Canada's too small for her." If that had come from anybody else, it would have "seemed ridiculous," he says, "but her? Like, of course."

Kidding aside, Chrystia was known among her American friends for her quirky Canadian pride. She encouraged Alison to visit her in Peace River, promising that she would pick her up in a combine. Alison, who was from San Francisco, had no idea what a combine was.

Chrystia also had a habit of pointing out the Canadian identities of famous people who might otherwise be thought to be American, like writer Margaret Atwood or songwriter Leonard Cohen.

Years later, Alison was participating in a trivia contest when the host started reading out a question that began, "This Canadian-American broadcaster ..."

"Peter Jennings!" Alison immediately shouted out. "My team was like, 'Oh my gosh, you're so insane,' and I was like, 'No, no, I lived with Chrystia Freeland.'"

Friends recall that Chrystia stood out among the predominantly privileged and wealthy student body for being exceptionally frugal and unconcerned with material possessions. Though she had been granted a Charles S. Noble scholarship by the province of Alberta, and though both Don and Halyna had done well for themselves professionally, money was tight, and Natalka says that it was a constant scramble for the family to pay tuition every month.

Robyn Fass recalls that Chrystia lived modestly. She "was not trying to pass herself off as having more than she did. I remember her having one pair of running shoes, and she would just wear those," Fass says, regardless of season or social occasion. "Other people would have done a big shopping trip with their mom before showing up at Harvard and have all this stuff. She didn't have a lot of stuff, and she wasn't trying to be fancy or preppy or fit in."

Toward the end of her freshman year, Chrystia landed a much-sought-after summer job as a writer and researcher for a travel guide series called Let's Go, produced by Harvard Student Agencies. The application process was competitive—two hundred people applied for fifty positions. Chrystia was chosen to put together the Italy guide, which had sold twenty-five thousand copies the previous year.

While it seemed like an amazing opportunity, it soon became clear that while Harvard Student Agencies would pay for students to get to their destinations, once there, they'd receive only a modest stipend to cover transportation, accommodation, and food.

The summer of 1987 was not an easy one for Chrystia, as she visited various Italian cities, submitting copy to her editors back home every ten days. She was not an early riser and struggled with daily six a.m. train departures. She was exasperated by the whistles and unwanted attention bestowed on her by Italian men, recommending in the guide that female visitors don "a pair of wire-rimmed glasses to reduce the catcalls to a livable hum."

She took the job seriously, but she couldn't afford to visit the restaurants and cultural hotspots that she was expected to report on. Instead, says Franklin, she'd interview people leaving museums that had expensive entrance fees and ask them what they had seen inside. "I think that she, better than anyone our age at that time, [understood] not having money and what that means and how you experience it. And I don't think that's changed for her."

For Chrystia, the experience was worth it, despite the discomfort. It offered a valuable glimpse into what life could be like as a correspondent reporting from abroad. "It made me a lot more self-confident. It made me much more independent and much more outgoing," she told the *South Florida Sun Sentinel* in an interview about the Let's Go series. "Constantly being a stranger in a strange country, you learn how to thoroughly take care of yourself and how to make friends really quickly."

These were lessons that would prove useful for her most formative year as a Harvard student—one that would be spent far from the university's dorms and dining halls.

FIVE

Behind the Iron Curtain

I N MARCH 1985, MIKHAIL GORBACHEV had been unanimously elected general secretary of the Communist party of the Soviet Union. In response to the superpower's mounting economic problems, Gorbachev instituted the twin policies of perestroika (the restructuring of the Soviet economic and political systems) and glasnost (greater openness and transparency). In the non-Russian Soviet republics, these policies had the unintended effect of stirring nationalistic senti-ment and encouraging discussion of issues that had long been taboo: history, culture, language, religion, and—eventually—sovereignty.

In Ukraine, talk of independence emerged tentatively, barely above the level of a collective whisper. But it was a topic that had been delib-erated loudly, for years, in the passionately political community of Ukrainian émigrés in western Alberta.

Despite her grandparents' convictions, Chrystia, along with many of her generation who were teenagers at the time, tended to think that independence "seemed as quaint a notion" as Michael Chomiak's "old-world hand-kissing."

"The USSR looked immutable," Chrystia would later write. "As for

Ukraine, well, as Margaret Thatcher put it on a visit to Soviet Kiev, it was no more a separate entity than the state of California."

At Harvard, Chrystia's interest in the world beyond Canada's borders grew. In her Russian history and literature classes, she continued to delve into the debate that had dominated her family's kitchen-table discussions, learning that some of the field's smartest and most eminent professors also believed that her grandparents and their friends were dreaming an impossible dream. Still, it couldn't hurt to find out for herself. When, in the spirit of glasnost, the Soviet Union began welcoming exchange students from the United States, Canada, and other Western countries, Chrystia leapt at the chance to return to Ukraine.

In October 1988, Chrystia arrived at the Taras Shevchenko National University of Kyiv, where she would spend her third academic year. Like Harvard, the university had a reputation for educational excellence and a history of progressive thinking. Its main building, distinctive for its bright red facade and Ionic columns and portico, was located in the centre of the capital, on Kyiv's bustling Volodymyrska Street, facing the city's botanical gardens to the west and the beloved Shevchenko Park to the east.

Kyiv was both beautiful and drab. After the Second World War, the city had been reconstructed in typical Soviet fashion: wide boulevards; majestic government buildings and hotels in Stalin empire–style; dreary, low-rise Khrushchovka apartment blocks; and many, many monuments to Vladimir Lenin, leader of the 1917 Russian Revolution.

Khreshchatyk Street, Kyiv's elegant main thoroughfare, was lined with the city's trademark chestnut trees. At the top of the street sat October Revolution Square (now Maidan Nezalezhnosti, or Independence Square). As the weather turned chilly, the women wore headscarves and thick wool overcoats, and the men swapped their fedoras for fur hats.

Wandering the streets of the capital, twenty-year-old Chrystia must have felt at once further away from her family than she had ever been—in order to place a call home, a line needed to be booked twenty-four hours in advance by an operator—and more connected to her history than ever before.

At first, Soviet officials welcomed her effusively, happy to see someone of Ukrainian ancestry on the exchange. But that wouldn't last. An unmistakable—if gentle—undercurrent of revolution had begun to flow through the city, and Chrystia, journalistic radar buzzing, was itching to investigate.

The powerful new national movements that had developed in other Soviet republics as a result of Gorbachev's reforms were notably slower to take shape in Ukraine. But by 1988, Ukrainians' faith in the Communist party was steadily eroding. The deadly disaster at the Chernobyl nuclear power plant just north of Kyiv two years earlier had left many angry and disillusioned. The economic situation was dire; store shelves were nearly empty, and when fresh fruits and vegetables did appear, shoppers questioned where they had been grown, suspicious that they were contaminated with radiation.

Fear of authority, too, was on the wane, following the deaths in rapid succession of the Russian strongmen who had preceded the reform-minded Gorbachev: Leonid Brezhnev in 1982, Yuri Andropov in 1984, and Konstantin Chernenko in 1985. Emboldened Ukrainians began to speak out about corrupt party officials, though they still had to contend with a hard-line leader, Vladimir Shcherbitsky.

The summer before Chrystia arrived in Ukraine, the country's first public demonstrations calling for the creation of a popular opposition movement had taken place in Lviv. They were dealt with swiftly; dogs were turned on the crowd, and protesters were beaten and arrested.

By the fall, the action had shifted to the capital. Chrystia caught wind that, together with environmental groups, the university's student club Hromada—which shared a name with the co-op her mother, Halyna, had founded back in Edmonton—was organizing an ecological demonstration on November 13 not far from campus.

Despite freezing temperatures, ten thousand people showed up. For hours, the crowd listened to speeches by celebrated Ukrainian literary figures, environmental activists, and dissidents. In many cases, the speakers were forced to shout (once it became clear that they were veering into political territory, the authorities moved in and shut off their microphones). Nevertheless, they argued passionately in favour of more political, economic, and cultural autonomy. Chrystia was intrigued and resolved to learn more about the fledgling movement.

David Marples, now a professor of Russian and East European history at the University of Alberta, was visiting Kyiv on a fact-finding research trip sponsored by the World Media Association at the time of the protest. He knew Chrystia from Edmonton and had lived for a time in the Hromada co-op.

Not long after the World Media Association group arrived in Kyiv, Chrystia turned up at their hotel, perhaps having gotten wind of their arrival and work. She was happy to see a familiar face, Marples remembers, and decided to tag along for an interview with one of the ecological demonstration's speakers, Oles Shevchenko, a well-known dissident and former political prisoner. The interview, perhaps naively, was held in one of the hotel's guest rooms. KGB agents, who were omnipresent for the entirety of the research trip, could hear the whole conversation through the paper-thin walls. When it was over, Marples and Chrystia escorted Shevchenko to the lobby, where they could see a fleet of KGB "taxis" awaiting him on the street. Afraid for Shevchenko, they called a regular taxi to take him home. It wasn't Chrystia's first encounter with the Soviet secret police—she and her family had been surveilled during their trip to Ukraine when she was twelve—and it certainly wouldn't be her last.

TODAY, EFREM LUKATSKY IS one of Ukraine's most famous photographers. He has worked for the Associated Press for more than thirty years, covering wars in Afghanistan and Iraq, conflict in Gaza and Chechnya, and the 2014 Euromaidan protests. His photos have been published by major media outlets, and he was the first Ukrainian to be named a finalist for the Pulitzer Prize.

But in 1988, he was a thirty-two-year-old mustachioed engineer working for Ukraine's Institute of Electric Welding. That fall, some of his amateur photography was featured in an exhibition hall in the Kyiv Trade Union House, which sat on Khreshchatyk Street facing October Revolution Square. One photo—of nationalist composer Leopold Yashchenko, a grey-haired dissident whose choir was that year the first to begin publicly singing Ukraine's national anthem— caused quite the stir. The head of the exhibition demanded Lukatsky take the photo down, but visitors defended it. The next day, Lukatsky arrived to find that someone had pierced Yashchenko's face with a pencil; he proudly brought in a new print to display.

For the duration of the exhibit, Lukatsky hung around the hall, occasionally taking a break from checking out visitors' reactions to stroll around the square. On one of these walks, he ran into a colleague from the welding institute, who introduced him to his companion, who happened to be Chrystia. She looked like the actress Jodie Foster, Lukatsky remembers—pretty, with eyes that sparkled with life.

Lukatsky invited them into the hall, where Chrystia eagerly viewed his work. He and Chrystia became fast friends. Lukatsky delighted in showing Chrystia his version of Kyiv and introducing her to his photographer friends. They talked about their futures: Chrystia still wasn't sure if she should become a lawyer or a journalist, while Lukatsky argued they should both pursue careers in media.

Lukatsky was part of a newly formed group called Pohliad (Viewpoint), whose aim was to document everyday life in Soviet Ukraine, warts and all. Comments left in exhibition guest books ranged from appreciation for exposing a "harsh but necessary truth" to demands that the photographers be shot and their photos burned.

Chrystia was profoundly moved by Pohliad's ability to capture a key moment in Ukrainian history, often at personal risk to its photographers. She was also well aware that, even with the "openness" encouraged by Gorbachev's glasnost policies, the photos would reach a wider audience on the other side of the Iron Curtain. But first, they had to make it out of the country.

At the end of December, her first semester complete, Chrystia flew to London, where she was going to spend Christmas with friends. In her suitcase were photos by Lukatsky and five other members of Pohliad who were willing to risk having their work carried across borders.

The first week of 1989 brought mild weather to London, a welcome respite from the Ukrainian winter as Chrystia walked along City Road, arriving at the modern building that housed *The Independent*, Britain's newest newspaper.

After waiting for three hours by the reception desk, Chrystia was finally ushered into the paper's tiny foreign desk office, where she laid out the Pohliad photos—women selling wares at market stalls, passersby examining an American car in Kyiv, a girl at a rock concert wearing heavy eyeliner and a "Hurray for glasnost" badge. The editorial team was impressed, and on January 14 the photos were published in a full-page spread.

Not long after, back in Kyiv, Lukatsky was summoned to a meeting at the welding institute with the head of his department, who promptly ran out of the room, leaving Lukatsky alone with a man in a grey suit who introduced himself as Alexander Ivanovich—a KGB pseudonym. The man tried to convince Lukatsky that Chrystia was a Western spy, calling the photos propaganda and insisting Lukatsky provide him with information on Chrystia's contacts. Lukatsky said he would think about it.

The next day, "Alexander" was waiting for Lukatsky as he exited the metro. "Well, have you thought about it?" he asked.

He had no information to give on Chrystia, Lukatsky replied, but the experience had helped him make up his mind about his future: he was going to be a photojournalist.

FOR CHRYSTIA, TOO, JOURNALISM was looking more and more like a logical and enticing career—an avenue through which to both explore and be part of the biggest geopolitical story of the time. On February 10, *The Independent* published an article she had written under the headline "Ukrainian Party Chief under Fire." It was her first byline in a major international newspaper (though they did spell her name "Krystia"). She described an "unprecedented split" in the ranks of the Ukrainian Communist party—some of the more sympathetic officials in the establishment were beginning to get fed up with Shcherbitsky's iron rule, and Moscow was losing patience with how the party seemed determined to "put the brakes on any reform."

While on exchange, Chrystia began to act as a local fixer for Western journalists passing through Ukraine, including Bill Keller, a *New York Times* correspondent in Moscow who would go on to become the paper's executive editor. "I don't remember how I found

Chrystia," he says, though "knowing Chrystia, she probably found me." Keller hired her for a few stories; the biggest one they worked on together was about a mass grave in the pine forests of Bykovnya, a village just east of Kyiv.

Under Gorbachev, the Soviet Union was slowly opening up about the terror inflicted on the Ukrainian people during the reign of Joseph Stalin and his secret police, the NKVD, in the 1930s and '40s. The official story was that mass gravesites like the one at Bykovnya and several others around the country held the bodies of Ukrainians killed by Nazi troops during the Second World War, but locals knew they were the victims of the NKVD. Now, nearing the end of their lives, they were ready to tell their stories.

"My Russian was pretty decent but villagers were more likely to speak freely in Ukrainian," says Keller. "Chrystia was more than a translator; she was a co-reporter, tracking down villagers who had been alive at the time, charming them, asking the right questions."

The story made the front page of the *New York Times* on March 6. That year, Keller won a Pulitzer Prize for his reporting on the Soviet Union. Eventually, the burial site would be declared a national monument to the victims of communism.

For Chrystia, the experience of contributing to the Bykovnya story was an example of the power journalism had to unravel long-held fictions and reveal truths that those in power would prefer remain in the shadows. "I saw how important Bill was to these people," she would later tell the *Toronto Star*. "I'm sure he was a large part of why I became a journalist."

On occasion, Chrystia's emotional investment in the future of Ukraine meant the line between journalism and activism blurred. That winter, she was invited to give a speech as the Canadian delegate of the Shevchenko Ukrainian Language Society, which, the *Ukrainian*

Weekly wrote, "turned into an impressive manifestation of Ukrainian national assertiveness and of protest against the reactionary policies of the Ukrainian Party leadership." Her talk, about the ways Ukranian Canadians were working to preserve their mother tongue, was greeted with warm applause, and she was subsequently elected to the organization's board of directors.

For Soviet officials, this was all too much. Up until now, the KGB had been a peripheral presence during Chrystia's time on exchange, but they were about to make her life a whole lot more uncomfortable.

MOSCOW'S SHEREMETYEVO INTERNATIONAL AIRPORT, at the end of the 1980s, was dark and dismal, with long lines and numerous rooms at the back of the customs hall designed to hold the many travellers detained for interrogation. On March 31, 1989, returning to Kyiv via Moscow after another trip to London, Chrystia joined their ranks. Customs officials pulled her aside and searched her suitcase, which contained various newspaper clippings, pamphlets, and videotapes she had collected in London, all related to Western coverage of Ukraine. She tried to argue they were for personal use, but that mattered little to the officials, who seized the material.

On campus, following the delivery of her speech, handsome Russian men had started appearing at the door of her dormitory. They would strike up a conversation and then quiz her about certain Ukrainian nationalists and Western technology. Soon, Soviet authorities began calling her, requesting that she meet with them. She refused. Displeased, the Soviets sent a telegram to the Canadian embassy in Moscow on April 21, chiding: "Your national is a well-known troublemaker and you should keep better control over your citizens."

News of Chrystia's adventures made it all the way back to her home province of Alberta. "City Woman in USSR Tells KGB to Get Lost," read an April 28 headline in the *Edmonton Journal*. It included an interview with Chrystia's mother. "Am I proud?" Halyna asked. "You bet."

In Kyiv, too, Chrystia made headlines. *Pravda Ukrainy*, the official daily newspaper of the Ukrainian Communist party, dedicated nearly two thousand words to her "abuse of hospitality." It included a laundry list of Chrystia's many "anti-Soviet" activities: violating travel rules in place for foreigners by leaving Kyiv to interview dissidents and translate for Western journalists, getting "carried away" by "meetings and protests of various amateur organizations . . . so much that she barely had time for university studies," and engaging "in political intelligence and interfer[ing] in the election campaign of the USSR people's deputies."

In January 2020, in the KGB archives in Kyiv, Duke University professor Simon Miles uncovered a top-secret report on Chrystia—code-named "Frida"—written by the KGB's Colonel A. Stroĭ thirty years earlier. It describes the lengths to which Soviet officials went to hamper Chrystia's "hostile activities," including increasing her coursework at university and inserting an informant into her social circle. According to the report, Chrystia was able to send information back home by using, with the help of a contact at the Canadian embassy in Moscow, privileged and protected diplomatic mail (which Jeremy Kinsman, a former Canadian ambassador to Russia, notes is a "strict no-no" for embassy staff). She "skillfully avoid[ed] outside surveillance" and knew her telephone conversations were likely being monitored. Stroĭ writes of Chrystia with grudging admiration, describing her as "erudite, sociable, persistent, and inventive in achieving her goals"—a "remarkable individual" with an "analytical mindset."

While a part of Chrystia must have delighted in the exhilaration of feeling like she was living in a John le Carré novel, her nerves were beginning to fray. On her last night in Kyiv, four men, two of them KGB agents, showed up at her dorm, threatening to confiscate her passport if she refused to answer their questions. Chrystia—five foot two and trembling on the inside—told them that her passport was the property of the Canadian government, and that they should back off.

It was time to go home.

CHRYSTIA'S ACADEMIC YEAR IN Kyiv coincided with a period of tremendous change in Ukraine. By the summer of 1989, there was a demonstration every week and her grandparents' views on independence were looking less outlandish and more prophetic. Lucan Way, who studied on exchange in Russia that same year, says that he and Chrystia returned home from the Soviet Union with a further appreciation of the capitalist establishment in the West that, while not perfect and certainly in need of reform, was largely preferable to the alternatives.

When *Pravda Ukrainy* published its accusations, Chrystia was certain that she would never be allowed to re-enter the Soviet Union. But it turned out she would be welcomed back that September to attend the founding congress of the People's Movement of Ukraine for Reconstruction (RUKH). The group that would lead the fight for Ukrainian freedom—its seeds planted at the ecological protest Chrystia had covered nearly a year earlier—finally had a name.

Far from being a persona non grata, Chrystia was treated by the Ukrainians at the congress "like a celebrity," says Karin Davies, who was at the time the London bureau chief for the United Press International (UPI) news agency and on assignment in Ukraine.

"They wanted to share their goals with the world, and they knew they needed her—a young woman from Canada—to translate for foreign journalists."

Chrystia's encounters with the secret police hadn't put a damper on her desire to further the cause of Ukrainian nationalism. As Stroï noted, she was persistent when it came to achieving her ambitions.

Taras Kuzio, at the time the executive director of the Ukrainian Press Agency, remembers meeting Chrystia that fall in London, where she had stopped en route to Ukraine. The agency gave her books and journals to bring with her to Kyiv, which she took "without hesitation."

"There was no sign of being in the slightest scared by Soviet border guards checking her luggage or getting into trouble with the authorities. She in the end had no difficulties at the Moscow airport and delivered everything we gave her," says Kuzio. "Undoubtedly, as with all Westerners travelling to the USSR, she was followed by the KGB. She must have been aware of this and was assisted by our Kyiv staffers in arranging meetings with oppositionists, intellectuals, and activists. But the KGB were never going to be successful in intimidating her."

Back at Harvard, Alison Franklin remembers Chrystia showing her pro-democracy material that she had brought with her from Ukraine via Moscow. While travelling in Germany, Franklin had crossed the border between East Berlin and West Berlin and had been subject to an extensive search by officials looking for clandestine items. "I remember how they turned me upside down and shook me," she says. She was dying to know how Chrystia had evaded detection.

Chrystia's secret? *Playgirl*, and its photos of nude men. Recognizing that the Soviet border guards had a lot in common with the rural "farm guys" Chrystia had gone to school with in Alberta, she'd lined her bags with copies of the salacious magazine, guessing correctly that the guards would be too embarrassed or disgusted to delve any deeper into her belongings.

IT WASN'T ONLY UKRAINE that was changing in the late 1980s and early '90s. Chrystia, too, had experienced a profound period of growth. She had arrived in Kyiv as an exchange student, but she would leave as a budding journalist—one who was willing to put herself at some risk to get a story out. As would be the case throughout her journalistic career, she wasn't afraid of being in the middle of it all; in fact, she craved it.

UPI's Karin Davies had been so impressed with Chrystia's translation work that she had given her a card and encouraged her to get in touch; Chrystia spent the summer of 1990 working in UPI's London office as an intern. In November, she submitted her senior thesis, "RUKH: The New Ukrainian Nationalism," and she graduated in January 1991.

In a 2013 interview with Little PINK Book, Chrystia was asked what she considered to be her biggest career mistake. "I wish I'd been a more serious student," she replied. "Now as I become older, I realize that those are times when you're allowed to just read and think and develop skills. I wish I'd developed that more."

It's a curious answer for someone who had developed more skills than many an undergraduate. Robyn Fass interprets her friend's comments to mean that while Chrystia did well in university, she juggled a multitude of activities outside the classroom and kept one eye trained on the outside world.

"I think she is imagining what it would be like to be solely focused on class work. There are some Harvard students, for example, who write a senior thesis at the level of a PhD dissertation. The students who graduate summa cum laude—that sort of thing," says Fass. "It might also be about the experience of just being a student, which is sort of a vacation, compared to the level of responsibility she assumed so young."

While that type of student experience might seem appealing in hindsight, no one can argue that Chrystia failed to make the most of her years at Harvard. It was there, after all, that she began to make some of the genuine, high-powered, and high-profile connections that would come to serve her so well in her political career. She befriended, for instance, economics professor Larry Summers, who would go on to become chief economist of the World Bank and US treasury secretary under President Bill Clinton. (They first met when she popped in to his office to inquire about the economic advice he had shared with the government of what was then the Soviet Socialist Republic of Lithuania.)

"She just really sought out and became very close to people who she thought were important. And that's, I think, a different way of treating school really seriously," says her sister Natalka.

At any rate, Chrystia excelled sufficiently at Harvard to be awarded a prestigious Rhodes Scholarship to pursue a master's degree at the University of Oxford. "I was in complete shock, in a total state of disbelief," Chrystia told the *Edmonton Journal*. Halyna, for her part, was "ecstatic, but not surprised."

At the beginning of 1991, Chrystia's immediate future seemed set. She had been chosen for a competitive Ukrainian Canadian Congress summer internship that gave young people the opportunity to shadow members of Parliament in Ottawa. And she planned on moving to England in the fall to continue her studies.

In the meantime, though, she had a few months to herself, and the story of Ukrainian independence was one she was determined to see through.

PART TWO

PAPER CHASE

SIX

A First Draft of History

FOLLOWING THE FOUNDING congress of RUKH, the People's Movement of Ukraine for Reconstruction, in September 1989, the fight for a free Ukraine continued to gain momentum.

In January 1990, hundreds of thousands of people formed a human chain stretching from Lviv to Kyiv, calling for independence; shops in Lviv sold out of blue and yellow fabric as protesters sewed Ukrainian flags, banned for years under Soviet rule.

In March, candidates from the democratic opposition, including RUKH leaders, won a quarter of the seats in Ukraine's Parliament, the Verkhovna Rada, housed in a white neoclassical building topped by a hundred-ton glass dome. Though the Communist party still held a majority, that summer, the Rada voted to declare sovereignty—a symbolic step but an important one nonetheless.

And in October, in what would come to be known as the Revolution on Granite, student protesters pitched tents on the cold slabs of October Revolution Square. As a result of the students' hunger strike, Ukraine halted its approval of Mikhail Gorbachev's proposed union treaty, which aimed to set out a new power-sharing arrangement between the Soviet republics. Gorbachev, caught between conservatives in his party who wished to reverse his perestroika and glasnost policies and progressives advocating for more aggressive market reforms, hoped the treaty would placate both and keep the Soviet Union intact.

Despite the growing political ferment, Ukraine—a country of 52 million people with vast agricultural and industrial resources—remained largely off the radar of newspaper editors in London and New York. The story of the Soviet Union had hitherto been covered through the lens of Moscow, where correspondents from all the major Western outlets were stationed. None of these outlets had staff correspondents in Kyiv.

In the spring of 1991, with her undergraduate diploma under her belt and a couple of months to kill before she was due to start her parliamentary internship in Ottawa, twenty-two-year-old Chrystia thought she would try to fill that gap. "It was a hell of a story, and nobody was reporting it," recalls Andrew Gowers, then the features editor of the *Financial Times* (*FT*) in London. "It was a plum to be plucked, and she was there to pluck it."

Bohdan Krawchenko, who had known Chrystia since she was a baby, was similarly drawn to Kyiv. He had been working as the director of the University of Alberta's Canadian Institute of Ukrainian Studies in Edmonton but decided to take a sabbatical and move to the capital. "I knew something was going to happen—I was pretty certain the Soviet Union was not going to work out," he says. "I wrote a book that ended with that [assertion], and everybody thought, in the 1980s, that this was slightly cuckoo."

In Kyiv, Krawchenko met a group of people who told him, "You can be part of this thing, stop writing about it." And he did, becoming the director of policy studies at the Council of Advisors to the Rada, whose members included former British foreign secretary Sir Geoffrey Howe, billionaire investor George Soros, and Zbigniew Brzezinski, who had served as national security advisor to US president Jimmy Carter.

Krawchenko lived in a spacious three-bedroom apartment on what was then called Lenin Street, right next to the city's opera house. That spring, he remembers, Chrystia walked through his front door and said, "Oh, you have a big apartment!" And she ended up staying for several months, forgoing the internship waiting for her in Ottawa. Parliament Hill would have to wait.

THE LONDON-BASED *Financial Times*, known for its business coverage and its light-pink paper, was first published in 1888. By the 1990s, David Kynaston writes in a brief history of the *FT*, it had become "one of the very few genuinely international papers."

It was also something of an old boys' club. Upon becoming the paper's foreign editor in 1986, British journalist Jurek Martin discovered that in the *FT*'s history, only two women had been appointed as foreign correspondents. "I consciously set out to do something about this," he says, "trying to look for really sharp and original talent—if you'll permit me to say it—in skirts rather than suits." Martin also hoped to ramp up the *FT*'s coverage in places where it hadn't before had a presence.

Toward the end of her time at Harvard, Chrystia had met Anthony Robinson, a former *FT* Moscow correspondent who was spending a year at the university on a Nieman Foundation fellowship. He remembers being impressed by her ability to speak both Ukrainian and Russian, the latter of which she had learned at Harvard, and connected her with Martin.

"When Tony brought Chrystia to me, I thought she was the sort of person who could hack it," says Martin. He hired her to be the *FT*'s stringer in Kyiv, a "non-staff job, but the kind you give to a person who you think could graduate onto the full-time paper if they do well."

In Kyiv, Chrystia obtained one of the first press cards issued by the Ukrainian foreign ministry. Over the next few months, she'd be joined by a handful of other Western correspondents, some of whom, like Chrystia, had grown up in Ukrainian diaspora communities.

"It was a small group, so obviously we all knew each other," says Chrystyna Lapychak, a Ukrainian American who worked for the *Christian Science Monitor*. "It tended to be mostly women, [though] there were a few men." She remembers one slightly bewildered Ukrainian member of Parliament describing the Western press corps: "He commented, 'They're all named Chrystyna, or Chrystia, or Marta, and they all run around wearing black.'"

The living conditions in Ukraine were much the same as when Chrystia had visited with her family for the first time in 1980. One correspondent remembers waiting in line for hours for what he thought was water, only to discover the liquid on offer was vodka. Another recalls stores with shelves empty of anything other than pickled vegetables.

Communications remained spotty. Fax machines were hard to find, and fax paper even more so. (Conveniently, one machine was located in the post office below Krawchenko's apartment; he would bring back fax paper when he travelled abroad.) Long-distance calls still needed to be booked in advance with an international operator, and the quality of the line was often so bad that journalists dictating their articles to their papers' copy takers couldn't be sure that the names of the Ukrainian people they were quoting would turn up correctly in print. And Westerners still had to contend with surveillance. "In those days, they listened in to our phone calls. I know, because I would hear them breathing," says Natalia Feduschak, who worked for the *Wall Street Journal*.

Nevertheless, Ukraine was a "terrific" place for young journalists to launch their careers, says James Hill, a Pulitzer Prize–winning British photographer who got his start in Kyiv. "There was an amazing story happening: a new country being born."

Life for Westerners, who benefited from an extremely favourable exchange rate, was inexpensive. A one-bedroom apartment with parquet floors and a balcony could be rented for less than fifty dollars a month, and a dinner of steak and potatoes, or borscht and dumplings, cost a few dollars. Food could be bought at private markets, which were out of reach for ordinary Ukrainians. Thanks to affordable flight and train prices, correspondents could travel frequently even though they weren't making a lot of money.

Being a twentysomething journalist in Kyiv was also tremendously fun. The expatriate community was tiny, so Chrystia and her colleagues would often find themselves at parties with Western ambassadors or the heads of foreign companies, usually held at someone's home.

"There was terribly cheap vodka and beer, and then the Ukrainians would come and chain-smoke and you'd have cigarettes put out in the cheese sandwiches," says Hill. "There were always twice as many people in the kitchen as it could really fit. It was unpretentious and casual, almost sort of student-like. People weren't going to fancy restaurants, because there weren't any."

Ukrainian politicians viewed the press corps as an important conduit to the West. The foreign ministry was welcoming and encouraging, providing journalists with passes to the Rada, where they could wander wherever they pleased, including the office of Communist party chairman Leonid Kravchuk.

"I live in Paris now," says Hill. "The chances of my rubbing shoulders with [French president Emmanuel] Macron on any kind of friendly basis, I'd say, are zero. That was not the case then. There was a far greater proximity—an unusual proximity—between journalists and people in power."

Throughout her time in Kyiv, Chrystia proved to be exactly the kind of journalist with whom people in power were keen to cultivate a relationship. Karl Bostic, an American who worked as a freelance producer for ABC News, says this was partly because she had the backing of the *FT*, but also because "she knew her stuff. She was very, very smart, and she had a laser-beam focus."

He continues, "The lawmakers had never governed before, and they had never had experience with the West before, so in many ways, she was kind of teaching them too. She was a bridge for them to the West, and they'd be bouncing ideas off her—'How should I do this, how should I express that?'—because they didn't know."

The fact that Chrystia was equally at home speaking both Ukrainian and Russian was also an advantage. Her language skills "made her access and her ability to communicate with the players in Ukraine much better than the rest of us, especially journalists who had to work through interpreters," says Hill.

He notes that Chrystia used her "feminine guile" to her benefit, charming politicians for whom speaking with Western female journalists was a novelty: "She likes to, I think, tell a story about coming from humble farmer roots. You can tell that one of her tactics is to sort of disarm people, and I think she used that as a journalist in Kyiv. You know, 'Nothing to fear here, I'm just a farmer's girl. You can tell me everything.'"

Chrystia herself would downplay the journalistic chops that made such an impression on her fellow correspondents. Speaking about her experience reporting in Ukraine at a lecture in Edmonton in 2000, she lamented the "hours, and hours, and hours" she was made to spend in waiting rooms: "Everyone act[ed] as if it was a huge and terrific favour they were granting me by giving me the privilege of talking to them."

While Ukrainian politicians relished the opportunity to get their message out to the world, she added, they weren't used to having something they said appear in print in the papers. Sometimes they were outraged; other times they would deny having given the quote in question at all. (In 1992, after Chrystia wrote articles that were critical of Kravchuk, he refused to speak with her or the *FT* in general for almost two years.)

Among the press corps, however, she stood out as being exceptionally plugged in. If there was a scoop to be uncovered, the person to do so would likely be Chrystia.

"We would stake out prominent Ukrainian parliamentarians after meetings and interview them in a hallway. Chrystia would always be amongst our cluster, but then of course she would always have their phone numbers and she would have her own, private, one-on-one meetings," says Bostic.

James Meek, a British journalist and novelist, says Chrystia was always "switched on, socially." He remembers strolling up the street toward the Rada together one day, Chrystia wearing her trademark oversized fur hat. Suddenly, she broke off their conversation to point out a young man who was walking in the opposite direction. "She said, 'Oh, there's Ed Balls.' I'd never heard of Ed Balls; I thought, who the hell is Ed Balls, and how does she know him?"

At the time, Balls was a London-based *FT* journalist who often visited Ukraine to report on Soviet demilitarization and economic reform. (For a while, he and Chrystia were romantically linked, as were many among the young *FT* reporters who formed a close clique in the 1990s.) Ultimately, Balls would become a senior Labour party politician, serving as chancellor of the exchequer under British prime minister Gordon Brown.

"But this was a decade earlier, when he was just, you know, a dude," says Meek. "This wasn't even somebody from the United States or Canada. She was very aware of who was advising who about what, and what was going on. That's how I knew she was moving in a certain direction."

Her former colleagues remember Chrystia as pleasant and courteous, the kind of person who would share her notes with others who happened to arrive late at a press briefing. But most would describe their relationship with her as friendly rather than being friends.

At the end of a long day, Bostic remembers, the majority of the press corps would go and compare notes at the Hotel Dnipro on Khreshchatyk Street. "Chrystia did not hang out or socialize with us. She didn't need to," says Bostic. "I remember being in places like Baghdad—the *New York Times* or *Washington Post* people don't hang out with other journalists."

When a group of photographers are looking to capture a particular scene, Hill says, there's always one spot from where, when the action is breaking, the angle is better than anywhere else. "I think Chrystia was often, in a journalistic sense, that person who was standing in the right spot, watching events unfold."

CHRYSTIA'S KNACK FOR FINDING herself in the right spot is illustrated by an incident that occurred at the city's Hotel Ukraina. She would long be remembered with admiration by Ukrainians for the role she played. On May 30, 1991, for her first *FT* story, Chrystia wrote about the ongoing union treaty negotiations. In a sidebar story, she reported on Stepan Khmara, a white-haired, outspoken RUKH MP who strongly opposed the treaty. He had become a national hero, she wrote, following his arrest in November 1990 on trumped-up charges of assaulting a police officer.

On Wednesday, July 17, Khmara stood up and walked out of the courtroom where his trial was taking place, calling the whole thing a "political farce." Despite the judge's order that he be rearrested, Khmara returned to room 311 at the Hotel Ukraina, which he had been using as an office. Coal miners from Chervonohrad, his hometown, stationed themselves in the hotel room's entryway as bodyguards, and soon the third-floor hallway was lined with about forty older women from Kyiv and western Ukraine, in dresses and headscarves, sitting and holding anti-communist placards. "It was almost like a women's battalion," recalls Bohdan Krawchenko.

The press corps, knowing that an arrest was imminent, set up a rotation system, so that one correspondent would always be in the bedroom with Khmara, along with his family members, colleagues, and a group of Ukrainian journalists (including Chrystia's old friend from exchange, photographer Efrem Lukatsky).

Chrystia's shift was scheduled for Thursday afternoon. It passed without incident, and Marta Dyczok, a Canadian correspondent for *The Guardian*, arrived to take over. Before Chrystia could leave, however, they received word from a Ukrainian colleague that something was about to happen, so she decided to stay and wait.

For a while, all was quiet, Dyczok recalled in an interview for the Oral History of Independent Ukraine project. As the hours passed, the hotel room, crammed with twenty-odd people, became increasingly hot and stuffy. Eventually, the phone line to the room was cut off. From the balcony, they could see police cordoning off the street below. A fire truck arrived and a safety net was set up. ("I'm still not sure

why, I guess they expected us to jump or something," says Dyczok.)
A crowd of people began to gather outside. Krawchenko was among
them, periodically shouting up to Chrystia for updates.

Inside, the coal miners ripped the bathroom door off its hinges
and placed it by the room's entryway as an extra layer of protection.

Finally, at around eight thirty p.m., dozens of armed "black beret"
troops—members of an elite special forces squad known as OMON—
stormed the hotel. They forcibly removed the women from the hallway,
pulling them by their hair, and then broke down the hotel room door
with an axe, spraying the inside with teargas. Reaching the bedroom
door, the OMON "burst into the room with their helmets and with their
shields and their batons," Dyczok says. "And I happened to be standing
next to Khmara, so I saw the baton go whack on his head, him falling
to the floor, and him being dragged out."

Lukatsky remembers Chrystia remaining calm, scribbling frantically in a notebook, a wet handkerchief secured around her face.

For the next several hours, Chrystia, Dyczok, and their Ukrainian
colleagues were stuck in the bedroom with no access to water or a
bathroom, unable to report back to their editors. "The phone lines
were cut off, which meant I couldn't file the story. I also couldn't phone
anybody to tell them what was going on," says Dyczok. "I couldn't
call the embassy, I couldn't call a friend, nothing."

But Chrystia, Krawchenko says, "had to get the damn story out."
Standing on the balcony, she pitched him her notes, which he then sent
to the *FT* using the fax machine in the post office below his apartment.
Chrystia's report on Khmara's arrest made it into the Friday paper,
earlier than any of her competitors.

Finally, at around one in the morning, local police opened the
bedroom door, and Chrystia was able to take full measure of the
destruction. In the bathroom, the toilet was smashed in, and there was

blood all over the hotel carpet. Carnations were strewn everywhere; Khmara's daughter had been celebrating her eighteenth birthday.

For the two foreign journalists in the room, used to reporting on violence but not being subject to it personally, it was a sobering incident, one that underscored the stakes for Ukrainians fighting for their freedom. "That was one of the most scary experiences in my life," says Dyczok, "because it was the first time I felt what it is like to be physically threatened and unable to do anything about it."

According to Krawchenko, Chrystia was "somewhat shattered but held well together. She was amazed by the strength of the women who had stood guard in the room to defend Khmara."

For Ukrainians, Chrystia's involvement that night underscored her commitment to their cause. "We saw Chrystia as one of ours," says Andriy Shevchenko, a journalist who would go on to become a Ukrainian ambassador to Canada. "We saw her as a warrior—in some ways, a superhero—with magic powers far beyond her Canadian passport."

AS SHE HAD DURING her time on exchange, Chrystia never hid how invested she was in the outcome of Ukraine's push for independence. And she wasn't shy about encouraging Canada do all it could to tip the scales toward freedom.

In 1989, on a visit to the Soviet Union, Canadian prime minister Brian Mulroney had announced plans to open a consulate in Ukraine. It was a decision that ran contrary to the policy of US president George H. W. Bush, who supported Gorbachev's attempts to shore up unity among the republics, fearing the instability that would be wrought on the international system should the centre fail to hold. Many in Canada's foreign ministry shared Bush's view.

Two years later, Canada's diplomatic representative in Kyiv, Nestor Gayowsky, had yet to be accredited and was still working out of a makeshift office in a hotel room. In a July 8, 1991, op-ed in the *Toronto Star* that foreshadowed her views as foreign minister on government bureaucracy, Chrystia didn't sugar-coat her feelings about External Affairs dragging its feet. She was embarrassed and angered, she wrote, by Canada's "vacillating foreign policy towards Ukraine." Instead of a "major economic opportunity," Ottawa appeared to see Ukraine "merely as the homeland of a vocal and irritatingly assertive Canadian ethnic community." She continued:

> While senior Canadian politicians have forcefully supported a beefed-up Canadian presence here, the External Affairs bureaucracy has done its best to suffocate Canada's fledgling consular presence with red tape. The consulate-to-be is under-staffed, under-funded and ignored. I have been told by Ottawa insiders that several months ago External even tried to reverse its decision to send a Canadian representative here ...
>
> Thanks to Canada's tremendous individual and institutional contacts with Ukraine, this is one of the few places in the world where Canadian businessmen can bank on a warmer welcome than Germans, and where Canadian diplomats are more assiduously courted than Americans. One hundred years ago, Canada welcomed the first Ukrainian settlers. Today, Ukraine is ready to repay us for our generosity. But no one can find the Canadian consulate in Kiev to deliver the cheque.

Chrystia's sources were correct—External Affairs was suffering from budget cuts, and "Kyiv came up on the chopping block," Gayowsky later confirmed to Marta Dyczok. Department officials also worried that appearing to support an independent Ukraine would bolster the Quebec separatist movement at home. But in the end, the office was maintained—cancelling plans for representation in Kyiv, on the centenary celebration of Ukrainian settlement in Canada, was deemed to be "politically unacceptable."

For the most part, over the summer months of 1991, Chrystia stuck with straight reporting, filing articles for the *Washington Post* and *The Economist* in addition to the *FT*. John Lloyd, then the *FT*'s Moscow correspondent, would visit Kyiv and Chrystia would whisk him around, introducing him to her contacts. Though she was "something of a partisan," says Lloyd, who would become a close friend and mentor, "she didn't write propaganda or anything close to it. It was quite rigorously neutral." He soon found himself flying in less frequently: "There was no reason to go, because she was so good."

Many young reporters who land in a new place, Lloyd says, may well get people to speak with them; they can capture the facts and the framework of the political situation. But it's not everyone who possesses a "partly indefinable sense of the way in which the society is moving. She got that."

Daniel Franklin, *The Economist*'s Europe editor at the time, says Chrystia provided the magazine with valuable intel that challenged the experts' projections of the future of the Soviet Union. "I sometimes felt I was getting a more balanced view, perhaps, than even, say, George Bush in the White House was getting, because his view would have been filtered through Moscow," says Franklin. "Whereas it was very obvious, from what Chrystia was reporting, that this wasn't tenable, this wasn't going to hold, this was coming apart."

· · ·

"THAT EXPERT RELUCTANCE TO think that the dominant paradigm could change," Chrystia would later write in a personal essay called "My Ukraine" for the Brookings Institution, "reached its apogee for Soviet Ukraine in August, 1991."

After a two-day visit to Moscow, Bush travelled to Kyiv on August 1, where he addressed the Rada. In what *New York Times* columnist William Safire nicknamed Bush's "Chicken Kiev" speech, the US president said Americans would support those pursuing freedom, democracy, and economic liberty—within the context of a reformed Soviet Union. He warned against "suicide nationalism" and said the United States would maintain the "strongest possible relationship" with Gorbachev's government.

For Chrystia, this was a moment of cognitive dissonance. "Listening to Bush in the parliamentary press gallery, I felt he had misread the growing consensus in Ukraine. That became even clearer immediately afterward when I interviewed Ukrainian [MPs], all of whom expressed outrage and scorn at Bush for, as they saw it, taking Gorbachev's side," she wrote. "The magnitude of the West's miscalculation, and Gorbachev's, became clear less than a month later."

On August 19, a group of communist hardliners who opposed Gorbachev's reform agenda—as well as his union treaty, fearing it would give too much power to the republics—attempted to overthrow the Soviet leader, placing him under house arrest in his dacha on the Crimean Peninsula. After three days, the coup failed and Gorbachev regained control, but it was too late. The old order was crumbling, and the Communist party had been fatally weakened, triggering a "stampede to the exits" by the non-Russian republics.

On August 24, in a special session, Ukraine's Parliament voted 321–2 to declare independence, subject to a referendum in December. Outside, by the steps of the Rada, a crowd of thousands waved blue and yellow flags, cheering and singing the Ukrainian national anthem that had for so long been outlawed by the Soviets.

Susan Viets, a Canadian correspondent for *The Independent* who had been the very first Western journalist to report from Kyiv, remembers the electricity of the moment and what it meant for those witnessing it. "I was trained very rigorously to look for two sides of the story—that you weren't supposed to get involved, et cetera. I think for diaspora Ukrainians there may have been a slightly different dynamic at play," says Viets. "But that was just an extraordinarily emotional period. As someone with no links to Ukraine, I was filled with an incredible sense of joy at what happened. I think we all understood at that point that the referendum would just confirm what had occurred on the twenty-fourth of August."

The coup and the declaration of independence were the exception that proved the rule when it came to Chrystia's uncanny sense of timing. While Gorbachev was holed up in his dacha, she had been travelling and was stuck in England, unable to get back to Ukraine in time for Parliament's vote.

But by September, Chrystia had returned to Kyiv, where she would stay for the next two years, reporting on the birth of a nation. She had decided to defer her master's degree at Oxford and persuaded her department to allow her to postpone her start date. "It was thrilling and rewarding—and scary—to be doing a first draft of history," she told Little PINK Book. "I was writing stories that I knew, if I hadn't written them, no one else would have."

The day before the referendum, back in Edmonton, Ukrainian Canadians lit candles at Saint George church and whispered a special prayer for their motherland, the *Edmonton Journal* reported. Halyna Freeland, while not praying, was glued to her TV set, "sitting on pins and needles," as she told the paper.

On December 1, 1991, 92 percent of eligible Ukrainians cast their vote for independence, and Leonid Kravchuk became the country's first democratically elected president. In a move that must have made Chrystia proud, Canada was the first Western country to recognize Ukraine as an independent nation, despite misgivings from the US and Soviet leaders.

"Both George Herbert Walker Bush and Gorbachev asked me not to do it, for different reasons—Gorbachev told me that he thought it would hasten the breakup of the Soviet Union, which in his mind was a disaster, and Bush because there were other important events taking place in eastern and central Europe, and he wanted to focus on those rather than being required to deal with Ukraine as well," said Brian Mulroney in a 2022 interview.

"So I told both of them, no, thank you. I appreciate your point of view and your opinion, but Ukrainians have been fighting for independence for hundreds of years. And I've got to recognize them right away."

Being present at the disintegration of the Soviet Empire would profoundly shape Chrystia's thinking, solidifying two of her core beliefs: that people can change systems and that conventional wisdom can be wrong. "The experts, including the CIA and a president steeped in foreign policy, turned out to be wrong and my émigré grandparents, who arrived in [Canada] in middle age and spoke English with a heavy accent, turned out to be right," she would later write in remarks prepared for the 2011 O. D. Skelton Memorial Lecture. "That experience delivered a powerful personal, as well as intellectual, punch."

Natalka Freeland remembers her grandmother, Alexandra Chomiak, sobbing at the news of the referendum results, not only because the dream she and Michael had kept alive since fleeing Lviv in 1939 had become reality, but also because her granddaughter was one of the journalists reporting it to the world.

Growing up, the reigning line from the teachers in Chrystia and Natalka's Plast and Ukrainian classes was, "Well, when the revolution comes ..."

"This is why you do Plast. This is why you march around in the Alberta sunshine in uniform learning Morse code in Ukrainian, which is not a skill that has ever been useful to me," says Natalka. "But it was because we were going to somehow help. All of us thought this was bogus—we really thought that [the Soviet Union] was permanent, the way people think of the US now. For it actually to be changeable was so stunning, and to be able to be a little bit a part of it—it really was what our whole lives had led up to."

Later that month, Chrystia and her colleagues in the press corps travelled to Minsk, where Kravchuk met with Boris Yeltsin, Russia's first popularly elected president, and the leader of Belarus to sign an agreement formally dissolving the Soviet Union.

Gorbachev, whose reforms had led to an outcome he had never intended, resigned on Christmas Day. "I am leaving my post with apprehension, but also with hope, with faith in you, your wisdom and force of spirit," he told the nation in a televised address. "We are the heirs of a great civilization and its rebirth into a new, modern, and dignified life now depends on one and all." That evening, the red Soviet flag, with its hammer and sickle, was lowered from its perch above the Kremlin and replaced with the white, blue, and red flag of the Russian Federation.

Halyna, too, would heed the call of the revolution. In 1992, she accepted an invitation from Kravchuk to head the Ukrainian Legal Foundation, which aimed to create a modern legal system for the newly reborn country. Ukraine would face its share of challenges in the years ahead, as a nation that had no democratic institutions attempted to transform itself into a democracy. But for the time being, Ukrainians, including Halyna, looked to the future with hope and excitement.

"When I was 25, I was married with two small children and was practising law. I thought this is what I'll be doing for the rest of my life," she told the *Edmonton Journal*. "This is the opportunity of my life ... [Ukraine] won't have a democratic society until there are changes to the legal system."

CHRYSTIA CELEBRATED HER TWENTY-FIFTH birthday just before leaving Ukraine for Oxford in the summer of 1993, two years later than planned. She had witnessed first-hand what American political theorist Francis Fukuyama called the "end of history"—what appeared to be, for a time, the triumph of liberal democracy over authoritarianism—and had made the most of the fertile training grounds Kyiv provided for young journalists. As she had done at Harvard, she built mutually beneficial connections with powerful and influential individuals who considered her to be someone worth spending time with.

In a 2012 interview with *The Walrus*, Chrystia recalled going for a walk in one of Kyiv's parks with George Soros, who was looking at the possibility of funding pro-democracy groups and wanted to pick her brain. It turned out to be the beginning of a decades-long professional relationship. Michael Ignatieff, who would go on to serve as leader of the Liberal Party of Canada, met Chrystia while in Kyiv working on a television series on nationalism; he was impressed by her humour and her ability to make sense of Ukraine's chaotic new beginnings.

Chrystia's former colleagues in the Kyiv press corps vividly remember the force of her ambition. "I think that everyone could tell that Kyiv was too small for her," says James Hill. For Chrystia, Ukraine was an important first step on the way to something even bigger.

Alex Shprintsen, a journalist who had first met Chrystia while freelancing for the *Los Angeles Times* in Ukraine, notes a Russian expression that translates well into English: "ambitsii bez amunitsii," or "ambition without ammunition." "People say it about those who have big designs for themselves, but really there's nothing behind it. Chrystia was the opposite. She was a person who had ambition, with ammunition."

SEVEN

The Wild East

S T ANTONY'S COLLEGE, located in North Oxford on a pleasant, leafy street in a residential neighbourhood, was a logical choice for Chrystia. Since its founding by a French merchant in 1950, the college had attracted distinguished professors and a cosmopolitan mix of graduate students interested in politics, economics, philosophy, and international history. In a coincidence that would surely have tickled any KGB spymasters keeping tabs on Chrystia from afar, St Antony's had developed a reputation for being a college of spies, due to its alleged connections to the British intelligence community during the Cold War.

"If you had any interest in the former Soviet Union or Eastern bloc, you would probably want to be associated with St Antony's," says Brett House, another Canadian Rhodes Scholar whose time at the University of Oxford overlapped with Chrystia's. "It's one of the grown-up colleges. You go to St Antony's if you're not interested in the smells and bells, boys' choirs and pomp and circumstance, and old libraries of Oxford. You go there because you've got an agenda, you want to get it done, and you want to be around like-minded people."

Through her Rhodes Scholarship, Chrystia was meant to be awarded $24,000 a year for tuition and other costs for a minimum of two years. Eager to quickly return to journalism, she opted to complete a one-year master of studies degree in Slavonic studies from 1992 to 1993, supervised by Harold Shukman, a British scholar of Russian history.

Though she was "quite geekishly" engaged with her studies, as she later told alumni magazine *Oxford Today*, Chrystia's attention lay far to the east of Oxford's beautiful dreaming spires. She travelled frequently throughout her academic year, supported, fortunately, by professors who were open to students being involved in a "once-in-a-lifetime moment" in their area of study: the rebuilding of the former Soviet Union.

Toward the end of her first term, Chrystia flew to Russia to help the *Financial Times* with its coverage of the country's parliamentary elections, reporting on the rise of the far-right extremist (and unfittingly named) Liberal Democratic Party, whose xenophobic and bombastic leader promised to "make Russia rich again."

She also met and interviewed Boris Nemtsov, the thirty-four-year-old governor of the Nizhny Novgorod region and a candidate in the election. Nemtsov, who had a photograph of himself and former British prime minister Margaret Thatcher displayed on his desk alongside old issues of *The Economist*, would later become a high-profile opposition leader and a fierce critic of Vladimir Putin. (In 2015, he would be gunned down on a bridge over the Moscow River not far from the Kremlin, in the most prominent political assassination since Putin had come to power.)

Chrystia's freelance work impressed the *FT* leadership, particularly Andrew Gowers, who in 1994 was promoted from foreign editor to deputy editor. He insisted that the paper hire Chrystia, "not on some precarious, contract-free stringer basis" but as a proper member of staff. In March, she became the *FT*'s East Europe correspondent, reporting to Anthony Robinson, her old contact from Harvard, who, as the paper's East Europe editor, was by his own admission "totally overwhelmed" by the seemingly impossible task of trying to make sense of the disordered re-emergence of so many nation-states in the region.

Over the next few months, Chrystia juggled writing her master's thesis with travelling through eastern Europe, reporting on everything from the popularity of Harlequin romance novels in Poland to the intellectual conversion of Romanian president Ion Iliescu, a former communist, to the virtues of capitalism.

Almost three decades later, Robinson still remembers a "cracking" fly-on-the-wall account Chrystia wrote of joining a group of executives from Nordex, one of Russia's richest privately owned companies, as they flew from Vienna to Kyiv on board a private jet. She opened with a description of the in-flight antics of Moscow's nouveau riche, eyebrow-raising to both readers and the aircraft's blue-eyed, blond-haired flight attendant, who, under normal circumstances, would be an "ideal air-borne geisha."

"I was delighted to get an intimate look at the workings of one of Russia's richest privately owned companies—and not unhappy about doing it over smoked salmon and Parma ham in one of the huge leather seats of this private jet—but for Gabi, our stewardess, the encounter with Russia's new capitalists was clearly less of a thrill," Chrystia wrote.

"First, our group of Russian executives, decked in the finest Armani suits but flashing gold teeth in their broad Slavic faces, stormed the aircraft and wrestled for possession of the nicest pieces of fruit in the pretty trays Gabi had carefully assembled. Then came the pillow fight. Then Gabi ran out of both Stolichnaya and Absolut. But the last straw was probably when Gabi was dragged into a bear-hug—and

required to offer her immaculately made-up face for a birthday kiss—
by Grigory Loutchansky, president of Nordex and capo of our group
of Russian commodities traders."

A few months earlier, in an example of the new post-Soviet way of
doing business, the Nordex executives had helped Ukraine stave off an
energy crisis. Russia had cut off Ukraine's supply of fuel but, placated
by the prospect of hard currency, allowed Nordex to buy $120 million
worth of oil to provide to Ukraine. In Kyiv, Chrystia shadowed the
businessmen as they attempted to secure the sugar, wheat, and metals
Ukraine owed them in exchange, which involved three days' worth
of smoke-filled meetings and banquets with emotional, inebriated
toasting, obscene jokes, and countless bottles of vodka.

"To get that story you had to be beautiful, bilingual, and be treated
as 'one of the gang' by a bunch of rough, tough ex-[Soviets]—who
clearly could not have imagined that this petite, bright-eyed, invited
fellow passenger was taking notes, or committing to memory, their
very non-*FT* business ethics and behaviour," says Robinson. "It
revealed not only a great talent, but also more than a little ruthlessness."

In October, Chrystia reviewed *Comrade Criminal: Russia's New
Mafiya*, a book by former *Toronto Star* Moscow bureau chief Stephen
Handelman that laid out in depressing detail the criminal networks
and corruption that had taken hold in Russia since 1991. "Instead of
capitalism, Russia has turned to 'frenzied profiteering'; instead of fairly
applied laws and contracts, Russia has corrupt officials and business
deals enforced through the barrel of a gun; and instead of democracy,
Russia's future will be one of authoritarian rule or criminal chaos,"
Chrystia wrote, summarizing Handelman's observations.

While Chrystia lauded Handelman for convincingly describing
how Russia was being run, in her view his book had one serious short-
coming: it failed to identify both who, exactly, the shadowy figures

controlling Russia's criminalized political economy were, and how
they were making their money.

"Who is using Russia's thriving stock market to take control of
the country? What is happening in the oil and gas fields of Siberia?
And who is controlling Russia's buoyant metals trade?" she wrote.
"It may be that no western reporter can penetrate the labyrinth of
Russian capitalism and live to tell the tale. But Handelman's book is
like a vivid account of the wild capitalists of 19th century America
that fails to mention the Rockefellers."

Before long, Chrystia—thesis submitted and master's degree
obtained—would herself be the reporter to take up the challenge.

AS 1994 CAME TO a close, so did John Lloyd's four-year tenure as the
Financial Times' Moscow bureau chief. While covering the first years
of Boris Yeltsin's presidency, Lloyd had done an extraordinary job of
establishing the *FT* as the international media outlet that the Russian
government and business class took most seriously.

At the last minute, the person who had been hired to be his successor pulled out, and the paper was left scrambling to find someone else.
As he had earlier that year, Andrew Gowers went to bat for Chrystia,
as did Martin Wolf, an associate editor and the *FT*'s chief economics
commentator.

"Obviously, normally nobody of that age would get a job like that,
however talented," says Wolf, but the paper's top brass felt strongly
that the *FT* needed a Moscow bureau chief who was fluent in Russian.
"I talked to them and said I thought this was a gamble well worth
taking, and that she was likely to be very good."

"The *FT* does not have a very long history of advancing women,
shall we put it like that," adds Gowers. "I think there were some people

who thought, *Are you crazy? Are you serious?* But it happened, and it paid dividends many times over."

At twenty-six, Chrystia became the youngest-ever journalist to be appointed to run the *FT*'s Moscow operation. But before delving into the next chapter of her career, there was something she had to do.

As she recounts in the prologue of her first book, *Sale of the Century: Russia's Wild Ride from Communism to Capitalism,* just before Christmas, Chrystia trudged through the winter slush to Moscow's Kazan railway station, which was filled with hordes of Russian train travellers, beggars, and guards bearing machine guns. Soon she was approached by a youngish Russian man—a "baby broker," as her father Don referred to him—who presented her with a small, dark-haired, ten-year-old boy. Adik, as he was named, had been adopted by Chrystia's father and stepmother, and Chrystia had been charged with his safe passage to Peace River.

Chrystia was struck by how excited and envious Russians were at the good fortune that had been bestowed upon Adik. The *FT* bureau's researcher, Katya, half-jokingly asked if she, too, could be adopted by Chrystia's family; even the gruff border agent at Sheremetyevo International Airport smiled as she waved Chrystia and Adik through customs control. Though it was barely mid-morning, they headed to the airport bar, where Chrystia had a beer and a cigarette, imploring Adik to keep the latter between them—her family didn't know about the habit. He agreed, but advised her to stop smoking, noting that he himself had quit the previous year.

Adik had had a brutal childhood and, once in Canada, feigned an inability to understand the Russian language. Over the holidays, both Adik and Chrystia's grandmother Alexandra, who was intimately familiar with the ruinous effects of tsarism and communism, questioned Chrystia's plans to return to Russia in the new year.

But as ever, Chrystia was intent on reporting from the heart of the action. At the beginning of 1995, Chrystia landed in a Russia that was tumultuous and exciting, full of promise and confusion—a veritable wild, wild East. The Soviet Union had collapsed, but no one was quite certain whether the country's final destination would be free-market capitalism governed by the rule of law or something else altogether.

Chrystia remained cheerful and optimistic about Russia's "transition," as journalists then referred to it. Moscow had undergone an astounding transformation, she wrote in the *FT*: "Soviet shortage has been replaced by capitalist excess, as queues have given way to a proliferation of designer boutiques, $200 a head restaurants and streets choked with stretch-limos and dark Mercedes." Russians were suddenly bestowed with new liberties, able to speak more freely, cast a vote, or make a profit.

But many were also worse off than they had been in the twilight of communism. In 1991, Boris Yeltsin and his team of youthful reformers—much tutored by Harvard professor Jeffrey Sachs and other Western economists—had initiated radical economic measures that they hoped would shock Russia into capitalism. Four years later, the average Russian faced soaring inflation, mounting wage arrears, widespread unemployment, and a steep decline in living standards, rendering an ailing and frequently inebriated Yeltsin profoundly unpopular.

The state's authoritarian tendencies, too, had failed to be completely swept away with communism. In December 1994, in a misguided attempt to shore up his approval ratings, Yeltsin had ordered Russian troops into the tiny, semi-autonomous North Caucasus region of Chechnya, with the goal of quelling its growing independence movement. The president expected to be able to proclaim victory over the

Chechen separatists within forty-eight hours; what followed instead was a barbaric twenty-month war in which up to 100,000 people, many of them civilians, were killed.

Chrystia's optimism would be sorely tested over the next four years. "As I watched Russia's jostling progress, I came to fear that Russia was taking a wrong turn," she wrote in *Sale of the Century*. "By the time I left, I could imagine Adik's saying, 'I could have told you so.'"

IN 1995, THE *Financial Times'* Moscow bureau was located on the first floor of a foreigners' building on Kutuzovsky Prospekt, a broad avenue named for the general credited with driving Napoleon's army from Russia in 1812. The small team that Chrystia headed up included British journalist John Thornhill, a Russian office manager, and a Russian researcher. Their four-room office was constantly humming as news wires arrived via a fax machine or a noisy teleprinter, and the wall by Chrystia's desk was soon covered with paper listing potential stories she wanted to dig into and interviewees she planned to contact.

Chrystia—a diminutive woman in her mid-twenties—was initially seen by the rest of the Moscow press corps as talented but somewhat inexperienced, according to Thornhill. Chrystia herself acknowledged that the *FT*'s editor, Richard Lambert, and his deputy, Andrew Gowers, had taken a substantial risk in sending her to Russia. As it had in Kyiv, the gamble would soon pay off, as Chrystia established herself as force to be reckoned with.

"There's a certain kind of person who tends to be a bureau chief in Moscow. They often wear bow ties and have horn-rimmed spectacles. They tend to be quite old, a little bit on the pudgy side—they've been there, done that. It's a 'very serious job' for a 'very serious man,'" says former *Economist* correspondent Edward Lucas, tongue planted firmly in his cheek "And there was Chrystia, who was half their age, half their height, and just scooping them again and again and again. It was like watching a flyweight boxer beating a heavyweight. She wasn't very adversarial about it; she just happened to be better in the end."

For the majority of her time in Moscow, Chrystia lived in an *FT*-owned flat at 12/24 Sadovo Samotechnaya Ulitsa, just a few kilometres north of Red Square and Saint Basil's Cathedral. Affectionately known to foreigners as "Sad Sam," the pale yellow, nine-storey building overlooked the Garden Ring, a multi-lane concrete boulevard that encircled the centre of Moscow (as Chrystia's predecessor John Lloyd notes, something further from a garden could not be imagined).

Built by German prisoners of war in 1949, Sam Sad was old and creaky in parts, but its flats had high ceilings, big windows, and beautiful, worn-out wooden floors. It housed foreign diplomats, military attachés, and businessmen, as well as journalists from various media outlets, such as the *New York Times*, the *Daily Telegraph*, the *Christian Science Monitor*, and the British Broadcasting Corporation.

It also had a dedicated KGB "listeners' floor," remembers Quentin Peel, then the *FT*'s foreign editor, who lived in the *FT* flat in the late 1980s with his wife and five children during his posting to Moscow. "That's where various anonymous-looking gentlemen would go up and listen to tape recorders and things, which during our time would have been mostly filled with us potty training our little ones."

The *FT* flat itself was large by Moscow standards. It had three bedrooms, a kitchen, and a spacious living room with bookshelves, which Chrystia filled with rows and rows of well-organized notebooks.

Though she was friendly with the other correspondents in the building, sometimes popping over in the evenings for a glass of wine and a chat, her closest friends were outside the press corps. Those relationships with other expatriates were helpful in a place where life often had an Alice in Wonderland quality to it, and it was hard to know quite who to trust. Anything, it seemed, could be bought and sold for a price, Chrystia wrote in *Sale of the Century*. Even foreigners were unable to avoid living entirely without corruption; while driving her car around the city, she was frequently stopped for imaginary traffic violations and asked to pay bribes.

"You could go to work every day and have an 'Oh my God, did that just happen in Moscow?' moment," says Maria Kozloski, an American investment officer who, with her husband, Lance Crist, worked for the International Finance Corporation, an affiliate of the World Bank. They lived a couple of blocks away from Chrystia.

"She's a real firecracker of a personality, great fun to socialize with and hang out with," says Crist. "We were all in our late twenties and early thirties—it's a formative part of anybody's life, wherever you are at that time. But also, [in Russia] there was this unbelievable historic moment. There were no rules. It was just a mind-blowing experience that we all still talk about today."

Moscow's lively social scene provided endless options for entertainment, ranging from standard expat activities (viewing a ballet performance at the Bolshoi Theatre, visiting Russian friends' dachas on the weekend, or attending barbeques at various Western embassies, for example) to the more far-out ("We did a lot of bizarre things; I remember I was a judge at an identical twin contest," says Wendy Sloane, an American correspondent).

But for Chrystia, the experience wasn't predominantly about "the adventure," says Julie Mindlin, another close friend. "She wanted to tell the stories; she wanted to get to the bottom of whatever this was."

In 1981, at the age of ten, Mindlin had left Russia with her family and settled in Canada. Years later, as part of her master's degree at the University of Toronto, Mindlin returned to Russia in search of work experience. The university had given her a list of fellow Canadians in Moscow, including Chrystia. "I rang up every single one of them—a lot of people weren't interested and didn't have any time for me. Chrystia responded right away, and we really hit it off."

After a stint working in the *FT* bureau, Mindlin completed her degree in Toronto and returned to Moscow in 1996, staying with Chrystia until she found a job, through John Thornhill's wife, doing direct sales at a Swedish cosmetics company. "I think some people would describe her as quite intense, and [she] may not have been easy to work with all the time because of that drive ... But for me, I felt an affinity with that," says Mindlin.

Working across multiple time zones, Chrystia's friends remember their weekdays as busy and demanding, with little time to relax. In the evenings, they would check in to see who was free to eat dinner together in one of their apartments or possibly a restaurant. Eating out was expensive, but they would often visit Il Pomodoro, a casual Italian restaurant whose owners imported many of their ingredients from home. Chrystia and Mindlin would go at least once a week and, over pasta and red wine, "just complain to each other about whatever was going on in crazy Russia."

Occasionally, they would go to see a movie together. Western blockbusters weren't always shown in Russian theatres; instead, some of the bigger hotels would play them on screens. But of course, in Moscow even this wasn't entirely straightforward. "If you went by yourself and you were a girl, they wouldn't let you in, because they thought you were a prostitute," says Mindlin. One time, she and Chrystia, dressed down so as to dispel any illusions, went to watch *Up Close & Personal*, a 1996 film starring Robert Redford as a veteran news director and Michelle Pfeiffer as the aspiring young journalist he takes under his wing. After working in different cities, the two eventually marry, and the future looks bright until (spoiler alert) Redford's character is killed covering a story in Panama.

The movie got mixed reviews—Roger Ebert called it "contrived and corny"—and Mindlin thought it was terrible ("Why didn't he just leave?" she asks). But when she looked over, Chrystia was in tears, moved by the portrayal of journalistic virtue and duty. "She was romantic about what journalism could do."

Chrystia was also familiar with the challenges of dating a partner who was based in another place. After she started with the *Financial Times*, a mutual friend had offered to set her up with fellow *FT* journalist Graham Bowley, a Brit who had worked briefly for the UK Treasury and then at a bank in London after graduating from the University of Oxford with a degree in economics. Friends describe him as a talented reporter and writer, and an overall lovely person—genial and modest, with a quiet sense of humour. According to John Lloyd, he is "a man of great patience, as well as intelligence."

Graham, as he would later recount at their wedding, was not particularly optimistic about the potential union. The friend had mentioned that Chrystia was a Rhodes Scholar and had attended Harvard, and Graham didn't think she'd be his type. He may have gone to Oxford, but he had also grown up on a farm in Leicestershire, in the East Midlands, where his father had worked the land all of his years, as Graham's grandfather had before him.

When they actually met, to Graham's surprise, Chrystia introduced herself as a farmer's daughter, which changed everything; they quickly built a connection based on that shared sense of identity.

With Graham based first in London and then Frankfurt, the long-distance relationship wasn't easy, says Mindlin. Graham worried about Chrystia, who "wasn't exactly in the safest place in the world, doing crazy things." Despite the kilometres, they made it work, visiting each other when they could. Over one Christmas break, Chrystia introduced Graham to the frozen "white desert" that was Peace River in the winter. Moscow, she wrote in an *FT* article about their trip, was "relatively balmy" by comparison.

Graham also met Helen Freeland, who, as she had done with the bagpipers at Halyna and Don's wedding, couldn't resist having a bit of fun. "When I started visiting my wife's Scottish-Canadian relatives in the wilderness of northern Canada, her gritty Glaswegian grandmother welcomed the English guest by raising a Scottish flag on a pole above the Peace River, humming 'Loch Lomond' and whispering under her breath, 'Not to forget Bannockburn,' the decisive battle in which the Scots drove out the English in 1314," Graham would later write. "In return, I whistled 'God Save the Queen,' and we smiled. It was a good-natured family squabble that never got out of hand."

Mindlin remembers meeting Graham in Moscow and feeling like it was clear he "absolutely respected and supported" Chrystia: "There was no competition ... Sometimes in relationships, even very strong successful women all of a sudden in the presence of their partner behave differently. But there was none of that, she was exactly the same. They just balanced each other."

TO BETTER UNDERSTAND WHAT was happening in Russia, Chrystia thought it was important to get out of Moscow. Occasionally, while travelling to far-flung provinces where it would be useful to have an extra set of eyes and ears, she would buddy up with *Washington Post* bureau chief David Hoffman, whom she had met at St Antony's while he was completing a crash language course in Russian. Chrystia would pick him up and they'd head to the airport to catch their Aeroflot flight, she in sneakers, he holding a thick file of research. Given that

Chrystia spoke better Russian, she played the part of translator. "We just clicked," says Hoffman. "I really felt like I was in the hands of somebody I admired and who was really good."

In the spring of 1997, Chrystia and Hoffman flew to Krasnouralsk, a town more than 1,500 kilometres east of Moscow. The first thing they did was make an obligatory visit to the mayor, who mistakenly thought they were a delegation coming from the United States. At city hall, a literal red carpet had been rolled out, and crystal glasses had been set up in a banquet room. "That was the real nature of what being a correspondent was at that time," says Hoffman. "If you went to the far provinces of Russia, you were meeting people who had never met Westerners before."

On another trip, they witnessed the desperate economic circumstances of Russian industrial workers while visiting a factory in the Ural Mountains that made metal pipes, once a signature export of the region. Plagued by aging technology and mounting debt, production was down significantly, and the factory manager told them workers were being paid in pickles.

For Chrystia and Hoffman, it was an eye-opening example of how capitalism was working—or not working—in post-Soviet Russia. "It was bizarre," says Hoffman. "It helped form some of my beliefs that this transition wasn't going to be very smooth. This was the learning experience of those years."

Another factor that contributed to this understanding was the war in Chechnya. In August 1996, Chechen separatists recaptured Grozny, the Chechen capital, and Russia's national security chief announced a ceasefire. For Hoffman, the conflict was the darkest part of his Moscow experience, and he was reluctant to report on it from the ground.

"I hated that war. I thought it was completely unnecessary. It was very brutal—reporters were killed as quickly as anybody else," he says, It was Chrystia who convinced him that they needed to go cover the war in person, rather than writing about it from a more comfortable perch in Moscow. "I remember us having a very tense discussion in which I basically said, 'I don't want to do this,' and she said, 'We must do this.'"

In Grozny, they found a ravaged, desolate capital. The city had no food, water, or electricity, and thousands of homes had been destroyed in the fighting. Tension hung in the air; previous truces between the Russian government and Chechen separatists had failed, and Hoffman feared that Russian troops could launch an offensive at any minute and "wipe out everyone in front of them." They toured an abandoned, ghostly oil refinery where Hoffman worried sharpshooters could be hiding in dark corners. Later, they passed a cattle farm where the bodies of dead cows lay strewn across a field.

"I was scared out of my wits. It was the worst, scariest war coverage I've ever been in," Hoffman says. "Chrystia really drove me ... and to her great credit, we got through it."

Chrystia and Hoffman also visited the village of Samashki, which had suffered one of the most vicious assaults of the conflict when, as Chrystia wrote, "Russian soldiers, many of them alleged to be drugged or drunk, unleashed a frenzied massacre on the village, killing and maiming hundreds of civilians." In her reporting, she lauded the bravery of the Chechen fighters who, despite being "outnumbered, outfinanced and outgunned," had resisted Russian rule—in an echo, she must have noted, of the Ukrainian struggle to break free from Soviet control.

DESPITE RUSSIA'S AUTHORITARIAN TENDENCIES and economic blunders, Chrystia would come to believe that what really sealed the fate of its rocky transition out of communism was what she called Russian capitalism's "original sin." As part of the Yeltsin government's mass privatization program of the early and mid-1990s, the state's most valuable assets, including some of the country's largest oil and gas companies, were sold off for a fraction of their real value—the "sale of the century"—enriching a tiny group of men who would come to wield outsized control over the future of Russia.

These seven original Russian "oligarchs"—Boris Berezovsky, Mikhail Khodorkovsky, Vladimir Potanin, Vladimir Gusinsky, Mikhail Fridman, Pyotr Aven, and Aleksandr Smolensky—came from varied backgrounds but all shared a hustling, entrepreneurial spirit. In the dying days of the Soviet Union, they built their fortunes, selling everything from computers to windows to copper bracelets. By the time Chrystia arrived in Moscow, they had become the country's top financiers, sporting $100,000 watches, travelling in Western luxury cars, and frequenting the city's most exclusive nightclubs.

In the mid-1990s, the oligarchs were eager to raise their profile in order to be able to pursue funding from Western banks and investors. They saw the *Financial Times*, with its wide readership and respected reputation, as a direct line to the West. This was convenient for Chrystia, who was determined to answer the questions that had stymied the *Toronto Star*'s Stephen Handelman and other reporters: Who was really pulling the levers of Russian power? What made them so successful? And how were their links to government corrupting Russia's budding capitalism?

Chrystia would eventually become known as the one Western journalist who actually had the oligarchs' direct phone numbers; everyone else had numbers that belonged to their secretaries or bodyguards. The oligarchs "clearly liked talking with her," says John Thornhill. "She charmed them with her excellent Ukrainian-accented Russian and they loved to boast about how important they all were without quite realizing—I think—that she was memorizing every detail."

Though she complained that the dress code of Russian women—"teetering stilettos, short skirts and carefully applied maquillage at all times"—was "laborious," it was one she adopted for herself when dealing with Russia's most powerful men.

"She was a wonderful interviewer. She would quite famously say that she put on her shortest skirt when she interviewed them. That's as far as it went," says John Lloyd. "She can be quite tough, but she can also be very charming ... leading people to tell her more than [they] would have done to, say, a male interviewer or an unsympathetic woman interviewer. Here was this young woman just desperate to know more and more about how clever you were."

Her access clearly didn't rest on charm alone. Maria Kozloski and Lance Crist remember how thoroughly Chrystia would prepare for her meetings with the oligarchs, mining her contacts and social circle for details to back up her suspicions and readying different angles to take depending on which way the conversation went. They found themselves wishing they could be a fly on the wall for her interviews.

"She would get in there, and they couldn't hide behind the language difference, they couldn't hide behind her ignorance—because she knew the drill. She knew everything. She was unassuming, and she caught them off guard," says Crist.

"These oligarchs, for all that they've done, a lot of them were super smart. It's almost like she was an intellectual counterpart that they were trying to compete with," adds Kozloski.

One of Chrystia's biggest scoops involved a pact between the oligarchs and Boris Yeltsin, forged on the ski slopes of Davos, Switzerland, at the World Economic Forum, the exclusive annual gathering of world leaders, CEOs, and billionaires. At the beginning of 1996, with Yeltsin's approval ratings in the single digits, it looked increasingly likely that the president's Communist party challenger could emerge victorious in the election scheduled for that summer.

This was an outcome that the oligarchs wanted to avoid at any cost. On the sidelines of the February Davos conference, they secretly agreed to use their fortunes—and their monopoly over Russia's news media—to roll back the communist threat. They also decided that Anatoly Chubais, who had helped mastermind the government's economic reforms, was the best person to run their campaign.

On July 3, 1996, in a seemingly impossible comeback, Boris Yeltsin was elected to a second term as Russia's president. While the Russian press had reported on how the oligarchs had been involved in Yeltsin's re-election campaign, the details of the "Davos pact"—including the fact that there was a financial side to the alliance—remained mostly unknown months after Yeltsin's win.

Chrystia caught wind of these details at an October dinner party she hosted at Sad Sam in honour of Andrew Gowers, who was visiting Moscow. One of her guests was Mikhail Zadornov, chairman of the Russian Parliament's budget committee, who stunned everyone by sharing that the oligarchs had hired Chubais and paid him $3 million.

A few days later, Chrystia met Boris Berezovsky in the reception room of his downtown club, which was owned by Logovaz, his car dealership. Berezovsky confirmed for the first time that the seven oligarchs had indeed paid $3 million to finance Yeltsin's re-election. With the help of Gowers and Thornhill, Chrystia interviewed the rest of the group and pieced the whole story together in a feature for the *FT*.

"It was her subtle wiles that made them feel comfortable talking about it," says Gowers. "She got close to these people, but not so close as to be unseemly."

The oligarchs were "hard men," says Peel, the paper's foreign editor. "[There was] absolutely no question they all had a bit of blood under their fingernails." But they also shared a certain inexperience around dealing with Western media, as Peel saw first-hand on a visit to Moscow in the fall of 1997.

In August, Aleksandr Minkin, one of Russia's top investigative journalists, had published a story that revealed that Alfred Kokh, the minister who had overseen the selling off of Russian state assets to the oligarchs, had been paid a $100,000 advance by a shadowy Swiss book-keeping firm to write a book about Russian privatization. As Chrystia began to dig into the story, she learned that the Swiss firm had several suspiciously close connections to Oneximbank, which was owned by Vladimir Potanin.

When Peel arrived in Moscow, Chrystia told him that she had gathered evidence that Potanin was "basically paying off" Kokh, and that she had arranged for them to meet Potanin, who also happened to own *Izvestia*, a Russian newspaper that was involved in a joint venture with the *FT* at the time, for an interview.

"She said, look, I want to pin him down on this, so when we go along, I want you to be the nice, diplomatic, polite blow-in from London who's going to be a little bit wide-eyed and say, 'Oh wow Mr. Potanin, tell me all about the things you're good at,'" says Peel. "And then about two-thirds of the way through the interview, I'm going to come in and say, 'I want to ask you specifically about this relationship, and I've got this evidence,' and so on."

The interview started off as planned, "nice and friendly and lovey-dovey, cups of coffee and whatever." As soon as Chrystia brought up Potanin's friendship with Kokh, the atmosphere cooled dramatically.

"Things get pretty frosty, she pursues it—but the naïveté of Potanin was that he never stopped talking," says Peel. "He kept saying, you know, 'Well, what's wrong that we go on holiday together?'"

Notebooks full of quotations, Chrystia and Peel headed back to the Sad Sam flat, "giggling" to themselves that Potanin had "obviously been really quite hostile and angry and uncomfortable but didn't stop talking."

Before they could even put a word to print, however, they received a phone call from David Bell, the chairman of the *FT*. Bell had himself received a call from Potanin's deputy giving him a heads-up that Chrystia was working on the story, in case Bell wanted to intervene, given the "importance" of Potanin and their joint venture. Bell told the man he had no intention of talking to Chrystia, and that he would read what she had written when it came out in the paper.

"The call prompted me immediately to start to bring the partnership to an end," says Bell, adding that the resulting story "shows her at her best. It is clear, forensic, balanced, and still packs a punch."

WHILE CHRYSTIA WOULD COME to know the oligarchs well—deciding early on in her tenure as bureau chief that she wanted to write a book about their role in Russia's transition—her relationship with them wasn't necessarily an easy one. Russia in the mid-1990s was still very much a man's world, and she was frequently dismissed and condescended to.

"She was treated by an awful lot of Russians, because of the Ukrainian connection, with pretty good contempt. She really did have to use her elbows," says Peel, adding that they would patronizingly call her a "little Russian." "And she would bristle. She had a certain battle to fight, and the fact that she felt quite passionate about Ukraine probably in many ways helped her. It put a bit of iron in her soul, and made her quite tough."

And while she was quick to use feminine charm, she was frustrated to find herself subject to "a barrage of sexual innuendo"—an unfortunate but common annoyance in a city where the classified ads openly sought out secretaries "without sexual complexes" and financiers frequently went on family holidays surrounded by what Chrystia called a "harem of mistresses."

American journalist Andrew Meier, who worked for *TIME* magazine, remembers her brushing off a sexist charge from Boris Nemtsov, then a deputy prime minister under Yeltsin, who intimated to Meier over lunch that she must be getting her information in untoward ways.

"She just laughed," says Meier. "She would always just kick off her heels and sit on her bare feet. One of the oligarchs did tell me that she did that and he thought she was coming on to him—but that's just her thing. She's very unpretentious, a little bit un-self-aware."

Even within the press corps, Chrystia had to contend with colleagues—mostly men—who were threatened by her confidence and intensity. "They saw her drive and ambition as a sign of competition," says Mindlin. "I don't necessarily think that was the case, although I do think that if she put her mind to [something], she would get it, and there may be bodies left behind. Not in a bad way—not like a 'stab them in the back' kind of way—but simply because she's better or willing to do more."

In Moscow's relatively small expat community, Mindlin says, these successes were very visible, irking some who might have felt they had "done their time, been there longer, should have been promoted and weren't."

She continues, "The way to battle that is just to be better than everybody else. This aura of confidence that she would ooze—I think that was part of the armour you had to put on, because you were judged every step of the way."

. . .

IN DECEMBER 1997, the people of Moscow were subject to the coldest winter temperatures on record. While the deep-freeze brought "skies of Fabergé-egg blue and the brightest sun this normally dingy city has seen all year," Chrystia wrote, Russia's economic outlook remained dim. By the summer of 1998, as Chrystia's time as Moscow bureau chief came to a close, Russia was lurching toward a financial crisis that would result in the government defaulting on its debts and devaluating the ruble. The impact was catastrophic, Chrystia wrote; hundreds of thousands of Russian workers lost their jobs, and long queues and bare shelves, bleak staples of Soviet times, returned.

Russians who had let themselves believe in the Kremlin's vision of a prosperous future under capitalism felt betrayed by the president, and Yeltsin knew his government couldn't last much longer. In an attempt to ensure his survival, he hired and fired several prime ministers over the next year. Finally, in August 1999, he appointed Vladimir Putin, a virtually unknown former KGB agent who had operated in East Germany, to the position. (Chrystia, by then stationed in the *FT*'s London newsroom, was asked by Richard Lambert during a morning meeting: "Do I really need to remember this one's name?") That fall, Russia renewed its deadly campaign against Chechen fighters, determined to reverse earlier losses. Putin's popularity soared.

On December 31, Yeltsin stepped down, making Putin the acting president. The oligarchs lined up to back the spy-turned-politician, and in March 2000, Putin was elected president. Chrystia called him the "ultimate political cypher," writing that, as with Yeltsin in the 1996 elections, "the young reformers and Western businessmen were pinning their dreams on a strongman of ambivalent or simply unknown ideological inclinations; again, they were prepared to forgive him the callous abuse of human rights in Chechnya; and again, they believed that—after all the votes had been securely counted— he would somehow prove able to shake himself free of the vested economic interests that had sponsored his rise to power. They were wrong about Yeltsin—all we can do is cross our fingers they are not equally as mistaken about his heir."

She continued:

> The biggest danger is that Putin, like his predecessor, is a man driven by power, not by ideology. Yeltsin's overriding political objective was to remain in command; Putin's is almost certain to be exactly the same, for the simple reason that he was handpicked by the Family, as Yeltsin's entourage came to be known, for precisely that quality. Yeltsin did not choose Putin out of friendship, or shared moral beliefs. He didn't pick the lackluster East German sleuth for his intellect, his public profile, or his parliamentary finesse. Putin was selected for one quality alone: Yeltsin and his clan judged him to be the man most able to hang on to political power, and in so doing to protect the interests of the Yeltsin family, which feared poverty and prosecution the minute its patriarch left the Kremlin.

Likewise, for Chrystia, the verdict was still out on Russia's flawed capitalist revolution. Though it had been corrupted by a weak, greedy government unable to uphold its own ineffective laws, the experiment, in her view, wasn't a complete failure. She wrote:

> At the beginning of the 1990s, the question was communism or capitalism. At the end of the decade, the question was what sort of capitalism Russia would have: an open, liberal system, with clear rules of the game and free entry to new competitors, or a corrupt,

monopolistic capitalism, in which a few powerful players, with close connections to the government, dominate the economy? So far, the answer is not very encouraging. But compared to the other choices Russians have faced over the past century—tsarism or communism? Stalin or Hitler?—the question itself is something of an accomplishment.

Still, Chrystia's time as bureau chief was another experience, along with growing up in a proud Ukrainian Canadian household and her time reporting on Ukraine's push for independence, that shored up her steadfast belief in democracy—a system and a way of life that as a journalist and, later, as a politician, she would fight for and defend unwaveringly.

In a prescient warning, she noted that Russia's age-old "imperial mission, its instinct to subdue its neighbors," seemed to be making something of a comeback. With Russia's second invasion of Chechnya, it looked as if "aggressive nationalism might again become the country's collective mission, the perfect balm for the battered national ego."

She concluded, "For Russia's sake, and for our own, I hope not, as I hope that Chechnya will turn out to be the last gasp of a dying messianic agenda rather than the first breath of a new one. If Russia is lucky, and if Russia is wise, now will be the moment when it abandons its messianic projects altogether. It would be a big break, in some ways a bigger one than the shift from communism to capitalism, but it is a necessary one."

EIGHT

The Newspaper Wars

I N THE FALL OF 1998, after moving from Russia to England, Chrystia took refuge at the Bowley family's peaceful farm in Leicestershire for a few weeks, working on the manuscript for *Sale of the Century*. Though she would later wish she had taken a year off to complete the book, Chrystia didn't want to jeopardize her new position with the *Financial Times*, and so she soon arrived at the paper's headquarters, located at One Southwark Bridge along the banks of the River Thames in London, ready to take on the role of UK news editor. Not for the first time, she would be greeted with skepticism, in this case from colleagues who questioned her lack of background in British news.

At the age of thirty, Chrystia oversaw a staff of about seventy editors and reporters, while being managed herself by news editor Lionel Barber, who had just been promoted after spending more than a decade working as a correspondent for the paper in Washington and Brussels. The two would have a difficult and fraught relationship over the years.

"I was immediately thrown into working with her, and many people said, 'Why the hell has she got this job, because what does she know about the UK?'" says Barber. "The *FT* does that to people who are very smart and are going to go places; they'll put them in jobs that are quite challenging. My view, working with her, was, yes, she didn't know all the detail of what was going on in Britain at all, but she had a fresh perspective, and she got journalists to do interesting things."

As Canada's finance minister during the COVID pandemic, Chrystia would draw on lessons learned during her time as UK news editor. "I remember [a colleague who had previously held the position] saying to me, 'You're an editor now, and you're going to have to make a hundred decisions a day, and hopefully more of them will be right than will be wrong. But the important thing is not to be paralyzed by feeling you need to be perfect. The important thing is to make the decisions, because otherwise the paper cannot be published at the end of the day,'" she told Bloomberg in 2021. "You just had to take the information that was coming at you, absorb it, analyze it as well as you could, and then make a decision on which story was in, which story was out, which quote was in, which one was out, and not be too scared of making the wrong decision."

In 1999, along with one hundred daily editorial decisions, Chrystia found herself with not one but two weddings to organize. In her apartment in Moscow, Graham had dropped to one knee and asked her to marry him. "After our first raptures," Graham would later write, "she leaned forward and added one condition. 'Yes, but if we have children, they will have to speak Ukrainian.' She looked quite severe."

The first celebration was held on the grounds of the Bowleys' farm—a "very lovely traditional British wedding with some distinctly Ukrainian touches," remembers John Thornhill. "Lots of hay bales, champagne, and emotional speeches."

The second took place at the University of Alberta's Faculty Club in Edmonton on July 4. Ahead of the celebration, Graham and his parents visited Peace River, where Graham's father, David, marvelled at the size of the local dual-wheel pickup trucks.

The wedding in Edmonton, attended by guests from Canada, the United Kingdom, and the United States, also featured a great mix of traditions, including, of course, Helen Freeland's bagpipers. Halyna had sourced the crowns, rings, and icons traditionally used in Ukrainian weddings in Kyiv. Alison Franklin, Chrystia's Harvard roommate, recalls that guests were festively dressed, with woven Ukrainian shirts and elaborate British fascinators.

"There was an icon bearer—maybe two—at their wedding," says Franklin. "I remember this because one of Chrystia's other freshman roommates was obsessed with the guidance from the priest to help the icon bearer not pass out. We were told that icon bearers do fall occasionally because it's a long service and a difficult position to maintain while also ensuring healthy blood flow."

According to Chrystia's friends, Graham would prove to be a wise choice—an important part of the formula that has allowed Chrystia to achieve the goal she laid out to Franklin at Harvard: maintaining a fulfilling, high-profile professional career while raising multiple children. As a partner, Graham would provide quiet, stable support, content to make changes in his own career to accommodate Chrystia's ambitions.

One such opportunity would present itself the year they got married, and soon they would leave London for a new chapter in Canada.

THE LONDON MEDIA SCENE, where Chrystia got her earliest experience in management, is known for its tendency to be fiercely competitive. But across the Atlantic, in Toronto, Canada's largest urban centre, a newspaper war of Fleet Street proportions was unfolding.

On October 27, 1998, with great fanfare, media baron Conrad Black had launched his new conservative-leaning broadsheet, the *National Post*. Colourful and splashy, with a predilection for tabloid-style commentary and racy photos of supermodels, it was ready to give the staid, stuffy *Globe and Mail* a run for its money.

With four major dailies—the *Post*, the *Globe*, the *Toronto Star*, and the *Toronto Sun*—Toronto was suddenly the most competitive newspaper market in North America. At the end of the 1990s, the papers were flush with resources and embarked on frenzied hiring sprees. Douglas Goold, a former editor of the *Globe*'s Report on Business section, remembers journalists sneaking into the back and side doors of the *Globe*'s downtown headquarters at 444 Front Street West: "Sometimes they would run into each other—you know, two people from the *Star* who didn't know they were both looking for jobs—and say, 'What are you doing here?' 'No, what are *you* doing here?'"

Before the *Post*'s launch, the *Globe* "was in a fairly comfortable place" with a wide audience, says Geoff Beattie, at the time consigliere to the paper's owners, the Thomsons, Canada's wealthiest family. "It didn't have a lot of competitive pressure against it, so it did well. But it wasn't on the forefront of what it needed to do digitally."

David Walmsley, who had left Black's *Daily Telegraph* in London to be an editor at the *Post* (and who would, years later, go on to become the *Globe*'s editor-in-chief), was more scathing in his assessment. "When I arrived from London, which is the greatest newspaper city in the world, I saw the *Globe and Mail* and thought every Canadian had died and gone to hell," he told the *Ottawa Citizen*'s Chris Cobb for his 2004 book about the newspaper war, *Ego and Ink*. "It was an absolute disgrace ... It was the most boring load of nonsense I had ever read. This was a paper that needed a very serious kick up the arse."

The Thomsons recognized that they could be outmanoeuvred if they didn't up their game—and this was a battle they were simply not prepared to lose. As the *Post* launched, the family hired Phillip Crawley, a seasoned newspaperman from Newcastle, England, with a tough-as-nails reputation, to lead the charge. While Crawley had a lot of respect for William Thorsell, the thoughtful, intellectual Albertan who had served as the *Globe*'s editor-in-chief for nearly a decade, he felt the paper needed a leader who could shake up its culture and give it a more competitive news edge.

Crawley enlisted the services of executive recruiting firm Spencer Stuart, whose headhunters focused their search in the United Kingdom, due to the size of its newspaper market and its strong pool of editorial talent. After meeting with various candidates in London, Crawley hired Richard Addis, the flamboyant former editor of the *Daily Express* tabloid, who had experience publishing flashier, edgier content—but who knew next to nothing about Canada.

Among the candidates flagged by Spencer Stuart was Chrystia, whom Crawley interviewed in London. With her background as *FT* bureau chief in Moscow, her business reporting chops, her education, and her Canadian roots, she impressed both Crawley and the Thomson family. "Here was this exceptional talent with incredible media experience that was working for one of the marquee business newspapers in the world," says Beattie, noting that the *FT* was owned by Pearson, a major competitor. "The decision very much was made as, let's get Chrystia into the Thomson Corporation and find a big role for her."

The headhunters suggested to Addis that he might consider Chrystia as a potential number two. After sharing a meal together, Addis offered her the role of deputy editor. "I didn't know her, but I liked her, and she had a tremendous drive and that Fleet Street ruthlessness that I liked," Addis told Cobb. "I decided very quickly that we could change things more quickly together than I could on my own."

Though she had only been the *FT*'s UK news editor for a few months, Chrystia viewed this as an exciting opportunity to operate at a higher level—and it didn't hurt that the position would be based in her home country.

"I always wanted to come back to Canada," she said at the time. "[The *Globe* is] Canada's national newspaper, and in a country like Canada which is so disparate and so spread out, the few national institutions that we have really do shape our country ... It's a privilege to be given a chance to participate in that."

CHRYSTIA AND GRAHAM RENTED a three-bedroom red-brick house on Tranby Avenue, a narrow, tree-lined street in Toronto's Annex neighbourhood. They didn't own a car, so most days, Chrystia would ride her bicycle twenty minutes south to the *Globe*'s Front Street office.

When Chrystia took up her post as the paper's deputy editor in the fall of 1999, she once again faced an uphill battle, as well as charges that she and Addis were outsiders being parachuted into the newsroom from abroad.

In the *Star*, Richard Gwyn wrote that the *Globe* had "emasculated itself" by appointing a Brit—whose only experience of Canada thus far had been a ski trip to Whistler—as editor, a sentiment shared by other columnists. Chrystia, born and raised in Canada, was nevertheless not an acceptable choice for deputy, wrote Anthony Wilson-Smith in *Maclean's*: "She's the sort of Canadian the New Globe likes: she left Canada after high school, went to university in England and the United States and has never worked here."

Inside 444 Front Street, too, there was reticence about the new management team. "Richard was an eccentric of the first order, and

Chrystia had no idea how to run much of anything," says one former *Globe* employee.

From the staff's point of view, reviews of her performance as a manager would be mixed. As in previous positions, she rubbed some colleagues the wrong way, and they considered her manner to be abrupt or even arrogant.

"I felt she was totally phony when she talked—I just got this 'I can't trust you' vibe," says Jan Wong, a former *Globe* columnist. "She was determined to rise, and so she managed upwards. As an underling, I felt nervous around her ... The best editors have their reporters' interests at heart, and I never felt that with her."

In *Frank*, the gossipy satirical Ottawa magazine, anonymous reports cruelly poked fun at Chrystia's size and youth, portraying her as a bimbo and referring to her as "Chrystia 'Britney' Freeland," after the pop star Britney Spears. Even the tenor of her voice was considered to be fair game; one report claimed she sounded like a "chipmunk on helium."

While the *Frank* coverage bothered Chrystia at first, she told Cobb she had been subjected to much worse from the Soviet press in the 1980s and was able to tune it out.

There were also some on staff who admired her, including Cathrin Bradbury, a managing editor at the paper. She remembers her first impression of Chrystia was one of tremendous—verging on chaotic—physical energy. But, she says, "it was tempered by this intellectual precision. So just as you might have thought, 'There's chaos here,' you'd be drawn in by her intellect, and there was nothing chaotic about that. It was very direct, unaffected, unpretentious, precise. She was very formidable as an editor."

As in Moscow, Chrystia found herself in an environment where women were in the minority, and didn't let that prevent her from embracing her femininity. "She had a uniform which stood out a little bit in those days: she wore very high heels, and very short skirts, and very tight tops, not the everyday getup in the mostly still white male newsroom," says Bradbury. "She was so unapologetic and so un-self-conscious that she made it comfortable to be a woman, when it often wasn't."

Colleagues remember that while she would frequently highlight her Alberta roots, she would very rarely mention her time at Harvard and Oxford. "She never bragged," says Fred Kuntz, then the *Globe*'s associate editor. "It was all about the content, always, never about her. If ever she told stories about herself, they were humorously self-deprecating, like the time she drove her dad's combine harvester into the pond."

Business coverage was not Addis's forte, so reshaping the *Globe*'s Report on Business section—which former columnist Leah McLaren describes as "at the time a repository of almost exclusively conservative middle-aged white men"—fell to Chrystia, who believed in putting the job first, even at the expense of her reputation or likeability. She made it a point to integrate the Report on Business, which had previously operated more or less autonomously, with the rest of the paper, pushing hard to have more business stories on the front page and to break more scoops. This annoyed male reporters, many of whom had been at the paper for a long time, and who resented "this young woman who didn't really know a whole lot about the Canadian business community, but sure knew a lot about what she wanted, and what would be a good story," says Andrew Willis, a Report on Business columnist. "Chrystia was brought in to be an agent of change, and was more than willing to embrace that, and didn't care if she toppled over a few people's well-established credentials in order to get edgier business writing."

In addition to welcoming her more defined editorial responsibilities, Chrystia also demonstrated a willingness to embrace the more
intangible side of improving the paper's brand. She worked hard at
being the face of the *Globe* and making it a part of the Toronto business community, attending and sponsoring events, accepting speaking
assignments, and sitting down with Bay Street executives and CEOs
to encourage them to write for the paper.

"She was really good at the follow-through—if I introduced her
to the head of Royal Bank, a week later I'd find out that Chrystia had
followed up with a letter, or arranged a lunch of her own, or done
something to try and make that person feel like they were part of the
Globe's community," says Willis.

Colleagues also remember that she had a knack for understanding
the technology boom of the late 1990s and how the internet could
potentially transform the news industry as well as other industries. She
also thought it was important to give coverage a personal touch. "She
talked about how her dad's combine now had a computer in it, and
could measure moisture and the quality of the grain produced in every
part of his field, tracking that with satellites," says Willis. "That was
the way she wanted to make stories real—tell a story about technology
by talking about what it means to a guy driving a combine." (One
of the biggest stories of the time was the rise of Canadian company
Research In Motion, which launched its first BlackBerry product in
1999—Willis notes that Chrystia "got to be pretty good friends" with
co-CEO Jim Balsillie.)

On top of managing her *Globe* duties, Chrystia kept a close eye on
Vladimir Putin's Russia. In 2000, *Sale of the Century* was published, first
in the United Kingdom and then in the United States and Canada, to
positive reviews; in the *New York Times*, American author Robert Kaplan
called it "one of the finest works of journalism on post-Soviet Russia."

That December, Chrystia returned to Moscow, this time a few months pregnant with her and Graham's first child. It was early in Putin's presidency, and he hadn't yet given up on cultivating good relations with the West. With that goal in mind, the Kremlin invited the *Globe*'s Russia correspondent, Geoffrey York, along with journalists from the Canadian Broadcasting Corporation (CBC) and CTV, to interview Putin in advance of his upcoming state visit to Canada. Chrystia moved with her typical alacrity to get herself added to the Canadian media list for the interview, which took place in "one of the ornate, high-ceilinged rooms of the Kremlin, with gold-gilded walls, parquet floors and plush, faux antique furniture," as she and York described in their write-up.

The correspondents had arrived mid-morning and were kept waiting until the early evening. Tardiness aside, Putin seemed to "have decided that the best way to defuse mounting Western concerns about the fate of Russian democracy [was] with a personal-charm offensive."

Over seventy minutes, Putin portrayed himself as a pragmatist, smiling and joking with his interviewers. He solicited suggestions on where to ski in western Canada and, unprompted, shared statistics on the number of Russian hockey players in the National Hockey League, aware of the enthusiasm many Canadians felt for the sport. At one point, he even rubbed Chrystia's pregnant belly and told her he hoped the baby would one day become a hockey star. Still, behind this "softer and cuddlier Kremlin chief," the steel remained.

"There is still a raging debate in Russia and the West about whether Mr. Putin is a would-be dictator or a progressive modernizer who will drag Russia into the 21st century," Chrystia and York wrote. "One thing is clear: he is determined to create a strong Russian state. Throughout the interview, he spoke of the need to strengthen the state, to force everyone to obey the law, and to 'consolidate' political power to assure parliamentary approval for economic reforms.

"The key question, of course, is whether a strong state would impose limits on freedom."

IN FEBRUARY 2001, in a maternity ward in a Toronto hospital, Chrystia gave birth to a daughter, Natalka. A few weeks later she was back at work, nearly as quickly as her mother Halyna had returned to law school. Friends chalk up the short length of her leave to her unshakeable commitment to her career, and also note that she was the breadwinner of the family; Graham, no longer staff at the *FT*, was writing freelance pieces while also working on a novel.

Chrystia wanted to continue feeding Natalka breast milk, but her office had glass walls, so Addis covered them up with wrapping paper for privacy. She pumped at her desk, collecting the milk in little bottles that would then be sent home to Graham. Sometimes she would take Natalka with her to industry events—Addis remembers the baby being sick on his dinner jacket while he took his turn caring for her.

Her colleagues' reactions were again mixed: some viewed the breastfeeding as a refreshing illustration of her being both a new mother and a high-powered newspaper executive; others felt the whole thing was a bit too in-your-face (reports of the breast pump even made the pages of *Frank*).

Jan Wong remembers Chrystia calling her into her office while she was pumping: "I felt really offended. Why? I'm all for breastfeeding, I'm all for women having babies. [But] this was a scheduled pump. You don't need to make me sit there and watch you pump, it's like making me go with you to the bathroom, because you're so important, and you're so busy, that you have to multitask."

In *Ego and Ink*, Chrystia describes being hurt by the negative reception. "I had a big job, and although nobody was holding a gun to my head, it was not the kind of situation where someone could fill in for me for six months. So I was happy to come back," she told Cobb. "I felt the criticism was quite misogynistic. There was one week when I was attacked for coming back too soon after my daughter was born and another where I was attacked for expressing milk in my office. What can you do? Damned if you do, damned if you don't. It was hurtful that people you work with would do that."

Whatever her feelings, becoming a mother wouldn't hinder Chrystia's career rise. On the contrary, the next big opportunity was right around the corner. Back in London, the *FT*'s new editor, Andrew Gowers, was looking for someone to run the paper's digital site, FT.com—and he knew just the person. In early September, two years after returning to Canada, Chrystia gave her notice at the *Globe*. But before she left, she would be faced with her most important management challenge yet.

On the morning of September 11, two planes crashed into the World Trade Center in New York City. Air travel was quickly halted, and with Addis stranded in England, where he was visiting family, Chrystia was suddenly in charge of the entire *Globe* newsroom.

"She was brilliant, she was decisive, she was fast," recalls Eric Reguly, who was then a columnist for the paper and is now serving as its European bureau chief. It's an assessment that Chrystia's colleagues seem to agree on across the board.

"The energy on that day, and then the days that followed, was like nothing I've ever seen. We did amazing—journalists everywhere did amazing work. And for the *Globe*, Chrystia was leading it," says Willis.

She immediately instructed several reporters to drive down to New York in different cars using different border crossings, to hedge against delays. "None of us had any money—somehow she found, like, thousands of US dollars. I don't know how she did it, but all of a sudden, within hours, there was a lot of money. She got us mobilized really fast," says Reguly, who with Jan Wong was able to enter New York via the border crossing at the Thousand Islands Bridge and start reporting from the ground.

Cathrin Bradbury remembers an editor colleague arguing that they should devote the entire paper to the story and put together special sections to complement the *Globe*'s coverage. Chrystia didn't hesitate, making the case to Philip Crawley and the Thomsons that the special sections required high-quality photographs and more use of colour than would be in a normal edition of the paper.

In the end, Chrystia told Cobb, she considered that week to be her finest hour at the *Globe*, and the paper's staff would likely agree. After she returned to the *FT*, and years later, as Canada's foreign minister, she would hang on to her framed copy of those front pages.

CHRYSTIA'S FRIENDS VIEWED HER decision to return to the *FT* as a logical next step. "[In Toronto,] I think she felt she was a largish fish in a small pond as a journalist," says the *FT*'s Martin Wolf. "Even if Chrystia had stayed and become editor of the *Globe and Mail*, I don't think that would have satisfied her."

Though friends say Chrystia herself considered her time at the *Globe* to be a success, many journalists who worked at the paper would disagree, pointing to her inability to manage tensions in a newsroom full of big personalities. Once again, some colleagues took umbrage at her youth and felt that as a manager, she was more interested in advancing her own career than supporting them in theirs.

Bradbury, who has herself been a manager in the news industry, counters that charge. "There are managers who manage their own careers in order to increase their power, for power's sake; in order to go on to the next bigger, better thing. Then there are managers who manage up and manage power in order to make better journalism," she says.

Bradbury remembers "epic fights" about the special sections and the money that would be required to produce them. Chrystia looked the "money people" in the eye and convinced them that the extra costs were warranted.

"You're not having conversations with the journalist maybe one on one about the story and letting them talk through how they're going to write it—maybe that falls off, and that looks like selfishness," Bradbury adds. "But what you're really doing is fighting for the room and the space and the respect their story deserves. And that's invisible. I do believe that if Chrystia 'managed up' or was seen to be doing things behind the scenes, that was the cause she was fighting for."

Chrystia's involvement with the *Globe* was short, but it came at a pivotal moment in the history of Canadian newspapers. Each day was a battle, and there were tens of millions of dollars washing around to be won or lost, depending on how the paper's editorial management handled things. Geoff Beattie, who became close friends with Chrystia, says she both enjoyed the responsibility given to her and received a lot of credit for taking it on, impressing both Phillip Crawley and the Thomson family with her performance.

"She worked extraordinarily hard, during a very short period of time," says Beattie. "It wasn't driven by ambition; it wasn't driven by her own need to climb up the ladder. It was driven by purpose ... and the purpose in this regard was to take the *Globe and Mail* and elevate it to a much better product."

According to Cobb, a few years later, many would deem the *Globe* to be the winner of the national newspaper war.

Business and Billionaires

O VER THE NEXT FOUR YEARS, Chrystia's career at the *Financial Times* would progress at a meteoric rate. After packing up their home in Toronto, Chrystia and Graham relocated to a flat in central London, eight-month-old Natalka in tow. Chrystia's mother, Halyna, who had still been working for the Ukrainian Legal Foundation in Kyiv, decided to retire and move in with the family to help Chrystia balance the responsibilities of motherhood and her professional life.

As editor of FT.com, Chrystia oversaw the redesign of the website and introduced a digital subscription model for the paper. The *FT* was one of the first newspapers to implement a paywall, which was largely viewed as a positive development; ten months later, FT.com was operating at break-even, with around forty thousand subscribers.

A year after her return to London, Chrystia was made editor of the weekend edition of the *FT*, charged with overseeing the Saturday edition of the paper as well as the *Weekend FT* magazine.

In May 2003, Andrew Gowers's deputy, John Ridding—who would go on to become the paper's current CEO—moved to Hong

Kong to launch the *FT*'s Asia edition. Gowers appointed Chrystia as his replacement. At thirty-four, she became the deputy editor of one of Europe's most influential papers and, inevitably, would soon widely be considered a future contender for the top post.

"Is *The Financial Times* manoeuvring to appoint its first female editor?" asked *The Times*' City Diary, noting that most *FT* editors' tenures lasted about ten years, "so Freeland should be about ready when it is time for [Gowers] to go."

When Queen Elizabeth II hosted Buckingham Palace's first "all-female power lunch," Chrystia was on the list of invitees, along with former prime minister Margaret Thatcher, Harry Potter author J. K. Rowling, and singer Shirley Bassey. Chrystia frequently attended the annual World Economic Forum conference in Davos, and was named by the forum a "young leader of tomorrow" in 2005.

Her workdays at One Southwark Bridge were long, but as deputy editor she found time to visit Russia and Ukraine. Her profile of one of the original seven oligarchs, Mikhail Khodorkovsky—by then Russia's richest man—won Best Energy Submission at the 2004 Business Journalist of the Year Awards. (Even Khodorkovsky's wealth couldn't guarantee his safety; after running afoul of Vladimir Putin, he had been arrested at gunpoint and sent to Moscow's Matrosskaya Tishina prison.)

At the end of 2004, in what would be known as the Orange Revolution, a wave of protests kicked off in Ukraine following a runoff vote in the country's presidential elections that was largely seen to have been rigged for Viktor Yanukovych, the candidate backed by the Kremlin. In a second runoff vote, which took place on Boxing Day, Viktor Yushchenko, Yanukovych's reformist, pro-Western rival, was declared the winner. It was, in Chrystia's view, a triumph for Ukrainian civil society.

Chrystia remained steadfast in her commitment to Ukraine's ongo
ing fight for independence and did what she could to highlight the
country's plight. That December, *The Guardian*'s Roy Greenslade
spent a day at the *FT*'s headquarters, shadowing news editor Ed Carr
as he outlined possible front-page layouts for the paper's different
editions. Carr suggested to Gowers and Chrystia that the Ukraine
situation should be front-page news in Europe and the United States,
but that it should "go inside" for the UK.

"Gowers and Freeland agree to everything but the Ukraine
placement, insisting it should have a front page spot in the UK too,"
Greenslade wrote. "Carr smiles, having predicted earlier that he was
likely to be overruled."

Aided by Halyna, Chrystia made good on her pledge that Ukrainian
would be spoken in her household. Graham, outnumbered and slightly
bewildered by Chrystia's "strict regime of induction into Ukrainian
orthodoxy," wrote entertainingly in the *FT* about being a stranger in
his own home:

> At first, I only slightly resisted. It wasn't just the wall-to-wall
> Ukrainian I found irksome. Our education was cultural as well as
> linguistic. The embroidered shirts with ribbons and lace! They are
> supposed to be the epitome of Ukrainian peasant manhood but I find
> them, well, slightly ridiculous, not to say feminine. (My wife usually
> mentions Morris dancing at this point.) And as for the food, I like
> varenyky, kovbasky, even holubtsi. But, at Rizdvo (Christmas), 10
> courses of pickled herring and cabbage! (And what's wrong with
> turkey and stuffing anyway?)
>
> As for the language, I really did appreciate its benefits. The whole
> Slavic world from Warsaw to Kiev to Novosibirsk would be open to
> Natalka in a way it would never be for me. The literature of Tolstoy

and Gogol! The poetry of Pushkin! And of course, a second language would be supremely useful in my daughter's future professional life.

I knew all this, yet nevertheless inside me there still existed some kind of atavistic revulsion to the foreign. Was it wrong of me to want my daughter to speak my native language? I admit I took a guilty pleasure whenever she seemed to prefer English to the Slavic rival. Also it was just so damned tiring to have everything repeated twice.

"What's that?" Natalka would say. "Tistochko," replied my wife.

"What's she pointing at?" I asked.

"C-O-O-K-I-E."

"Oh ... coo ..."

"If you say the word, I'll kill you!"

"Tistochko," I said. "Tatu, kazhy tistochko!" smiled my wife.

"Cookie," I whispered petulantly.

"Grahaaam!"

I received assistance in these culture wars from my parents. They are sturdy dairy farmers from the English Midlands. They couldn't disguise the fact that all they had ever wanted for a grandchild was a little English Jack or Emma. Often I caught my mother substituting white sliced bread for our stodgier Ukrainian variety (usually involving caraway seeds), or buying Heinz ketchup, or slipping a bowl of Frosties onto Natalka's lap.

However, when it became clear that little Natalka's English was losing its Midlands lilt in favour of a southern British accent, Graham relented:

My own linguistic and cultural defences kicked in. No disrespect to real Londoners out there, but suddenly I understood how my wife felt.

Now, I take it all back. I need her help in this new cultural battle of my own. So give me borscht, varenyky and holubtsi! And my embroidered shirt! And, proshu, enroll me in the nearest Ukrainian class, shvydko.

Jesting aside, the presence of Natalka's "baba"—grandmother—was crucial for allowing Chrystia and Graham to thrive professionally, particularly when, at the end of 2004, Graham became the Brussels bureau chief for the *International Herald Tribune*, based in Belgium Monday through Friday and returning to London on the weekends.

Halyna "provided extraordinary amounts of support for [Chrystia] in child care, which I thought at the time was very imaginative and very clever—I would have given my back teeth to have that kind of support myself," says Gillian Tett, at the time another up-and-coming *FT* journalist in her thirties. "It was definitely something which helped her a lot as she was building her career, because she wasn't doing what the rest of us were doing, which was panicking every five minutes about how to get home at six o'clock."

In the summer of 2005, Chrystia gave birth to a second child, whom she named after her mother. As with Natalka, Chrystia took barely any discernible time off, quickly returning to her editorial duties.

DAVID BELL, AT THE time the *FT*'s chairman, remembers Chrystia with great warmth. "She was a very good deputy editor—shrewd, fair, and always with good ideas for stories," he says. "She worked very well with Andrew Gowers at a time when the *FT* was under some pressure."

To media colleagues outside the paper, Chrystia looked like a journalistic juggernaut, just unstoppable. The problem, however, was that while her star was on the rise, it was inextricably hitched to Gowers's wagon—and that wagon was on an increasingly wobbly ride. Amid a gloomy global economic outlook, the paper faced lagging UK sales and uncertainty around what a collapse in advertising income and the rise of the internet would mean for the future of newspapers.

"On the editorial floor lunches, foreign travel and taxis—perks that journalists take for granted—have been strictly rationed," reported *The Guardian* in 2003. "Even pens and notebooks appear in short supply. Before Christmas some staff were told that the stationery cupboard would not be replenished until the new year, leaving reporters to pick up freebie supplies at press conferences."

Despite Gowers's best efforts, by 2005 the situation had not improved. Over the previous three years, the *FT* had lost sixty million pounds, and UK readership, already in decline under former editor Richard Lambert, had fallen by 30 percent.

Throughout Gowers's tenure, as she had under Richard Addis during her time at the *Globe and Mail*, Chrystia showed herself to be a faithful and devoted deputy.

"Chrystia was extremely loyal," says the *FT*'s John Lloyd. "Everybody was grumbling about [Gowers]—you know, the usual stuff in journalism—but she would never hear a word against him ... just, 'Andrew's doing fine,' and 'It's a tough job.'"

Lionel Barber, who was then the *FT*'s managing editor in New York, was becoming increasingly frustrated with Gowers's performance. He gives Chrystia credit for sticking by Gowers, though he says she was loyal "sometimes to the point of infuriation."

When Gowers decided to split the role of *FT* news editor into a job share held by two journalists on the grounds that it was too strenuous for one, Barber, who had held the position himself, "went completely nuts."

"I asked to speak to Andrew; he wouldn't speak to me, so I had to speak to Chrystia," recalls Barber, who at the time was about to board a flight. "This conversation started in the airport, and it went on to the tarmac and into the plane. Finally, I'm just going, I can't be dealing with this! And she was still trying to persuade me."

By October, Pearson, the *FT*'s parent company, had decided a change at the top was required. In early November, an official statement announced that Gowers would be departing. His replacement? None other than Lionel Barber.

Immediately, speculation swirled around Chrystia's future. Within a couple of weeks, she agreed to take Barber's old job and become the *FT*'s US managing editor, based in New York City.

Barber's decision to shuffle Chrystia to the United States was something of a Rorschach test. Chrystia's friends and allies say the move was seen as a clear demotion—Lloyd calls it a "luxurious exile," noting that the position was "prestigious, but not what she wanted, which was the editorship."

He explains, "It meant that she was no longer in the running, essentially; it was saying, 'You're out of it,' as far as he was concerned. He didn't want her around. He certainly didn't want her as deputy editor, because he knew pretty well that her activity, her intelligence, her sheer talent, and her ambition would be a threat to him."

Gowers says Chrystia was devastated about what had happened; he remembers many tearful meetings around this time. In retrospect, he says that politically, both for him and for Chrystia, the move to make her deputy editor may not have been the right decision.

"I appointed Chrystia, I was very happy about that—that put a lot of people's noses out of joint," says Gowers. "But I also got a deputy who was too similar to me, in the sense that she wanted to shake things and break things, and it wasn't appropriate to have a 'shake things and break things' approach. We were in a little bit of a sort of mutual admiration echo chamber. Then I had my parting of the ways with the *FT*, and she was up shit creek, basically."

To others, like Jurek Martin, who had first hired Chrystia to be a stringer in Ukraine, Barber's decision was a "decent and honourable solution" to the fact that, due to her close association with Gowers, she couldn't stay on as number two.

Barber maintains he has "huge respect" for Chrystia, but emphasizes that he got appointed to sort out a mess.

"I had a very clear view of what had gone wrong at the *FT*, and look, Chrystia was part of the leadership. She wasn't ultimately responsible—Andrew was, because he was the editor. But the respect I had for Chrystia meant that I gave her my old job, and gave her a little empire in America, so to speak," says Barber.

"The idea that somehow it was an insult—I mean, that's ridiculous, frankly. It's not the case. Was she a bit bruised? Probably, yeah. But I had a mission, which was to make sure that the *FT* was going to be sustainably profitable and successful ... She was going to be part of my team, but at one remove. She couldn't have possibly stayed in London. It would have been impossible."

IN THE SPRING OF 2006, a few weeks after Chrystia officially took over as the *FT*'s US managing editor, Chrystia, her mother, Halyna, and Graham, along with Natalka, five years old, and baby Halyna, not yet one, moved into a three-bedroom apartment located on the eighth floor of a pre-war building in New York's Union Square neighbourhood. The apartment's facade was constructed in Beaux Arts style, and the living room had four large arched windows that gave the family a great view of various Fifth Avenue parades. Canadian and Ukrainian art pieces from Halyna's collection decorated the walls, and children's toys and books soon covered almost every available surface.

The *FT*'s office was located at 1330 Avenue of the Americas in midtown Manhattan. Though US managing editor wasn't the role she had envisioned for herself, Chrystia was determined to make lemonade out of lemons. Colleagues from the time remember her infectious energy: she was perpetually in a hurry, flying through Times Square on her way to meetings or awards dinners in her Asics GT-2000 running shoes (a change in style from the precarious stilettos of her Moscow days).

As head of the *FT*'s US operation, she was in charge of a team of forty or so in New York, as well as the *FT* journalists who were based in various bureaus around the country. Her duties included managing the general strategic overview of the paper's US coverage, the recruitment and retaining of talent, and being the "face" of the *FT*. The latter responsibility was where she really shone, developing, as Jurek Martin would put it, a "Rolodex beyond the dreams of avarice."

Chrystia would soon find herself in close proximity to the wealth and influence of the upper echelons of New York society, a world she was familiar with and comfortable inhabiting, after years of covering its Russian equivalent. She drew on old connections, convincing economist Larry Summers to write a column for the paper. She became a staple on the American talk-show circuit—*Charlie Rose*, *Morning Joe*, *Real Time with Bill Maher*—moving in circles with chief executives, investment bankers, ambassadors, and billionaires, with the aim of turning her access into journalism.

"She would be out until eleven o'clock at night at Lynn Rothschild's party meeting everybody who mattered in New York, [or] flying down to Washington to do a piece on television," says Geoff Beattie, who introduced her to power players like BlackRock CEO Larry Fink and former US treasury secretary Robert Rubin. "She became everybody's kind of favourite dinner guest."

As host of the *FT*'s *View from the Top* video series, Chrystia was a "fabulous, focused networker" who interviewed "anybody who was somebody on Wall Street, and also in politics," says Barber, including investor (and future US commerce secretary) Wilbur Ross, then–World Bank president Robert Zoellick, then–NBC Universal CEO Jeff Zucker, and then–Google CEO Eric Schmidt. The series wasn't totally free from internal pushback—some felt it was too soft—but it was generally popular and deemed to be a success.

"Chrystia made it her business to be in rooms with senior people, and that was quite an advantage to the *FT*," says Andrew Edgecliffe-Johnson, at the time the paper's media editor. "I think if you look at her contribution to the *FT*'s journalism in the US, a lot of it was about, 'Hey, I'm in a position where I can open some doors, let's go and open them.' And she was pretty collegiate about it ... I don't think she was seen as somebody who was stealing other people's thunder."

Gowers, who had joined investment bank Lehman Brothers as its head of corporate communications in London, kept in touch with Chrystia after his departure from the *FT*. One time, when he was in New York, she invited him to dinner with George Soros.

"Oh, and [Nobel laureate and former World Bank chief economist] Joe Stiglitz was there as well, how nice is that?" says Gowers, chuckling at the memory. "It was in a bistro-y place on the West Side, nothing special. And there they were, holding court, with Chrystia sort of waving the conductor's baton. It was too much."

All this was a far cry from the Peace River farmlands of her childhood. To keep herself grounded, Chrystia would speak with her father, Don, every few days by phone, and bring her daughters to Alberta for visits on holidays. Little Natalka and Halyna weren't allowed to watch television at home, and Barbie dolls were banned from the apartment (though the Barbie video game escaped Chrystia's "feminist fatwa").

Still, there was no avoiding the Hunger Games–style madness that came with navigating the New York City school system. In a new column for the *FT* called "The A-Train," Chrystia wrote:

> Begging powerful and imperious people for access is, I am sad to admit, an unavoidable part of my day job as a journalist. It turns out also to be a crucial skill in what, over the past few months, has been my unexpected moonlighting career—the quest to get my two-year-old into nursery school.
>
> Urban legends are usually just that but, speaking from the trenches, I can report that the struggle for pre-school and kindergarten places in Manhattan is every bit as absurd as you may have heard. Children under two are evaluated at "play" by squads of earnest, notebook-toting teachers. Parents agonise over making the right impression at interviews and choosing the perfect phrases in the essays they are required to write about their tots and their family's child-rearing philosophy. Savvy mothers and fathers enlist influential friends to lobby school directors and admissions officers— one acquaintance admitted to prevailing on Kofi Annan to write in support of her daughter's elementary school application, though I haven't heard of the now former UN secretary-general actually being deployed for pre-school.

Chrystia's A-Train columns are peppered with references to figures as varied as Nora Ephron, Adam Smith, Niccolò Machiavelli, and Leo Tolstoy, as well as nods to her childhood in rural Alberta and her love of wine and carbs. Her writing from this time is instructive on her views on immigration (pro), globalization (pro), and the judging of public figures based on their personal lives (against).

In one March 2008 column, Chrystia pondered whether it was better to be nasty or nice. Nastiness had "been in the ascent," she wrote, noting that in the recent Democratic primary race, US presidential hopeful Hillary Clinton's campaign had opted for "strategic nastiness" in an attempt to slow down challenger Barack Obama. She expressed sympathy for Eliot Spitzer, who had been forced to resign as governor of New York following allegations that he had repeatedly used the services of a high-end prostitution ring:

> To get a sense of how deeply he is hated, consider this. At a dinner this week I suggested to a couple of senior private equity executives that maybe Spitzer was getting a bum rap. After all, shouldn't we once and for all decide that the sex lives of our politicians don't have much bearing on how they do their day jobs? I haven't found the men in this world to be particularly politically correct, at least off the record, so I expected my position to be applauded. Not at all—when it came to their erstwhile scourge, these guys were pleased to be as prim as Puritans.
>
> As a friend of mine who used to be a partner at Goldman Sachs told me: "He was so sanctimonious and he used to believe in the perp walk. If you want to judge people, you had better be whiter than white."
>
> I often feel pretty stained myself, which may be the personal source of my Spitzer sympathy, and my general belief that niceness is usually the wiser course.

The columns, which Chrystia often finished in the early hours of the morning in her apartment while still in her pyjamas, are also infused with the long-held feminist mores she had inherited from Halyna. Throughout Clinton's campaign to be the 2008 Democratic presidential nominee, Chrystia made it clear that she had serious reservations about Clinton's suitability as a feminist role model, calling her an "imperfect standard-bearer for the cause of female advancement in the US."

As Obama appeared poised to clinch the nomination, Chrystia wrote that feminists shouldn't be too heartbroken at Clinton's loss:

> Even her harshest critics admit she is smart, tough, disciplined and incredibly hard-working—but none of those sterling qualities negates the biographical fact that the US's first credible female contender for the White House owes her national political career to marrying the right guy.
>
> In using her marriage—notably her eight years as first lady, which were often invoked as evidence that she would be "ready on day one"—as her launch pad, Mrs Clinton has more in common with the wives and daughters who inherited high office in dynasty-friendly regimes in south-east Asia and Latin America.

When it came to feminist icons, Chrystia posited, maybe women of her generation preferred "sisters who have done it for themselves"—like German chancellor Angela Merkel, Ukrainian prime minister Yulia Tymoshenko, or British prime minister Margaret Thatcher—to "damsels in distress or wronged wives."

This argument extended to Sarah Palin, the conservative, gun-toting governor of Alaska and mother of five chosen by Republican presidential nominee John McCain to be his running mate. While many feminists decried Palin's right-wing views, such as her anti-abortion stance and her belief in creationism, Chrystia admired the fact that Palin was a "genuinely self-made woman, who broke into politics without the head start of a powerful husband or father." Edward Luce, the *FT*'s Washington bureau chief, remembers covering Palin's acceptance speech at the 2008 Republican National Convention in Saint Paul, Minnesota, with Chrystia on September 3. The crowd cheered the address, but Luce was left unsettled. "This was the first real glimpse of Trump-ism. I was getting a slight goosestep-over-my-grave kind of feeling. And I looked to Chrystia, and she had tears in her eyes," he says. "I understood why; it wasn't anything about the ideology that moved her, it was the biography of this person, and the identity with her, fleetingly."

Chrystia's writing in the *FT* during the New York years also focused on the challenges faced by many women of her generation while trying to reconcile "two true loves—for work and for family." That she was managing to do so, with two small children at home and a husband with a demanding career of his own, didn't seem to be, in her opinion, a particularly laudable accomplishment. Tempted to attend a lecture by her parent-teacher association entitled "Crazy Busy—Overstretched, Overbooked," she changed her mind when reflecting that her immigrant grandparents, Michael and Alexandra, were "far Crazy Busier" than she was and "didn't spend much time complaining about it."

In a 2007 column ahead of Mother's Day, Chrystia, far from resenting Halyna's absences during her childhood, paid tribute to her mother for pushing the boundaries of what was expected of women:

As we take our Hallmark-sanctioned annual moment to honour our mothers, I am especially grateful that my own is one of that pioneering generation of women who fought for the right to lead a life stretched by "insane expectations" rather than one hemmed in

by gender constraints. The life choices that my generation seems to
see as a burden were, for them, hard-won opportunities.

Professional women nowadays don't have to fight quite so hard:
we are like second-generation immigrants, the native-born citizens
of a country our mothers had to struggle to enter. That is a fortunate
position, but I sometimes wonder whether, as in immigrant families,
the first generation doesn't worry that we've gone soft.

That year, Chrystia had particular cause to reflect on her mother's
achievements. Not long after the family arrived in New York, Halyna
was diagnosed with cancer. She chose to spend her final days at home
in the family's Fifth Avenue apartment.

"On her deathbed, my mother cursed sometimes and took what
pleasures she could—mostly, in the end, reading middle-brow crime
novels. But her main concern was with other people. Some of her final
instructions included: stop drinking bottled mineral water, because
it harms the planet; be gentler with my six-year-old and find a sport
that suits her; and give my prenatal books to our pregnant babysitter,"
Chrystia wrote in the *FT*.

Friends and relatives flew in to say their goodbyes. Halyna's sense
of humour failed to diminish with her health, says Chrystia's friend
Lucan Way, who remembers Halyna joking darkly about the size of
her tumour. To her sister Chrystia Chomiak, Halyna admitted that
her true height was four feet, ten inches—not four eleven, as she had
allowed Chrystia to believe.

On July 7, at the age of sixty, Halyna passed away, just two years
after her mother, Alexandra, who had died at ninety. It was a tremendous blow to her entire family.

"I wish I could say that the richness of my mother's life and the
grace of her leaving it have left me at peace—and I think I expected

that they would. I was wrong," wrote Chrystia, who had lost a lifelong anchor. "Even as, in the words of her oncologist, my mother's body 'melted away,' I realise now how sheltered I was by her fierce love. I'm coping for now by thinking that this is her final lesson to me—the vast gap she has left behind is the kind of shape I have to try to fill to become a good mother myself."

OVER THE NEXT COUPLE of years, with help from Ukrainian relatives and babysitters, Chrystia and Graham managed to cobble together child care, though she freely acknowledged in the *FT* that "balancing kids and career is a high-wire act, fraught with risk, anxiety and the occasional painful tumble." Graham had been hired as a reporter for the *New York Times* and was also working on a book about a tragic disaster on the world's second-highest mountain, K2, in which eleven climbers died in an avalanche. In 2009, while researching the book, Graham himself made the trek to K2's base camp, after first arriving in Islamabad and dodging fighting between the Pakistani army and Taliban forces on his way to the Himalayan mountains. That same year, Chrystia gave birth to her and Graham's third child, Ivan.

"The truth is that all of us would love to have a traditional, stay-at-home wife, and it is the working girls who yearn for one even more fervently than their rumpled (no one to do the ironing!) husbands," she wrote in a column about recent research into families' attitudes toward mothers working outside the home. "The news that our children seem actually to be benefiting from changing work patterns—even if we parents are feeling more stressed—is enormously reassuring for an occasionally guilt-ridden working mother like me. And it leads me to suspect that I am not the only mother whose personal solution to the work-life balance dilemma is to try to avoid neglecting my kids—but to embrace abysmally low house-keeping standards."

At work, Chrystia's pace never slowed, as she interviewed everyone from feminist icon Gloria Steinem to newly elected US president Barack Obama. She, too, had secured a book deal, initially to write about the similarities she had observed among the world's super-elite—the "plutocrats"—despite their varying origins. After the financial crisis hit in September 2008, she briefly questioned the project's viability: "I was convinced that the crisis indicated that we had hit the high-water mark of plutocracy, and that it was all going to fall apart after that," she told *Rotman Management Magazine*. But then she began to notice that, far from being decimated by financial ruin, the one-percent class had actually grown in size, wealth, and influence. With *Plutocrats: The Rise of the New Global Super-Rich and the Fall of Everyone Else*, Chrystia aimed to understand the origins of this phenomenon—and its consequences.

Still, as the first decade of the 2000s drew to a close, Chrystia found herself increasingly adrift. For the first time since beginning her career, she was without supportive leadership—without a guiding beacon to answer to, as one friend put it. Shut out of important editorial decisions being made by Barber's trusted team in London, and with Barber making it clear there would be no vacancy in the paper's top post for a long while, it was harder to see a path forward at the *Financial Times*.

Chrystia and Barber's relationship continued to deteriorate, to the point where they were barely speaking. Chrystia, who was finding it more and more difficult to do her job, told Gowers that she felt Barber was "out to get" her.

"She was under endless criticism—'Why haven't you done this?' and all that. He was just trying to drive her out," says Gowers. "I think it was the worst case of deliberate expulsion of talent that I saw in my entire time at the *FT*."

At the beginning of 2009, after four years as the paper's editor, Barber felt it was time to shuffle his top team. He wanted to move Gillian Tett, then an assistant editor who had extensively covered the financial crisis, into the US managing editor role, so he proposed creating a new position for Chrystia: Washington editor.

While it would have taken her out of management, at least for a while, Barber thought it was a pretty good offer; the way he envisioned it, Chrystia could write a column, be her own brand, and network to her heart's content.

In his book *The Powerful and the Damned: Private Diaries in Turbulent Times*, Barber wrote that Chrystia had done a good job in her role, but that he nevertheless suspected she perhaps wanted his job instead. He says he couldn't resist putting that in, as a joke, but that what he didn't want was to have "somebody just waiting for me to drop off my perch, and just staying forever in the New York post... And also, frankly, there were some questions I had about how effective Chrystia was in managing that network."

Coupled with the recent death of Halyna, the tension at work had left Chrystia in a bad emotional state. Her friends, inside the *FT* and out, felt that she was essentially facing constructive dismissal; the move to Washington would have been a clear demotion. "She was offered a job she couldn't take," says Martin Wolf. "This was very, very upsetting."

Chrystia, however, wasn't without options. She was a big fish— even in the large pond that was New York City's media scene—and it was time to move on.

TEN

Next

I N 1851, PAUL JULIUS REUTER arrived in England from Germany, where his first foray into the news business involved training a fleet of carrier pigeons to send information between Aachen and Brussels, Belgium. From his new office in London's Royal Exchange building, he used the telegraph to transmit stock prices across the English Channel. This venture eventually became the venerable Reuters wire service, one of the largest international news agencies. Reuters journalists, based in nearly two hundred bureaus, produce news stories and images that are then reprinted or repackaged by papers and magazines around the world.

In 2008, in a $16.6 billion takeover, Reuters was acquired by the Thomson Corporation, which had shifted its focus from newspapers to the global information industry, providing digital financial, medical, and legal data to paying clients. With the acquisition of Reuters' resources, then-CEO Tom Glocer said in a press release at the time, Thomson hoped to position the new company—Thomson Reuters— as the "world's leading source of intelligent information to businesses and professionals."

Geoff Beattie, who had been named Thomson deputy chairman in 2000 and whom Glocer credits with being the "co-architect" of merging the two companies, says that Thomson Reuters found itself in a situation similar to that of the *Globe and Mail* during the newspaper war: in need of major talent as it engaged in the "fight of its life" with its main competitor, Bloomberg.

As Glocer remembers it, Beattie came to him and said: "I know this absolutely dynamite journalist, she would be great for Reuters. And we have a good chance of getting her, just because of what's going on at the *FT*."

On February 28, 2010, the *Wall Street Journal* reported that Chrystia was in "advanced discussions" to leave the *Financial Times* for a senior position at Thomson Reuters. A day later, it was confirmed: nearly twenty years after her byline first appeared in the *FT*, Chrystia would be bidding farewell to the pink paper for the newly created position of global editor-at-large at Reuters. (At her goodbye party, Jurek Martin recalls, she singled him out in the back of the room as the editor who had given her her start. "I had to admire her facility at making that sort of connection and flattering the right people," Martin says.)

"Reuters was never the type of media outlet that well-known journalists with prestigious newspaper and magazine credentials were clamoring to work for. But that seems to be changing," wrote Joe Pompeo in *Business Insider* at the time, listing the marquee names Reuters had recruited and calling Chrystia "perhaps Reuters' biggest coup yet."

The company's headquarters were located in a gleaming thirty-storey building in Times Square, close enough to Chrystia's apartment that she could walk or jog to work in under half an hour, sometimes taking meetings in her running gear. As global editor-at-large, she was charged with elevating the Reuters brand as it attempted to expand from its more traditional role as a newswire. Along with writing columns that appeared on Reuters.com, the *New York Times*, and the *Globe and Mail*, she hosted live business events and conducted interviews for a new Reuters video service, Reuters Insider, which Beattie and Glocer hoped would give her a platform on par with those enjoyed by CNN stars Christiane Amanpour and Fareed Zakaria.

Felix Salmon, then a finance blogger for Reuters, likens Chrystia and Graham's apartment to Grand Central Terminal; Chrystia hosting journalists and business contacts for a meal that she had cooked herself, Graham carrying things in and out of the kitchen, a Ukrainian relative or babysitter scooping children's toys out of the way.

Chrystia remained a fixture on the American talk shows—in a 2011 profile, *New York Magazine* called her "a regular on the Davos–Aspen–Charlie Rose circuit," noting that she often hopped multiple times zones in a week. Many in the Reuters newsroom were bemused by all this jet-setting, and didn't necessarily see a connection between Chrystia's networking and the goal of advancing Reuters' reputation as a media powerhouse. As a joke, one editor put together a supercut of her interviewing various world leaders at Davos, referring to each as her "very good friend."

But ultimately, she had been hired for her magnetism and her Rolodex, and she believed her presence at conferences like the World Economic Forum would help legitimize Reuters in the eyes of influential politicians and corporate executives. "In a weird way, they give you a little more respect when they see you in those contexts," she told *New York Magazine*. "Rather than being the reporter pest or the reporter vermin, which is how we sometimes get treated, I think they see us more as real people."

Despite the enthusiasm she brought to the role of editor-at-large, as the months went by, Chrystia found herself frustrated and disappointed that Reuters simply didn't appear to have the reach or resources necessary to be a prominent player in the media scene.

"She was doing it all herself. Nothing was coming in through the door that wasn't Chrystia's personal connection," says one former Reuters employee who worked closely with her. Reuters Insider "was a disaster and it folded ... nobody watched it. She was holding up her end of the deal—she was getting George Soros and [then–director of the International Monetary Fund] Dominique Strauss-Kahn to appear at Reuters events—but Reuters was not pulling its end of the bargain and amplifying those voices."

The former employee remembers Reuters bringing in outside social media consultants for the Strauss-Kahn interview to try to get a hashtag trending on Twitter in order to crowdsource questions. It failed—nobody other than Chrystia had a wide enough following to attract the necessary audience. "I noticed that she felt—and frankly I felt, because I was sold the same vision—that Reuters wasn't as committed or able to carry out this jump to the next level of beyond just the wire service that had been described to her when she joined."

Also at issue for Chrystia was how reluctant the organization, not known for being particularly nimble or innovative, appeared to be when it came to embracing the digital revolution. The Reuters free consumer-facing website was notoriously bad—the former employee calls it the "exhaust system of the newswire"—and had always come second to Reuters' real money maker, the Eikon terminal, which provided companies with financial news and data on a subscription basis. Basic tasks, like inserting hyperlinks and embedding videos into articles, were almost comically challenging; at one point, an obituary for George Soros, who was still very much alive, was published erroneously, and it took hours for someone to manage to unpublish it. In addition to being hampered by primitive and clunky technology,

Glocer says, the website was always "somewhat confused" about who, exactly, it was seeking to serve: A general news audience? An international audience? A financial audience?

In order to dig into the problems with Reuters' digital strategy, the executive team asked Chrystia to write a memo, in which she laid out her vision for changes to the company's news business, including the need for substantially better technology to power the Reuters website and the introduction of an opinion section to attract distinguished and recognizable names who hadn't previously considered writing for Reuters.

According to Jim Impoco, then Reuters' enterprise editor, the memo hit the nail on the head. "She was brilliant, absolutely spot on. I was just blown away by her insights, just how quickly she figured out a good path forward. But you know, being Chrystia . . . what she was thinking was not completely unknown to people, she doesn't exactly have a poker face. What she really thought of [then–editor-in-chief] David Schlesinger and the body of work was completely evident—people knew she had nothing but disdain," he says. "She did not mince words at all in the memo. It was pointed, critical, and one hundred percent accurate."

Despite the fact that Chrystia had the support of chairman David Thomson and other fellow Canadians on the Thomson Reuters board, Impoco believes her candidness hurt her in the race to replace Schlesinger, who in 2011 moved on to be chairman of Thomson Reuters China. "She was set to become editor-in-chief of Reuters . . . how could she not get the job, with Beattie and all these people in her corner?" Impoco says that he and Chrystia "were both shocked that she didn't get it."

In February, Stephen Adler, who had joined Reuters the previous year from *Businessweek*, was appointed editor-in-chief, and in April, in what colleagues describe as a consolation prize, Chrystia was made head of Reuters' digital operation. In echoes of her relationship with Lionel Barber, she found herself under the direction of a manager who "did not trust her as far as he could throw her," according to Impoco. "He saw her as a threat ... he was painfully aware of the fact that she was connected to top Canadian executives."

As digital editor, Chrystia's main project would be the reimagining of the organization's website. Ryan McCarthy, who was hired as deputy editor of Reuters.com from the *Huffington Post*, says a website that moved as fast as the Eikon terminal, and that presented stories in a way that went above and beyond the information sold to wire service clients, was a "no brainer," but that at the time "there were people who basically didn't want Reuters to have a website." He once overheard an executive ask in a meeting whether or not they could sue people who tweeted out news they received from the terminal.

While Reuters understandably didn't want to cannibalize its business by giving away its news products for free, colleagues say Chrystia convinced both Stephen Adler and David Thomson that a competitive, consumer-facing outlet was necessary to land big interviews and showcase Reuters' extensive newsgathering capabilities. It was a feat that had been attempted before, and it wasn't going to be straightforward.

"The way it was presented to her by the Canadians was, 'This is not going to be forever, you'll be there in the wings, you're next,'" says Impoco. "What happened was they put her in charge of this digital project and then made it impossible for her to succeed."

CHRYSTIA WANTED TO RUN the project, known internally as Reuters Next, like a start-up inside a sprawling media conglomerate. She assembled a team of talented journalists, many, like McCarthy, who had previously worked at the *Huffington Post*. The team was based on its own floor, which was located several storeys below the newsroom and only accessible to Reuters Next employees.

At the time, "it felt like there was a lot of momentum," says Anthony De Rosa, Reuters' social media editor. "People were writing about us, and talking about us—it was great. It felt like there was a lot of energy in the newsroom ... Chrystia was like this force of nature that was helping drive the whole thing." From the start, it was an incredibly ambitious project: along with redesigning Reuters' front-end into a first-class website and developing corresponding mobile apps, the team was also tasked with building an entirely new, custom content management system from scratch—goals that could potentially each take years, says Daniele Codega, Reuters Next's design director, who was hired in early 2012. A launch date was set for that fall, which he says was "completely unrealistic. Everybody knew it, but everybody wanted it." He remembers Chrystia telling him often that a date that felt somewhat challenging would be important for "rallying the troops," especially given the organization's traditionally glacial pace of change.

Codega put together an elegant new design, lauded in the media after it was previewed, that would allow editors to organize news items into different stream-based channels, such as politics, business, and technology. But the project ran into a serious roadblock.

"Reuters Next was never a disaster from the journalistic side," says Felix Salmon, citing the quality of the team Chrystia had put together. "The disaster was on the tech side."

Because Chrystia thought it would be more effective to bypass Reuters' in-house technical team, the management consulting firm that had been hired to shepherd the project worked with outside tech vendors, which led to resentment inside the company. Progress stalled, as the smallest decisions got mired in bureaucracy and egos clashed; the Reuters Next rank-and-file were putting in long days, not entirely sure what they should be doing or who they were actually reporting to. In the meantime, millions and millions of dollars were spent, and the launch slipped further and further into the future.

As the calendar flipped, it was clear to many on the team that the project was reaching the end of its lifespan, and that whatever buy-in Chrystia—who in early 2013 was given the title of managing director and editor, Consumer News—had initially been able to rally from management was now in short supply.

In May 2013, it was announced that Andrew Rashbass, then the chief executive of the Economist Group, had been hired as CEO of Reuters' news business. "I remember meeting Andrew and essentially being interviewed by him for an hour—it felt like I was being grilled," says Jim Roberts, the executive editor for Reuters digital. "It was clear that his questions came from a point of skepticism about Reuters Next, about giving away consumer news."

Around the same time, Roberts notes, some board members who had been supportive of both Chrystia and Reuters Next stepped down, including Geoff Beattie and Roger Martin, then the dean of the Rotman School of Business at the University of Toronto (who Chrystia would later say has played a "voice-of-God" role in her life).

For Roberts, it wasn't entirely a surprise when, at the end of July, Stephen Adler called him into his office and told him Chrystia was gone. "And I mean gone," Roberts says. "No farewell, I didn't get to say goodbye. She and I had no conversation before she left; it was like, whoa, not only she's leaving, she's already gone."

. . .

IT TURNED OUT CHRYSTIA hadn't just left Reuters, but journalism entirely. Felix Salmon remembers walking into the Reuters Next office with some colleagues and seeing her on the television from Toronto, where she'd announced she would be running to be the Liberal Party of Canada's nominee in an upcoming by-election.

Chrystia's decision to depart—which would be heavily analyzed in the months to come—sent shock waves through Reuters HQ, and the fallout would soon be felt by her former team, who knew the writing was on the wall for their project. "At that point we were already way behind schedule, way over budget, shit was going wrong left, right, and centre," says Salmon. "The minute that she went, it took us all about ten seconds to realize that was the end of Reuters Next. Without her, there was no way this thing was going to work."

Less than two months later, in a September 18 email to staff, Rashbass announced that he had decided to cancel Reuters Next, which he considered to be "a long way from achieving either commercial viability or strategic success."

A week after Rashbass sent his email, BuzzFeed News published an article examining the events that had led to the project's failure, entitled "How Chrystia Freeland Hastened Reuters Next's Demise." In it, reporter Matthew Zeitlin cited unnamed sources accusing Chrystia of being more focused on beating competitors rather than how advertisements—and thus ad revenue—would fit into the design.

"I don't understand what they were thinking, 'Let's not run any ads, let's spend millions and see what happens.' The idea that it had to be monetized caught them by surprise," an anonymous source told Zeitlin.

But as former Reuters Next employees point out, it was never obvious that the executive team expected the website to be a major revenue centre. "When I joined the project, nobody was talking about ads. Nobody cared—the point was to make this the crown jewel of Thomson Reuters, and kind of utilize that influence and that exposure to maybe indirectly drive revenue to the other businesses, not differently from what Bloomberg does," says Codega.

Impoco agrees, saying that before Rashbass was hired, Reuters Next was envisioned as a showcase for Reuters' improved journalism. "It was going to be a loss leader," he says. "She went in thinking, 'We need to basically increase revenue on the terminal side, and this is going to do that by becoming our north star, our public face.' There's a big difference between that, and 'Go in there and figure out how you're going to make money.' Reuters was losing ground to Bloomberg by the week and was punching well below its weight. She maintained that better journalism would increase awareness and bolster sales. Then a new boss waltzes in, rolls his eyes, and insists that everything has to make money."

Colleagues also find it difficult to gauge to what degree Chrystia was responsible for the timeline delays, which also contributed to Rashbass's decision to pull the plug. Perhaps, some suggest, she could have more adeptly managed the dizzying array of stakeholders or had better alignment with internal Reuters teams. But others praise her for getting buy-in for the project in the first place.

"This is a huge ship, and even moving it an inch actually is a colossal achievement," says McCarthy. "It takes someone with real charm and verve to go to the Reuters board and get them to sign off on something like that . . . I've seen other media execs try and do the same thing, and not even get out the front door."

In retrospect, he adds, she was faced with what was perhaps an impossible task. "Could you completely revolutionize a $13 billion company's digital presence in two years, given the state of it? Or is that a ten-year project that really shouldn't be on anyone's balance sheet?"

It's a hard question for McCarthy, or anyone, to properly answer. When it comes to Chrystia's management style at Reuters, however, the reviews are largely positive, contrasting sharply with her years at the *Globe and Mail*.

That's not to say she didn't have her detractors, particularly in the Reuters Toronto bureau, where, just before Christmas in December 2011, two dozen employees were informed that they were being let go, with the majority of the jobs to be moved to what was then known as Bangalore, India. More than a decade later, emotions are still raw for several employees of the Toronto digital newsroom, who felt that Chrystia, despite being the head of digital at the time, and Canadian, to boot, was uninterested in the fate of their newsroom. Leah Eichler, a senior editor, remembers meeting Chrystia in Toronto and presenting her with a list of ideas to keep the operation running. "She's looking at me and after five or six minutes she just says, like, 'Leah, stop talking.' I was like, 'Why?'" Eichler says. "She said to me, 'It's never easy when the invading army overthrows the ancien régime.'"

But many who worked under Chrystia in New York remember those years fondly, noting her positive energy, hands-off decision making, and willingness to provide opportunities for career growth. Like at the *Globe and Mail*, she was perceived to be talented at managing upwards, which for her team was an asset, because it shielded them from "a lot of bullshit," says Codega.

"When I worked for her, it was the thing I valued the most, because I was on the internet throwing bombs, and every so often someone would phone up her bosses and say like, 'Can you fire Felix?'" says Salmon. "And I would never hear about it. She would just take all of that flack, and make it go away."

Codega, who had immigrated from Italy and had many conversations with Chrystia about political events happening in his home country, adds that a skill of Chrystia's he particularly admires is an ability to "modulate herself" to be able to relate to people, whether it's a "kid from Italy," a CEO of a multibillion-dollar corporation, or a Russian oligarch. That ability was key to the success she attained in her journalistic career, as it would be for her second act as a politician.

PART THREE

THE ROOM WHERE

IT HAPPENS

ELEVEN

Making the Leap

T HE SEEDS OF CHRYSTIA's journey from journalism to politics were planted in 2011. As part of that year's international conference circuit, she travelled to Banff, Alberta, in October to take part in a panel at the Banff Forum, an annual gathering where business, political, and academic leaders meet to discuss the public policy issues facing Canada.

Katie Telford, at the time in her early thirties and working as a senior consultant for StrategyCorp, a policy strategy firm in Toronto, was in the audience. Telford's first foray into politics had been as a page in the Ontario legislature when she was in seventh grade, inspired by her neighbour, then–Ontario NDP premier Bob Rae, and she had since held a series of impressive positions. At twenty-five, she had been named chief of staff to Gerard Kennedy, Ontario's education minister; she later ran his campaign during the 2006 Liberal party leadership race to replace Paul Martin, whose minority government had been defeated by Stephen Harper's Conservatives in a general election, ending twelve years of Liberal rule. When former cabinet minister Stéphane Dion won the leadership race and became leader of the Official Opposition in the House of Commons, Telford worked in his office for two years, rising to become his deputy chief of staff.

Though she had ventured briefly into the private sector, government was never far from Telford's mind. Watching Chrystia from the crowd, she turned to her husband and said, "It's women like that, that we need in politics."

Back in New York, in addition to managing her Reuters duties, Chrystia was hard at work finishing the manuscript for *Plutocrats*. Her columns from the time explore her interest in rising global income inequality—what she would eventually call her "chief obsession"—and how to make the economic liberalism favoured by Western governments work for everyone.

Capitalism, Chrystia believed, is "the best prosperity-creating system humanity has come up with so far. But that doesn't mean it doesn't need to evolve. The high-tech, globalized capitalism of the 21st century is very different from the postwar version of capitalism that performed so magnificently for the middle classes of the Western world. That's why a lot of people, including many hard-driving capitalists, are trying to figure out how to retool the institutions of capitalism for our time."

As she had done with the oligarchs in *Sale of the Century*, with *Plutocrats*, Chrystia aimed to zoom in on who, exactly, made up the ranks of the ultrawealthy. In a February 2011 cover story for *The Atlantic* called "The Rise of the Global Elite," she laid out the research she had collected for the book, arguing that in the aftermath of the financial crisis and its lopsided recovery, it was impossible to ignore the growing concentration of wealth in the hands of the very few—not the one percent, but the 0.1 percent—spurred by a revolution in information technology and the liberalization of global trade.

Through my work as a business journalist, I've spent the better part of the past decade shadowing the new super-rich: attending the same exclusive conferences in Europe; conducting interviews over cappuccinos on Martha's Vineyard or in Silicon Valley meeting rooms; observing high-powered dinner parties in Manhattan. Some of what I've learned is entirely predictable: the rich are, as F. Scott Fitzgerald famously noted, different from you and me.

What is more relevant to our times, though, is that the rich of today are also different from the rich of yesterday. Our light-speed, globally connected economy has led to the rise of a new super-elite that consists, to a notable degree, of first- and second-generation wealth. Its members are hardworking, highly educated, jet-setting meritocrats who feel they are the deserving winners of a tough, worldwide economic competition—and many of them, as a result, have an ambivalent attitude toward those of us who didn't succeed so spectacularly. Perhaps most noteworthy, they are becoming a transglobal community of peers who have more in common with one another than with their countrymen back home. Whether they maintain primary residences in New York or Hong Kong, Moscow or Mumbai, today's super-rich are increasingly a nation unto themselves.

The effects of globalization had largely been positive, she believed, especially in lower-income countries, but she warned that its benefits had been shared unevenly.

Earlier in 2011, Chrystia had been invited by Morris Rosenberg, deputy minister of Canada's foreign affairs department, to give the annual O. D. Skelton Memorial Lecture in Ottawa, in which speakers were encouraged to examine big questions concerning Canada's international relations. Though she had spent most of her career outside of the country, Chrystia was still a known quantity in Canadian intellectual circles. (In addition to her friendships with David Thomson, Geoff Beattie, and Roger Martin, she considered former prime minister Paul Martin a mentor, and Mark Carney, then governor of the Bank of Canada, was a family friend and would become godfather to her son, Ivan.)

In her lecture, Chrystia referenced her time reporting on Kyiv's push for independence in 1991; she remembered witnessing the "humbling of the experts" who failed to imagine that the breakup of the Soviet Union was possible and the "vindication" of her grandparents, whose faith had never wavered. This, and the professionals' failure to predict the bursting of the global financial bubble or the anti-government protests that swept through much of the Arab world beginning in 2010, were examples of people's perpetual struggle with paradigm shifts. Post 2008 and post 1989, she argued, the international community needed to put the economy at the heart of foreign policy.

How to organize the world economy, she said, had "been a rising concern since the collapse of communism, and the subsequent adoption of some version of capitalism by almost all of the Western world."

But for me it was the meltdown of 2008 which moved the challenges of the global economy from being a concern of Wall Street, or of Bay Street, or of the City of London, to a concern of the foreign ministries around the world. The financial crisis showed us that globalization is not only an engine for international economic growth, but a source of grave and really global risks. Healing the global economy, I think, is now the world's most urgent priority, and it's not a job that can be done on the national level.

Nuclear weapons were the dominant concern of the Cold War, fighting actual wars was the dominant concern of the post-9/11 era.

Today, the most important mission of foreign ministers and heads of states is figuring out how to rebalance the world economy, and fight the protectionist impulses which are an inevitable reaction to the recession.

Sooner than she might have thought, Chrystia would be presented with a chance to do more than just diagnose the problem and to try her hand at solving this vexing challenge.

A YEAR AFTER THE Banff Forum, in October 2012, *Plutocrats* was published to positive reviews. David Boies, the famed litigator—and one of the many super-elites featured in *Plutocrats*—and his wife, Mary, hosted a book launch at their home in New York. According to a *Toronto Life* profile of Chrystia written by Jason McBride, Don Freeland had finished up his harvesting responsibilities a few days early and flew in for the party. Chatting with Geoff Beattie, who planned to host a similar launch for *Plutocrat*s at a restaurant in Toronto the following month, Don "half-jokingly suggested" that Beattie extend an invitation to Justin Trudeau, the forty-year-old MP from the Quebec riding of Papineau, who had just announced his bid for the Liberal leadership, with Katie Telford as his campaign manager.

Supporters hoped Trudeau, with his charisma, energy, and famous political pedigree, would be a boon for the Liberal party's fortunes, after a disastrous performance in the 2011 federal election under Michael Ignatieff left the party in third place behind Stephen Harper's Conservatives and Jack Layton's New Democrats. Critics, however, argued that Trudeau, a former snowboard instructor and schoolteacher, was inexperienced in the realm of politics, and that he lacked the intellectual heft of his father, Pierre Elliott Trudeau, who had been Canada's prime minister for nearly sixteen years. To counter this narrative, a key element of his team's strategy would be to recruit heavyweight candidates who could help bring credibility to a future Trudeau government.

When the invitation to Chrystia's Toronto book launch arrived, Telford remembered how impressed she had been in Banff the previous fall. She and Trudeau decided to attend, along with Gerald Butts, who had been a close friend of Trudeau's since their time at McGill University and who would become his top advisor.

Trudeau and Chrystia, similar in age and both parents to young children, got along right off the bat. The prospective leader, who had already signalled that a key focus of his agenda would be income inequality and the challenges facing the middle class, found much of interest in *Plutocrats* (according to the *Toronto Star*, it would become his "campaign bible.") But despite having a good chat, Chrystia didn't really think she'd see Trudeau again.

Meanwhile, as everyone mixed and mingled, Telford ended up having a long conversation with Chrystia's father. She can't remember if she told him the Banff story or if he offered up the thought unprompted, but at one point Don said, "My daughter should run."

"I totally agree," Telford replied. "Do you think she would?"

"I think you should try," said Don.

Afterwards, Trudeau, Telford, and Butts piled into the car that would drive them to their next event. "You know, her dad said maybe she would run," Telford said. Trudeau looked at her and responded, "That would be great—you should make that a project for us."

Over the next few months, Trudeau's team and Chrystia kept in touch, calling and messaging each other and tentatively exploring the idea. While the whole thing seemed somewhat implausible, given

Chrystia and Graham's established life in New York, Chrystia had many questions for Telford, who saw a glimmer of an opening and felt the mission wasn't completely a fool's errand.

At Reuters, the Next project had stalled, and with it, Chrystia's career. Her friends remember her being noticeably unhappy during this time. "She thought she'd made a bad career decision by going to Reuters—she had been given this understanding that she was going to run it, and then it didn't happen. I think she felt like she was kind of at the end of what she could achieve journalistically," says Lucan Way. She had also been feeling for some time that it might be time to go home. "Canada has always been an integral part of Chrystia's identity. As an undergrad she talked constantly about Peace River and expressed strong attachment to Canadian values of multiculturalism. This is very much part of who she is. I remember that the assumption was always that she would eventually return to Canada—even if she spent substantial time abroad."

As well, friends note, an interesting thing had happened between the writing and the promoting of *Plutocrats*. While Chrystia had approached the project strictly from a journalist's standpoint—the book itself includes very little prescription—Trudeau's overtures got her thinking about what it would be like to be able to implement solutions to the massive problem of global income inequality.

"I feel like the politics thing kind of fell into her lap," says Chrystia's sister, Natalka. "I think with [Trudeau] it was sort of like, 'Oh yeah, you care so much about fixing inequality? Come do it with us! You care about making the world a better place? Let's do it.'"

Still, Chrystia had major doubts, and to Trudeau's team the answer was looking like a no more than a yes for months. Graham had recently returned from two reporting stints in Kabul, Afghanistan, and some semblance of routine had returned to their household. The kids were against the idea of Chrystia entering politics, and the salary cut would be significant.

As would become her signature way of making decisions in government, Chrystia consulted widely. Though some in her circle were wary, advising her there was no rush, with three children at home, many were supportive of the idea.

The *Financial Times*' Martin Wolf knew it was a high-risk proposition; there was no way to predict whether or not she would enjoy politics, what her working relationship with Trudeau might be like, or if the Liberals would even form a government in the near future. But he nevertheless advised her to take the gamble, because he believed she had certain talents that would enable her to succeed. "She's a genuinely warm human being, and she actually likes people," he says. "She has infinite energy and is really well informed ... she's very sensible and intellectually disciplined."

John Lloyd remembers that he and Wolf could sense that a large part of Chrystia wanted to be in the public service—something that Trudeau had made clear to her was an important motivating factor for him as well—rather than a succession of high-paid, prestigious media jobs. "She wanted to give something back, if you will. That's a trite thing to say, but I don't think it was trite to her."

By the summer of 2013, whether or not to make the life-changing decision to leave journalism for a potential career in politics remained mostly a hypothetical choice, given that the next federal election wasn't scheduled to take place until 2015. But a decision by Bob Rae, then the Liberal MP for the riding of Toronto Centre, would present Chrystia with an opportunity to make the leap earlier than expected.

In April, Trudeau had won the Liberal leadership race in a landslide victory. In mid-June, while in Ottawa to speak at a National Union of Public and General Employees convention, Chrystia met the new leader for a casual breakfast on a Saturday morning. Trudeau told Chrystia that Rae would be stepping away from federal politics, triggering a by-election in Toronto Centre. And, he asked, would she be interested in replacing him?

Chrystia gave the offer serious consideration for a month before telling Trudeau's team that, regretfully, she couldn't do it; it didn't seem to be the right move for her family. Natalka, then twelve, had written "an impassioned essay on why the job would be a bad idea," reported Jason McBride in his *Toronto Life* profile. McBride described what happened next:

> Freeland eventually confided in Trudeau about her uncertainty and, to her surprise, he was sympathetic. "I've had a lot of male bosses," Freeland said, "and I had never talked about my personal life that way with one. Most women would say, 'Never tell a male boss you're not going to do something because of your kids. That's the ultimate no-go.'" As it happens, Trudeau had once written a similar plea when his father wanted to move the family from Ottawa to Montreal. He offered to talk to Natalka. "He took the argument seriously," Freeland said. "It wasn't just about calming me down or winning me over. It was clear he meant it, and I thought, this is a really good guy."

Graham, for his part, was supportive and thought she should do it. The kids eventually relented, after Chrystia promised that if two out of the three of them wanted her to quit, she would. Don, meanwhile, was sending her nightly emails, encouraging her to run.

"I grew up in Alberta in the age of the Alberta Heritage Trust Fund, which provided generous scholarships. And I got a whole bunch of them," Chrystia later told the *Globe and Mail*. "My dad said to me,

'Canada has invested a lot in you. You might win, you might lose. But you owe it to Canada to give it a try.'"

In an interview with Ezra Klein published in the *Washington Post*, Chrystia acknowledged that there was some credibility to the argument that politics had become "dirty and trivial and petty"—an arena where it had become almost impossible to do good work. But in deciding whether or not to enter the fray, she had to ask herself whether she believed in the concept of democracy. The answer, of course, was an unequivocal yes: "I've lived in countries without democracy. I've watched people sacrifice to create democracy. The way it looks and is lived now often isn't that appealing. But I'm idealistic. And I feel if I can try and have a voice as a directly elected politician that's an important and powerful way to make your city or country a better place."

A final consideration loomed large for Chrystia as she made her decision: the memory of Halyna and her years spent trying to improve the lives of others, whether it be the marginalized rural women of Alberta or Ukrainians yearning for democracy. When Halyna died, Chrystia's sister Natalka says, it was as if a baton had been passed and it was now up to Chrystia to continue the work that had been so important to their mother.

"She was really all about being in the trenches and being committed to actually doing stuff for people," Chrystia told *Toronto Life*. "I thought, 'Okay, here's your chance to roll up your sleeves and make the world a better place, to do something for Canadians.' I felt I would be too much of a schmuck if I didn't do it."

TWELVE

The Battle for Toronto Centre

T ORONTO CENTRE, A MULTICULTURAL and densely populated downtown riding, had been a Liberal party stronghold since 1993. In 2013, there were more than ninety thousand electors living within its borders, which stretched roughly from Lake Ontario north to the Mount Pleasant Cemetery, and from Avenue Road and Yonge Street east to Bayview Avenue. It had a history of stately and eminent representatives, including Bob Rae, former Liberal defence and foreign affairs minister Bill Graham, and former mayor of Toronto David Crombie.

A candidate running on the premise of wanting to make the economy work for everyone couldn't choose a more appropriate riding. In a *National Post* column about the upcoming by-election, Jonathan Kay wrote that Toronto Centre was a "world-class case study in income inequality." It contained some of the city's richest neighbourhoods, like posh Rosedale, with its multimillion-dollar mansions, and also some of its poorest, like St. James Town and Regent Park, where residents struggled with poverty, inadequate housing, and unemployment.

On July 27, the *Globe and Mail* reported that, in the wake of Rae's departure, Chrystia had quit her job at Reuters and would be seeking the Liberal nomination. In a column in the paper a couple of days later, Chrystia laid out her motivations for running, citing her growing conviction that the world was experiencing a "profound, global economic shift, comparable in its scale and scope with the industrial revolution," and her worry that prevailing economic forces would fail to "easily or naturally deliver the widely-shared prosperity which is the bedrock of western liberal democracy." She suggested some initial areas of focus:

As University of Ottawa economist Miles Corak has shown, social mobility is one of the casualties of rising income inequality and the hollowing out of the middle class. We must do everything we can to lean against that trend, particularly investing in public education, starting in preschool. Second, we need to become the world's most attractive destination for entrepreneurship. As traditional middle class jobs vanish, we need to build a platform that makes it easy for driven, inventive Canadians to take risks and create new ones. Third, we need to find ways to realign business incentives with public ones. Toronto is leading the way here, with initiatives like the MaRS Centre for Impact Investing, but there is a lot more to be done.

To Ezra Klein at the *Washington Post*, she readily admitted that she wasn't an economic genius, and underlined the monumental nature of the task of reshaping the global economy:

I'm not Keynes or Teddy Roosevelt or FDR. I don't have fully formed in my mind the answer. I also think—and this is a really core conviction of mine—that there are some issues in politics where there is, at least for me, an easy yes/no answer. Full, equal rights for gays and lesbians—that doesn't require deep thinking and elaboration of policy. That's an easy one. For me, a woman's right to choose. But how we find ways to share the fruits of globalization and the technological revolution more widely is really hard. I think it's a 25-year project for a lot of people thinking and writing and proposing. And it'll require a lot of trial-and-error by politicians. And I can see people's eyes roll every time I say that. But it's true. It'll take a lot of time.

Though Prime Minister Stephen Harper had not yet set a date for the Toronto Centre by-election, it was already being touted by commentators as a high-stakes harbinger of things to come; a decisive showing by either Justin Trudeau's Liberals or Thomas Mulcair's New Democrats would bode well for the winner's prospects in the 2015 federal election. Chrystia told the Canadian Press that she considered it to be a "very consequential moment." First, though, she would have to win the Liberal nomination.

After being elected Liberal leader, Trudeau had committed to open nomination processes for all ridings in the country, which would leave the decision of who to nominate as the Liberal candidate up to party members, with no interference from the party leader or his team. This assertion would immediately be tested, as critics charged that Chrystia had been specifically chosen by Trudeau—a "parachute candidate" reminiscent of Harvard academic-turned-politician Michael Ignatieff, whom Conservatives had successfully painted as an out-of-touch outsider who "didn't come back for you."

"The Toronto Centre contest, which really isn't one, recalls the bad old days of the once-great Grits, when earnest and hard-working locals were pushed aside—and out-of-touch aristocrats made their entrance, trumpets heralding their arrival, and the leader's minions throwing rose petals ahead of them. The aristocrat, in this case, isn't Michael Ignatieff, although you could be forgiven for remembering him right about now," wrote Warren Kinsella in the *Toronto Sun*. "It is Chrystia Freeland, who (like Ignatieff) has lived and worked for years in the US, who (like Ignatieff) passed some time at Harvard, who has written books (like Ignatieff) about Russia and the plight of people from a lower station in life, and who (like Ignatieff) is being heralded as a political star by the finest minds of deepest Rosedale."

When Rae had announced that he would be stepping down, it was widely assumed that George Smitherman, who had served as Ontario's deputy minister and as the member of provincial Parliament for Toronto Centre, would have a lock on the federal nomination. Smitherman himself had every intention of seeking to replace Rae—that is, he says, until one "fateful weekend day" in the summer of 2013.

"I met up with my former assistant and friend, Gerald Butts, to be told, really, that somebody I'd never heard of, and whose name I couldn't remember after I went home, was going to be the anointed one in Toronto Centre," Smitherman says. "[My] first introduction to Chrystia Freeland was to hear that she'd be snuffing out my political dreams in Toronto Centre."

Todd Ross, a long-time community leader with deep roots in the riding, had already put his hat in the ring, after having received personal reassurances from Trudeau that the nomination race would be open. Diana Burke, a former RBC Royal Bank executive, also announced her candidacy.

Referring to Smitherman's "forced retirement," the *Post*'s John Ivison wrote that open nominations had fallen at the first hurdle:

How much faith should anyone place in his other democratic reform pledges—loosening the grip of the Prime Minister's Office; introducing changes to the electoral system; banning partisan government advertising? Personally, I think it's entirely sensible for the leader to reserve the right to parachute "star" candidates into safe seats. But when your whole unique proposition is that you are an agent of change, it behooves you to live up to your own heady rhetoric. "Doing politics exactly the same way as Jean Chrétien" doesn't quite have the same ring to it.

Bill Graham, the well-respected, long-time Liberal who had been interim leader of the party in 2006, became one of Chrystia's co-chairs, along with then–Toronto Centre MPP Glen Murray, former Ignatieff deputy chief of staff Sachin Aggarwal, and communications guru Amanda Alvaro, who had worked on several Liberal campaigns.

Graham, who died in 2022, distinctly recalled Trudeau stressing the importance of getting Chrystia into the House of Commons. But he said it wasn't a "cakewalk" of a race and that Chrystia's nomination wasn't a foregone conclusion, given her limited profile in the riding. Chrystia herself maintained that Trudeau had made it clear she would need to win on her own merits.

"The truth is that she was given little more than some good advice, a soft signal of support from the leader, and a handful of introductions, including to me," says Alexis Levine, Chrystia's campaign manager. "No money, no staff, no communications materials, nothing. She was dropped into an open nomination against candidates that had been organizing for years."

Because the party sets the deadline for signing up members ahead of the vote, and campaigns didn't always know when this deadline would be, teams needed to work fast. By the cut-off date of August 20, around twelve hundred Liberal members had signed up to vote

As she'd done during top-level journalism posts throughout her career, Chrystia enthusiastically put in the time and work required to make her goal a reality. "I've rarely seen a candidate work harder, knock on more doors, make more calls," says Levine. "She took nothing for granted; she called every single eligible voter in the riding association; she worked morning until night, and she somehow still made time for her kids."

The nomination itself took place on September 15 at the Toronto Reference Library. Chrystia and her team set up shop in a small hair salon across the street, where the names of potential voters were listed on charts on the wall.

In the library, each candidate was given twenty minutes or so to address the assembled members. Chrystia was nominated by Bill Graham and seconded by George Smitherman, who by then had been won over by her capacity to connect with the riding's residents.

Smitherman rejects any comparison of Chrystia to Ignatieff, saying there are two kinds of parachute candidates: those who can fit and those who can't. "Toronto Centre is a very special place, you just cross the street and it's a whole new range of issues and the like," he says. "It's not everybody that could get dropped in there and actually meet the naysayers head on by demonstrating openness, capability, warmth, understanding, empathy—and she had a lot of those things to rely on."

After the speeches, Levine remembers, Chrystia returned to the salon and worked relentlessly until the polls closed, calling members and encouraging them to turn out to vote. Once the votes had been counted, the candidates were informed of the result: Chrystia would be Toronto Centre's Liberal party nominee, having collected five hundred of the thirteen hundred ballots cast. Ross, who had come in second, made a motion to make the results unanimous.

"She didn't just sit back and say, 'Oh, they'll take care of me.' She put a lot of effort into it, and that resonated really well with people," says Ross, who came to see Chrystia as a fitting successor to the "statespeople" type of politicians who had represented the riding in the past.

Afterwards, Chrystia and her team celebrated with a victory party at a restaurant above the Bloor-Yonge subway station. The last few weeks had been a blur for Chrystia; in addition to working to secure the nomination, she'd sorted out schools for the kids and purchased a $1.3 million semi-detached home in Summerhill.

But the hard work wasn't over: a few blocks south, at the Central YMCA, the New Democrats had chosen feisty columnist and activist Linda McQuaig, author of *The Trouble with Billionaires: Why Too Much Money at the Top Is Bad for Everyone*, as their candidate in the riding. The stage was set for what commentators referred to as a battle royal between the two parties—and between two former journalists with very different visions of how to tackle the thorny issue of income inequality.

ON OCTOBER 20, STEPHEN HARPER announced that the Toronto Centre by-election, along with three others—in the Montreal riding of Bourassa and the Manitoba ridings of Provencher and Brandon-Souris—would be held on November 25, 2013. Chrystia, frequently in a bright red quilted North Face puffer jacket that Graham had bought her, threw herself into greeting potential voters at subway entrances and knocking on as many doors as time allowed (often, her team had to cut conversations short to keep her moving). Over the course of the month, the manner in which she ran her campaign was pure Halyna: energetically and as positively as possible. Both she and McQuaig found that Toronto Centre residents were concerned with housing, transit, and jobs, and also ready to talk about "big ideas, whether it's the income gap in Canada, the environment or foreign affairs," reported the *Toronto Star*'s Susan Delacourt.

Though it wouldn't have surprised people who had seen Chrystia network her way through an international conference or regale a dinner party, Bill Graham and the rest of her team were impressed with the ease and speed with which she seemed to transition into a natural retail politician. Whereas Rae, her predecessor, was "brilliant," with an "extraordinary brain," he was quite reserved, Graham said, while Chrystia "actually likes people." A part of the job Graham enjoyed the most was speaking with constituents from different walks of life and learning about the myriad cultures that were represented in the riding, and he saw in Chrystia the same sort of attitude. "She's got an actual warmth to her, and a bit of a twinkle in the eye that sort of suggests something a little bit mischievous," he said.

The self-assuredness colleagues like the *Globe*'s Cathrin Bradbury had noticed about Chrystia during her years as a journalist was on full display during the campaign, and her team soon came to appreciate her determination to be unabashedly herself.

Ahead of a pub event scheduled to introduce her to a host of campaign volunteers, Chrystia met Amanda Alvaro in a nearby office, wearing a red sheath dress and her grandmother's pearl necklace. "She looked great," says Alvaro. "But then I looked down, and she was wearing this rather hideous pair of running shoes."

Alvaro's job being communications, she asked Chrystia if she planned on changing her shoes. "She kind of looked at me, in a look that I would come to know, [in] bewilderment, like, 'Why? This is my outfit!'" says Alvaro. "I didn't want to ruffle the feathers of the candidate, so I was like, 'I guess we're rolling with this, and I'll have to deal with it later on.' And I'm thinking to myself, 'Oh, but I *will* deal with it.'"

They arrived in the pub, which was packed wall-to-wall with people excited to shake Chrystia's hand. At some point, someone suggested she say a few words, so she began speaking to the crowd. The problem was, given her height, no one was really able to see her properly.

Alvaro quickly scanned the room, hoping to find a solution. Before Alvaro could even turn back around, Chrystia had hopped up on top of a table, where she proceeded to deliver her address to the fired-up room. "I'll never forget that moment, because I looked [up] and thought, you couldn't have done *that* in heels," Alvaro says. "That is so her, because she recognized what mattered was not what was on her feet; what mattered was that she could get on her feet, to a place where she could be seen and relatable and approachable to every single person in that room ... When you get to know her, you realize she just doesn't have time for the fluff."

As Chrystia embarked on her second career, she did encounter a learning curve. She had to remind herself to trust her team and to not micromanage every element of the campaign. Ben Bergen, who volunteered as a candidate's aid (which, he explains, meant the two spent the campaign period "melded together"), says that at first, she was a bit of a fish out of water. "In campaigns you basically stand up an entire company within thirty days, and the candidate is not necessarily the CEO of everything," he says. "So I think that was maybe a bit of a shock to her, that it wasn't this grassroots campaign, it really was a machine that kind of powered her."

The skill of letting go and being comfortable delegating tasks is one Chrystia would need to work on throughout her time in politics. Natalka Freeland jokes that, as Chrystia's younger sibling, she is entitled to call her sister bossy, though that's not quite the right word. "She's assertive," Natalka says. "She wants everything done, she wants it done a certain way, but by and large I think her go-to is to freakin' do it herself rather than boss someone else into doing it. I think there is a certain type who, what they want to do is tell other people what to do. She just wants to do it, and she wants to do it her own way."

On the campaign trail, Chrystia's guiding principle was to assume that the other side always had "positive intent." She has nodded to PepsiCo CEO Indra Nooyi several times in interviews for putting her on to this approach, but it's one she seems to have absorbed from a young age—when sorting out her room-sharing situation with Alison Franklin at Harvard, for example. In a *Politico* essay entitled "How I Gave Up on Snark to Become a Canadian Politician," Chrystia came out in defence of smarm:

> If you are a professional critic—a prosecutor, an investigative reporter, a short-only investor, an opposition politician doing battle in Question Period—you need to be a snarker. Your tone is a matter of personal style; you may choose to dress your iron fist in a velvet glove. But your central purpose is negative, critical, to find fault and to deliver judgment—in short, to snark.
>
> If your job is to build something, however—if you are an entrepreneur, a mayor, an architect—you need to be a cheerleader, a believer, a seeker of consensus, rather than a finder of fault. Personal style aside, your guiding imperative is to be creative, constructive, to find a way to make things work, rather than to look for reasons they can't—in short, to smarm. No wonder the snarkers and the smarmers are naturally at odds . . .
>
> And on this one, I'm with the smarmers. A society whose dominant tone is snark is ultimately one that is politically disengaged. A

culture that is mostly about pointing out how vile, venal, stupid and hypocritical political leaders are, and how ineffective if not downright harmful government is, is a culture in which people will conclude that there is no point in being politically involved, even with as slight a commitment as voting.

As the race for Toronto Centre heated up, columnists noted that Chrystia's campaign jibed with Trudeau's "more sunny, float-above-fray approach," while McQuaig channelled a more critical, no-holds-barred style. The NDP wasted no time before putting out ads criticizing Chrystia for the columns in which she had professed admiration for Sarah Palin and Margaret Thatcher, as well as for purportedly shipping "good middle-class jobs" overseas with the shuttering of the Toronto Reuters newsroom. McQuaig adopted "from Toronto, for Toronto" as her campaign theme, and the NDP made much hay of the fact that Chrystia hadn't lived in Canada for a decade.

It was a line of attack that Natalka had worried might be thrown at her sister, especially given Ignatieff's experience. But she says that Chrystia, for her part, took umbrage at the assumption that newcomers to the city would be unable to make a meaningful contribution. "She was like, 'That's right, I haven't been in Toronto for generations, and gosh, I thought the point of Canada was we don't say you get special privileges because you've been here longer. We say if you're here and ready to roll up your sleeves and work, then we're happy to have you,'" says Natalka.

As voting day approached, Toronto Centre continued to receive coverage in the media, notably for sparking what many considered to be a much-needed debate around how to alleviate the squeeze being experienced by Canada's middle class. (McQuaig, for example, called for a hike on corporate taxes, while Chrystia said she didn't support raising taxes in a time of slow growth.)

Despite the breathless analysis in the media, the odds were low that the NDP, which had put forward an impressive showing, would succeed in staging a major upset in such a safe riding. Throughout the campaign, Chrystia maintained a comfortable lead over McQuaig, bolstered by Trudeau's frequent appearances on the hustings.

On November 25, reported Anne Kingston in *Maclean's*, Chrystia's day "included the obligatory early-morning transit stop meet-and-greet, casting her ballot with her children in tow, thanking her many volunteers and a final swing around the riding with Justin Trudeau, which included a photo-op at a Tim Hortons."

That night, hundreds of Liberal supporters gathered in the Jack Astor's restaurant at Yonge-Dundas Square to wait for the results. As Kingston described it:

> By 10:30 p.m. a Liberal victory seemed assured—with Freeland making history as its first female MP. "We stayed positive, we stayed focused on what the people of Toronto Centre wanted," a jubilant Freeland, her voice hoarse, told the boisterous, filled-to-capacity room. The turnout was so large that dozens of volunteers were forced to mill outside the front doors, hoping for entry. Standing behind Freeland on the stage, in what might be a symbolic gesture, was Bob Rae, whose sudden retirement this summer paved way for Freeland's surprise entry to political life.

Graham's parents, David and Barbara Bowley, who had flown to Toronto for the occasion, described the atmosphere as electric: "We were so excited that she won, it was wonderful," David told a local British newspaper. "We were packed in like sardines, it was so busy and hectic but brilliant." Chrystia's daughters, Natalka and Halyna, were also on hand to witness their mother's entry into politics, although their brother, Ivan, only four, stayed home.

In the end, the Liberals took 49 percent of the vote, an increase from the 41 percent Rae had won in 2011. The NDP, for their part, had their best-ever performance in the riding, winning 36 percent, while the Conservatives won just 9 percent and the Green Party 3 percent.

Chrystia had survived the first two hurdles in her high-stakes career gamble: winning the Liberal nomination and then being chosen as Toronto Centre's representative. But it was clear to those in her circle that she had her sights set on something much bigger.

"There are politicians that I've worked with that are very focused on what's happening locally, what's happening in the riding," says Alvaro. "That's not to say she's dismissive of that, but even from the very beginning, she had a much bigger view of why she was there. And it was not to shake hands at doorsteps. It was to one day become exactly what she's become. And that was evident, if you were close to her and you watched her."

As Chrystia celebrated the fruits of her labour over a whirlwind few months, though, the work of being on the inside of one of the political systems she'd so often analyzed as a journalist was just beginning.

THIRTEEN

Getting to Work

C ANADA'S MAJESTIC PARLIAMENT BUILDINGS, built in Gothic revival style, sit on a gently sloping hill in the country's capital overlooking the Ottawa River. On January 27, 2014, Chrystia, wearing a wide smile and one of the red sheath dresses that would become so recognizable to Canadians, entered the House of Commons as an MP for the first time, arms linked with Liberal party leader Justin Trudeau on her right and Liberal MP Carolyn Bennett on her left. The combine-driving farmer's daughter from Peace River, who from such a young age had wanted to be in the room where things happened, had arrived on Parliament Hill, and she was ready to get to work.

Along with appointing Chrystia co-chair of his new Economic Council of Advisors, Trudeau named her the Liberals' international trade critic. Through her reporting, she had come to believe that the uneven effects of globalization and trade had led directly to rising polarization in Western societies, as countless middle-wage, middle-income jobs were shipped overseas, hollowing out the middle class. From her perch in opposition, she would be in a position to encourage the government to adopt policies designed to mitigate those effects.

In her first statement to the House, though, Chrystia chose to focus on another pressing challenge, one that would define the lens through which she viewed international relations in the twenty-first century: the battle between democracy and dictatorship raging in autocracies around the world. In her view, the most urgent example of this struggle was taking place in Ukraine.

During the 2004 Orange Revolution, a wave of people-power had swept Viktor Yushchenko to victory, and many hoped that the Ukrainian president would reform the country's economy and orient it further toward the West. Yushchenko, however, failed to live up to expectations and was unable to rein in the corruption plaguing Ukraine. In 2010, his 2004 pro-Kremlin rival, Viktor Yanukovych, won the presidency, this time without having to cheat. But in late 2013, when Yanukovych decided to back away from a promised trade deal with Europe, protesters once again filled Maidan Nezalezhnosti, or Independence Square, decrying the president's attempts to strengthen Ukraine's ties to Russia. The Euromaidan Revolution, as it came to be known, soon turned violent and bloody. Government forces, supported by Moscow, used batons, tear gas, stun grenades, and, eventually, live ammunition against the crowd, which despite freezing temperatures swelled to the hundreds of thousands. In February 2014, with more than a hundred people dead, Yanukovych fled to Russia.

In her address to the House while these events were unfolding, Chrystia asserted that what happened in Ukraine mattered to the world, and called for targeted sanctions against Yanukovych and his allies, expedited Canadian visas for the Euromaidan protesters, and the dispatching of high-level observers. As in the *Toronto Star* op-ed she'd written as a twenty-two-year-old stringer in Kyiv in 1991, she argued that the situation in Ukraine presented an opportunity for Canada to punch above its weight, in the spirit of former prime minister Lester B. Pearson.

"Right now, everyone in that part of the world is watching Ukraine very closely to see what the outcome will be, and to see if people like us, democratically elected officials in democracies, will not only talk the talk but walk the walk, and whether we believe in democracy enough to support it when it is at risk."

WHILE CHRYSTIA'S PRIORITIES AS trade critic were clear-cut, being a politician would take some getting used to; it also added a new layer of complexity to the perennial question of how to manage child care. While she travelled back and forth to Ottawa, Graham, still with the *New York Times,* would spend most of the workweek in Manhattan, flying back to Toronto for the weekend. Again, it was the deep multi-generational ties of the Chomiak family that held everything together.

As her grandmother Alexandra had once supported her mother, Halyna, two of Halyna's sisters—Marusia, who lived in Edmonton, and Natalka, who lived in Winnipeg—now decided to help Chrystia, taking turns living in the Summerhill home when Parliament was in session.

"For my mother, it was a personal decision to support me. But for my aunts, there was a political element too," Chrystia explained in a 2019 *Chatelaine* feature written by Leah McLaren. "It's been a huge strain on them and their husbands and their kids. I'm really conscious of that and eternally grateful. But my aunts agreed it was an important thing to do and that they would support me to make it possible."

In Ottawa, too, Chrystia was aided by an aunt: Halyna's cousin Larissa Blavatska, who had recommended that Chrystia apply to UWC Adriatic when she was in high school. After a long career as a

Canadian diplomat, Larissa had retired and was living in an apartment a brisk fifteen-minute walk from Parliament Hill.

On Monday mornings, Chrystia would take an early flight from Toronto to the capital, heading immediately to the Hill for a packed day of meetings. While in Ottawa, she would sleep at Larissa's, usually after arriving on foot shortly before midnight. On Thursday evenings, she would fly back to Toronto, and would do constituency work on Fridays. Larissa, who took great pleasure in her niece's company, never heard Chrystia complain about being tired: "I read somewhere someone's definition of genius; it's the person who lasts five minutes longer. And she does."

In Toronto, Chrystia and her team mostly worked from her kitchen table, rather than from her constituency office. Ben Bergen, who after the by-election campaign became her executive assistant, says that when dinnertime arrived, Chrystia or her aunts would feed young Natalka, Halyna, and Ivan—and sometimes Bergen, too. After the children went to bed, he and Chrystia would work for a couple more hours, often over a glass of wine or two. A few times, when Chrystia was scheduled to take an early flight, her political staffers helped with school drop-offs.

Though it made for long days, "we made sure to be supportive," says Bergen. "That's how you build capacity for women to be involved in politics."

Beginning with her time in opposition, Chrystia made a conscious decision to blend her personal and political lives, purposely integrating her children into her workdays and doing almost all of her socializing at home to be near her family. One spring evening, for example, she hosted David Frum, a former speechwriter for US president George W. Bush who was then a senior editor at *The Atlantic*, at the house for dinner. Natalka and Halyna were busy doing homework and practising their musical instruments, so Frum and Ivan, then five, headed outside for a "man versus machine competition" on the sidewalk—Frum on foot, Ivan on a scooter. "We had a lot of fun, and by the time we returned to the house he had expended enough energy to sit peaceably in place all the way through the meal," says Frum.

"She just pulls you into her life, but it works. I think it was wildly disarming, but also extremely effective," says Bergen.

Along with the logistical contortions that came with Chrystia's new life as a politician, learning to navigate relationships in the House of Commons after two decades as a journalist would also present a challenge. Throughout her by-election campaign, she'd frequently highlighted her belief that a more positive tone was desperately needed in the political sphere, to prevent ordinary citizens from being turned off by the entire enterprise.

But, as she would discover, not all of her parliamentary colleagues were on the same page. Bob Rae, who lived a couple of streets over from Chrystia, had gotten to know her during the campaign and continued to visit the family at home after her election. He remembers that Chrystia found her arrival in Parliament difficult and wasn't sure if she had made the right decision. In giving her advice, he didn't mince words, comparing the House of Commons to the cutthroat environment of the Serengeti plains. "You've got these wildebeests who are going across, and you've got a bunch of tigers and lions and snakes and crocodiles who are looking out for the littles ones, and the weak ones, and the ones they think they can get," he told her. "It is not for the faint of heart, and what you did before is of absolutely no relevance to them. And they're not interested in the substance of what you're saying, they're interested in destroying you and your reputation."

Chrystia got a taste of this almost immediately, exactly a week after Andrew Scheer, then the Speaker of the House of Commons, called on MPs from all sides of the aisle to "elevate the tone" of Question Period, the time set aside each day for the opposition to put questions to the government.

On February 4, during Question Period, Chrystia rose to ask the government about a new International Monetary Fund (IMF) report that warned that sluggish productivity growth was eroding Canada's competitiveness. But before she could quote from the report, she was drowned out by jeers and heckling from Conservative MPs across the aisle. After Scheer called for order, Chrystia attempted to continue and was once again shouted down.

Following the exchange, in an echo of the nasty criticism Chrystia had been subjected to in the pages of *Frank* magazine during her time at the *Globe and Mail*, Matthew Millar, a correspondent for the *Vancouver Observer*, tweeted: "Put your 'big girl' voice on for #QP @cafreeland ... the Hon. Members' water glasses are shattering."

The behaviour of the Conservative MPs and Millar's subsequent tweet didn't sit well with many media commentators and politicians. The *Toronto's Star*'s Susan Delacourt called it a "disgusting little episode," telling CTV's Don Martin that it was "obviously the pitch of her voice that was being made fun of." Conservative cabinet minister Michelle Rempel Garner tweeted: "Can we all agree that commenting on an MP's gender in a derogatory fashion does not further a political position in any meaningful way?"

Even Sheryl Sandberg, then the chief operating officer of Facebook and author of the 2013 best-selling book *Lean In: Women, Work, and the Will to Lead*, lent her support. The Lean In Facebook group, liked by hundreds of thousands of users, posted a video of the exchange and said: "We applaud Canadian MP Chrystia Freeland for leaning in and speaking up—despite heckling and interruptions. Let's make sure all of the women sitting at the table are heard!" Sandberg, who had known Chrystia since they were both undergrads at Harvard, commented: "This is an amazing story—go Chrystia!"

The next day, in the *Observer*, Millar apologized for his tweet and for perpetuating the "continuing issue" of gender discrimination in the male-dominated world of politics. Chrystia, for her part, turned the incident into fodder for a Liberal fundraising blog: "Don't let the Conservatives shout us down," she implored. "Let them know Canadians insist that women's voices be heard, including in the House of Commons."

Parliament wasn't the only place she would make her voice heard. That month, as the crisis in Ukraine continued, Russia played host to the 2014 Winter Olympics, which were held in the coastal resort city of Sochi—a $50-billion-dollar extravaganza that Vladimir Putin hoped would bolster Russia's credentials on the international stage. Instead, Putin's actions in the dying days of the Games would make him a pariah to the West.

Fifteen years earlier, Chrystia had called Putin the "ultimate political cypher," writing in *Sale of the Century* that the question facing Russia under its new president was "whether a fresh fanatical faith will seize the national imagination. The oldest and most durable one is still lurking in the national psyche and of late it has been making something of a comeback. Russia's imperial mission, its instinct to subdue its neighbors, has always been the country's most powerful and most successful ideology." Would the aggressive nationalism that informed one thousand years of Russian history again become the country's guiding imperative?

That winter, the West would finally have its answer.

Shaken by Yanukovych's ouster, and fearing that the pro-Western transitional government that had taken his place would attempt to bring Ukraine into the European Union (EU) and the North Atlantic

Treaty Organization (NATO), as had been the case in other neighbouring former Soviet republics, Putin convened a secret all-night meeting of his security chiefs. As the meeting broke up in the early hours of February 23, the Russian president ordered his colleagues to prepare for the takeover of Crimea, the peninsula in southern Ukraine where Soviet hardliners had held Mikhail Gorbachev hostage in his dacha during the 1991 coup.

On February 26, the Canadian government sent a delegation of four Conservative MPs, including Foreign Minister John Baird, and four representatives of the Ukrainian Canadian community to Ukraine with the goal of aiding its transitional government. No opposition MPs were invited along, despite Chrystia's argument that it would send a much stronger signal of support were the mission to include representatives from all political parties.

A few days after the delegation departed, the Liberal party sent Chrystia to Kyiv anyway, where she stayed with her uncle Bohdan— Halyna's younger brother—and his wife in their apartment. Yet again, she wrote in her "My Ukraine" essay for the Brookings Institution, Ukraine was fighting for its political soul—and for its national survival.

"The capital was, almost literally, grievously wounded. The air was thick with smoke from bonfires, reeking with the stench of burning tires. The once-elegant Khreshchatyk was a grimy tent city, the avenue itself denuded of its cobblestones because protesters had pulled them up to throw at the armored special forces who were firing tear gas and live bullets at them," she wrote. "But Kyiv also felt invigorated and united. The city was experiencing the kind of we're-all-in-this-together feeling familiar to anyone who lived through the London Blitz, or 9/11, or other times of national crisis and tragedy."

In response to Russia's invasion of Crimea, Stephen Harper

announced that Ottawa would withdraw its ambassador to Moscow and suspend its preparations for the next meeting of the world's leading industrialized nations, known as the Group of Eight (G8), scheduled to take place in Sochi in June.

In Kyiv, Chrystia argued Canada and its allies should go further; she advocated for targeted financial sanctions and travel restrictions on Putin and his entourage, as well as for a discussion around Russia's continued membership in the G8. In interviews, Terry Glavin wrote in the *Ottawa Citizen*, she was offered a "wide-open shot" at the Conservatives but didn't take it. As she told the CBC: "It's really important for me right now as a Canadian MP outside Canada in a country which is in grave jeopardy to present a united front with the government ... I will say that people here in Ukraine are grateful for Minister Baird's visit. They are delighted that the Ukrainian flag flew in Ottawa today. I've heard people say that they are pleased about the recall of the ambassador ... there's no dissent between me and the Liberal party and the prime minister and the foreign minister on Ukraine right now."

On Putin, however, she didn't hold back, arguing in a *Financial Times* op-ed that a Russian victory in Crimea would jeopardize the progress made by the world's newest democracies since the fall of the Berlin Wall and the breakup of the Soviet Union more than two decades earlier. "It will embolden dictators and discourage democrats. It will strengthen those who argue that the only right is might and erode efforts to create a rule of a law that extends beyond national borders," she wrote. "Mr Putin's goal is to dismember Ukraine. We cannot allow him to succeed."

By mid-March, Canada, the United States, and their allies had imposed sanctions on Russia and formally excluded it from the G8.

On March 24, Chrystia was in her kitchen, preparing lunches for the kids to bring to school. From her Twitter feed she discovered that, partly in retaliation for the sanctions, the Kremlin had banned her and twelve other Canadians from entering Russia. While others might have considered it a badge of honour, she was saddened by the news. "I think of myself as a Russophile," she wrote in her Brookings essay, noting that she spoke the country's language and had studied its history. "I loved living in Moscow in the mid-nineties as bureau chief for the *Financial Times* and have made a point of returning regularly over the subsequent fifteen years." And there was more than sadness to contend with; as an astute observer of history, she feared that what was happening in Ukraine would turn out to be the start of a new Cold War—or something even worse.

FOURTEEN

The Power of Positive Politics

F OR ALL OF 2014, the Liberal party had led in the polls, with the Conservatives close behind and the New Democrats trailing in third place. But ahead of the next federal election, scheduled for October 19, 2015, the Liberals' fortunes looked uncertain. Justin Trudeau's popularity, it seemed, had peaked months earlier, taking a hit after his rivals painted him as green and inexperienced (a widely viewed Conservative ad, first released in May, famously asserted that the Liberal leader was "just not ready"). Despite the fact that Chrystia had already attained a degree of public visibility rare for a new MP, doubt began to creep in. Faced with the potential of years in opposition wilderness, she wondered if the decision to give up her life in New York had been a mistake.

"I remember having a moment with her where it was like, 'Oh, God, we might not win this one,'" says Amanda Alvaro. "I think everyone gives up something to run, but ... she had moved her whole family, she had left a career that she was not just good at, but [in which she was] really thriving. She had made this plunge into politics, and she was primed to do something really extraordinary. We were standing there just feeling ... like, 'Wow, this might not happen.'"

On August 2, Stephen Harper announced that he had asked Canada's governor general to dissolve Parliament, triggering an eleven-week election campaign—the longest federal campaign in modern Canadian history. Because of a boundary redistribution, Chrystia would be running in the new riding of University-Rosedale, after being acclaimed as the Liberal candidate the year before. Another star recruit for the Liberals, Bill Morneau—the chairman of Morneau Shepell, Canada's largest human resources company—would run in Toronto Centre.

Despite her misgivings, Chrystia donned a new pair of red running shoes, climbed on her red bicycle, and once again threw herself into campaigning, becoming one of the Liberal party's go-to spokespeople—and an increasingly valuable member of Trudeau's inner circle.

Brian Clow, who had been working as Ontario premier Kathleen Wynne's issues manager at Queen's Park in Toronto, took a leave of absence to run the Trudeau campaign's war room. He remembers that one August morning, barely three weeks into the campaign, the team caught wind that Joe Oliver, the Conservative finance minister, would be giving a talk at the private, men-only Cambridge Club in Toronto later that day. Wanting to draw attention to the event, they called Chrystia and asked if she'd be willing to hold a press conference at the club.

In a wood-panelled lobby on the eleventh floor of the Sheraton Hotel, Chrystia confronted the club's owner, Clive Caldwell, about the appropriateness of a finance minister giving a private briefing to an exclusive group of Bay Street finance types. "It ended up being a bad day for [Oliver]," who cancelled the event, says Clow, noting that not everyone would jump at the request to show up at a men's club with a couple of hours' notice. Chrystia was "always willing to step up and participate and help the team."

And whatever the polls were showing, Chrystia believed in what she was doing—in the ability of politicians to positively affect the lives of Canadians—enough to convince others to join her.

In 2014, Maryam Monsef, a twenty-nine-year-old Afghan Canadian activist, had finished second in the race for mayor of Peterborough, Ontario, and had since rebuffed repeated approaches from the Liberals to run federally. A phone call from Chrystia changed her mind.

As Monsef sat in her room at home, she felt comfortable asking Chrystia questions she hadn't been ready to ask others who were encouraging her to run. Her biggest concern was how a career in politics might affect her plans to start a family. Chrystia was candid, Monsef remembers. "She said something to the effect of, 'The worst feeling in the world is when you have to get to Ottawa, but you've got your little one clinging to your legs, not wanting you to leave, and you've got to go, because you're serving your country,'" says Monsef. But Chrystia was proof that, however difficult, being both a mother and a politician was possible.

"This woman picked up her entire family and moved from New York back to Canada so that she could do this, because it's so important. And here I am with an opportunity to do that, I don't have to move, I can just serve the community that has given me so much," Monsef remembers thinking. "She just made such a great case for why doing it is important, why the timing is right, why I'm the right candidate ... she was one of the last people I spoke with before I decided to run, and that conversation will stay with me forever."

As the 2015 federal election campaign kicked off in August, many polls pegged Thomas Mulcair's New Democratic Party as the front-runner, with the Conservative party in second and the Liberal party in third. Ahead of the first televised leaders' debate, hosted by *Maclean's* magazine on August 6, Harper's spokesperson, Kory

Teneycke, told the CBC that expectations for Trudeau had "probably never been lower for a leader going to a debate." He continued: "I think if he comes on stage with his pants on, he'll probably exceed expectations."

But as the country would see, and his opponents would discover time and time again, it was a mistake to count the youthful and charismatic Liberal leader out. Trudeau held his own against Harper and Mulcair in the debate, as he would in those that followed. After a September 17 *Globe and Mail* debate on the economy, commentators praised him as an assertive and effective communicator who didn't seem fazed by the verbal attacks thrown his way. He confidently highlighted his party's economic plan, arguing that the way to kick-start the economy would be to run modest deficits in order to invest in infrastructure spending.

"Was he convincing? Not always," wrote David Parkinson in the *Globe*. "But he did better than his two opponents in explaining the rationale behind his policies. He presented himself as the only man of the three with something meaningful to offer. And he looked like he knew what he was talking about."

By September, the NDP surge appeared to have slowed and the party was outflanked on the left by the Liberals, who looked more and more like the party with the greatest odds of beating Harper. Though the election period was long, gruelling, and bitter, as parties sparred over hot-button issues like the economy, immigration, and identity politics, Trudeau ran a largely upbeat campaign, energizing crowds of young voters and enthusiastically posing for selfies with supporters.

In the days leading up to the October 19 vote, the Liberals' momentum continued to build. On election day, the Liberals won a decisive majority government, crushing the NDP and bringing almost a decade of Conservative government in Ottawa to an end. It was a remarkable political comeback, both for Trudeau personally and for the Liberal party, following its humiliating third-place finish four years earlier. After winning just 34 seats in 2011, the party now held 184.

"Sunny ways, my friends. Sunny ways," Trudeau told his elated supporters in Montreal, in a nod to a nineteenth-century speech by former Canadian prime minister Wilfrid Laurier calling for a less divisive approach to political conflicts. "This is what positive politics can do."

At a rally in Ottawa the next day, in front of a cheering audience, Trudeau delivered a message to Canada's allies abroad who may have worried that the country had lost its "compassionate and constructive voice in the world" during Harper's tenure. "On behalf of 35 million Canadians," Trudeau said, "we're back."

A small transition team, which included Katie Telford and Gerry Butts and was led by former deputy minister Peter Harder and McCarthy Tétrault CEO Marc-André Blanchard, was responsible for helping to prepare the incoming Liberal government for the job of governing and for ensuring a smooth handover of power. The group immediately set to work, meeting for the first time in Ottawa the day after the election in a federal office tower on Slater Street. Along with reviewing classified briefings and policy recommendations from the public service, one of the transition team's top tasks was to help the prime minister–designate select the ministers who would make up his new cabinet.

Away from the prying eyes of the media, Harder and Blanchard conducted initial interviews with each would-be minister, spacing them out so that candidates wouldn't run into each other. The interviewees—including Chrystia, who had been elected in University-Rosedale with a solid 50 percent of the vote—knew they were being considered for a possible cabinet position, but not for which one. Over forty-five minutes or so, Harder and Blanchard asked them a series of questions designed to determine their suitability, vet their judgment, and weed out any conflicts of interest (or potentially embarrassing skeletons).

Blanchard recalls that while there was no "pre-set decision" in terms of who would fill each ministerial post, Trudeau was "pretty clear" from the outset that he intended to make Bill Morneau his finance minister—though even then the team did consider Morneau for other positions.

While Chrystia initially hoped, given her business journalism background, she would be given the finance portfolio, the transition team unanimously agreed that she should oversee Canada's international trade file, surmising that her experience living and working in the United States and Europe would be helpful.

"It was clear that she has a style that plays very well with the prime minister," Harder says. Some ministers, like political veteran Stéphane Dion, who was appointed minister of foreign affairs, for example, were chosen with the goal of "bringing peace to a party that had been divided." Chrystia, however, was "very much in the other category of people who represented the direction that the prime minister wished to take his government and his party. And her ministerial responsibilities reflect[ed] that."

Once the transition team had agreed on the makeup of the cabinet, the candidates were called back to a second meeting, this time with Trudeau, where they were informed which post they were being offered.

Chrystia, having learned of her assignment, took the hush-hush nature of the process seriously. She reiterated to Ben Bergen that the news must be kept secret, for fear of jeopardizing her appointment. (Bergen remembers her assiduously avoiding questions from then–*National Post* columnist Andrew Coyne, whom they had run into one day at the Summerhill branch of Terroni, an Italian restaurant chain.)

On the morning of November 4, the members of Trudeau's new cabinet met at Ottawa's Delta Hotel and, looking around, finally discovered who their ministerial colleagues would be. The ethnically diverse cabinet, whose ranks included a former astronaut, a former regional chief of the British Columbia Assembly of First Nations, a Paralympic Games medallist, and the first Sikh to command a Canadian Army Reserve regiment, would make headlines around the world for its fifty-fifty gender split—fifteen women and fifteen men. It was, Trudeau said, a cabinet that looked like Canada.

Chatting excitedly, the soon-to-be ministers boarded buses that drove them to 24 Sussex Drive, the official residence of Canada's prime minister. Soon, they prepared to walk the short distance to Rideau Hall, the official residence of Canada's governor general, where they would be sworn in.

Maryam Monsef, who had been appointed minister of democratic institutions, remembers the electric and euphoric atmosphere of the day. The public had been invited to greet the new ministers, and crowds of celebratory well-wishers lined the grassy pathway as they made their way to Rideau Hall. The weather—crisp, clear, and sunny—couldn't have been more perfect. For the Liberals and their supporters, it was as if a dark cloud had been lifted.

"That walk, the excitement, the hope, just the energy of Canadians who came out who believed in democracy, who were excited and hopeful about the future—I will never forget that day," Monsef says. "And Chrystia, the most badass of them all, in red. We're all wearing our black and white or whatever. But she's wearing red. It was brilliant."

In the Rideau Hall ballroom, Trudeau, Chrystia, and their colleagues were officially sworn in, taking their oaths of office. After the ceremony, the prime minister and his cabinet gathered for photos with Governor General David Johnston. Johnston sat front row, centre, with Trudeau immediately to his right. On Trudeau's right was Chrystia, beaming in her sheath dress and pearls. According to Harder, the positioning was meant to send a "deliberate message" about the important role that she would play in Trudeau's government. It's an uncanny bit of foreshadowing—the position of the prime minister's right-hand woman is one she would find herself in time and time again.

Another photo from that day is symbolic as well; in it, Chrystia sits among her colleagues during the swearing-in ceremony, and on her lap is six-year-old Ivan, in a blue button-up shirt and a bow-tie, giving his mom a kiss. Being both a parent to small children and a high-profile Canadian cabinet minister wouldn't be easy, but Chrystia was determined to show the country what her mother Halyna had demonstrated to her—that if you have enough drive and energy, and a village to rely on, balancing your "two true loves" is possible.

FIFTEEN

Trial by Trade Agreement

O NCE IN GOVERNMENT, Chrystia continued to spend the majority of the week in Ottawa, where her ministerial office would
eventually employ a team of around twenty, led by Brian Clow, who
became her chief of staff. Often, she would travel between Toronto's
downtown Billy Bishop Toronto City Airport and the Ottawa
International Airport several times a week. "Thank God for Porter
[Airline] flights," says Clow. "She may be their most frequent flyer."

The frugal mindset that Harvard friends remember from Chrystia's
undergraduate days stuck with her in government. For the most part,
she continued to stay at her aunt Larissa's apartment not far from
Parliament Hill. (At one point, according to Ben Bergen, she inquired
about having a futon set up in her office so she could sleep there.)
A year after the Trudeau government's swearing-in, the *Hill Times*
reported that she was the thriftiest member of the cabinet, expensing
just $401.78 since the beginning of October 2015 for accommodation in
Ottawa, an average of about $33 a month (Monsef, Defence Minister
Harjit Sajjan, and Natural Resources Minister Jim Carr spent the most,
averaging around $2,000 a month).

As a cabinet minister, Chrystia was no more of a morning person than she'd been when reporting for Let's Go in Italy, grudgingly catching six a.m. trains. Political staff who have worked with her say she is not someone who is going to be up at the crack of dawn unless she has to be. "She loves staying up super late, but hates getting up early, [though] she does it," says Bergen—her natural energy enhanced by a steady stream of caffeine, with cappuccinos being her drink of choice.

"Some days would be non-stop—I could start getting phone calls and text messages at seven a.m.," says Clow, noting that the team often worked late into the night, though not unreasonably so. "It would be very rare that we'd be talking after ten, but up until ten, fair game."

When at home in Toronto, Chrystia would also go dark for several hours in the evening, taking care to preserve the family time that was so sacred to her—former employees recall that a certain amount of effort was put into arranging flight schedules that would allow her to have dinner with her kids. As it had been when she was in opposition, her Summerhill home was the focal point for department staff, who would work at her kitchen table for hours (sometimes to the obvious annoyance of Graham, back in town from New York).

To sustain herself while on the demanding schedule of a cabinet minister, Chrystia watched her diet, often turning to soup from the Parliament Hill cafeteria. "She doesn't really believe in processed crap," says Bergen. "She's the kind of person who would eat a pork cabbage roll that was made by her aunt, rather than a Big Mac. Not that she's some sort of nut about it, but she eats real food—like, she would eat butter over margarine."

In Ottawa and Toronto, she continued to exercise when she could, famously running or biking to meetings in a T-shirt and leggings, staff following in an Uber or taxi. She still didn't own a car, and when she did employ the chauffeur services available to all cabinet ministers, she would request a francophone driver and sit up front in the car's passenger seat, using the time to practise her French language skills. "Everything is at kind of a frenetic pace with her. It's often about trying to do way too much in way too little time," says Bergen. "For her, it was about squeezing every last drop out of anything."

It was that farmer's daughter mentality at work, with a premium placed on planning and efficiency—if you don't grow, fertilize, and harvest the crops in the summer, you'll regret it in the winter.

UNLIKE A COUPLE OF his recent Liberal predecessors—John Turner, for example, who argued during the 1988 federal election that the Canada-US Free Trade Agreement Conservative prime minister Brian Mulroney had negotiated with the United States was a threat to Canadian sovereignty and amounted to selling out; and Jean Chrétien, whose position during the 1993 federal election was that sections of the North American Free Trade Agreement (NAFTA), signed the previous year by Canada, the United States, and Mexico, must be renegotiated—Justin Trudeau made it clear during the campaign and upon taking office that he, like Chrystia, regarded international trade as a necessary tool for improving the prosperity of the Canadian middle class.

In early 2016, Canada was poised to sign onto two ambitious trade pacts, each worth billions of dollars. Just days ahead of the 2015 federal election, the Harper government had announced that Canada and eleven other Pacific Rim countries had reached a deal—the Trans-Pacific Partnership (TPP)—that would establish the world's biggest free trade zone. Though the deal was negotiated by the Conservatives, the signing and ratification of the TPP would fall to the newly elected Liberals. Despite their pro-trade stance, both Trudeau and Chrystia made clear they would not be committing to the TPP automatically, stressing the need to consult stakeholders and better understand the details of the deal.

With the second pact on Chrystia's docket—the Canada–European Union Comprehensive Economic and Trade Agreement (CETA)—there was no such hesitation. While Chrystia's mandate letter from the prime minister instructed her to "consult on Canada's potential participation" in the TPP, the first task listed under "top priorities" was to "implement" CETA, which would give Canada access to a market of 500 million consumers, create middle-class jobs, and generate billions of dollars in bilateral trade and investment. With protectionist rhetoric heating up south of the border in the 2016 US presidential election campaign, as Republican candidates in particular promised to do whatever it took to protect American manufacturing jobs, Europe was looking like a particularly attractive trading partner.

Negotiations between Canada and the then twenty-eight member European Union had been under way since 2009, and an agreement in principle had been reached under the Harper government in October 2013. "This is a true, high-level, 21st-century trade agreement, which is going to open up tremendous economic opportunity for Canadians," Chrystia told the Canadian Press in an interview.

Getting the "gold-plated" CETA across the finish line was a crucial policy priority for the Liberals, one that would take up the majority of Chrystia's time as trade minister. In theory, with the agreement more or less complete, it should have been a relatively straightforward task—according to Chrystia, a case of "dotting the i's and crossing the t's."

That didn't quite end up being the case; instead, as EU commissioner for trade Cecilia Malmström put it, she and Chrystia would be confronted with the negotiation from hell.

After the 2008 financial crisis, with many European countries facing economic disaster, newly elected centre-right governments enacted painful austerity measures, deepening social inequalities. Across the continent, countries witnessed a rise in isolationist and anti-globalization sentiment—from both the right and the left sides of the political spectrum—which manifested itself in anti-trade protests that drew tens of thousands of demonstrators, giving elected officials pause when it came to signing international agreements like CETA. In particular, critics were passionately opposed to a controversial mechanism in the deal known as the investor-state dispute settlement (ISDS), designed to protect businesses from arbitrary decisions by governments. (As an example, in 2022 a tribunal ordered the Italian government to pay hundreds of millions of dollars to a British oil company, after determining Italy had breached its obligations to the company by enacting an offshore oil drilling ban.) They feared the mechanism would give foreign companies unbridled influence, allowing them to override domestic labour rights, health standards, and environmental laws.

According to Malmström, it didn't help that Europe was also negotiating a trade agreement—the Transatlantic Trade and Investment Partnership—with the United States, whose powerful corporations had proven to be adept at securing favourable outcomes in ISDS disputes. Post-financial crisis, "there was this feeling that only the big companies and the banks had been bailed out, while the normal, ordinary people on the street had suffered," says Malmström. "And here comes America with its big companies, and they're going to impose their standards, and their chlorinated chicken, and their GMO issues on us." Suddenly, ISDS became "the most pronounced acronym in Europe."

As a result, European Union officials quietly approached Trudeau's government and requested that CETA's ISDS clause be reviewed. Faced with her first negotiating hurdle, Chrystia "understood immediately that, whether we like it or not, this is a must," says Malmström.

Over the course of 2016, the negotiations would be plagued by numerous other unanticipated complications. ("This is Kafka," reads one entry in Malmström's diary from the time.) In a June referendum, the United Kingdom voted to leave the European Union, sending shock waves through the continent and beyond. In the *Globe and Mail*, Campbell Clark argued that CETA was suddenly a "lesser prize" for Canadian businesses: "One-third of Canada's trade with the EU is with Britain, so [CETA] is now about two-thirds as valuable as it was last week."

Malmström recalls that she and Chrystia were both "shocked and saddened" by the vote, but that, ultimately, the United Kingdom's decision to leave didn't affect their resolve to get a deal done—there were still twenty-seven countries in the European Union with which to negotiate.

And indeed, they really would be negotiating with each one: in an attempt to quell rising opposition against trade, the European Union decided in July to give each one of its members' regional and national parliaments a final say on the ratification of the deal. This meant that one country could theoretically hold CETA hostage. Romania and Bulgaria, for instance, at one point threatened to veto the deal if Canada failed to lift a visa requirement for citizens wishing to visit the country; according to Malmström, Chrystia managed to convince Trudeau to agree to do so.

In the face of populist turbulence across Europe, Chrystia and Malmström agreed that strengthening ties between Canada and the European Union was more important than ever. "We believe the right choice is for partnership and prosperity, not division and isolation ... Now is the time to build bridges, not walls," they wrote in a joint *Globe and Mail* op-ed.

The two trade leads had built a close rapport, speaking every day during the height of negotiations—sometimes several times a day— no matter the hour. At their first meeting in Davos, they "instantly had a connection," says Malmström. They were the same age, and even looked alike, both wearing glasses and sporting similar haircuts (though Malmström is almost a foot taller). They took to calling themselves "sisters-in-trade." Together, they set out to clear the path to ratification of obstacles one by one, though it often felt like a game of whack-a-mole.

Chrystia's strategy involved meeting with key leaders in European countries that had issues with CETA, to address their concerns and hopefully persuade them that ultimately the deal would be beneficial for both parties. Together with her department officials in Ottawa, Chrystia "went step-by-step, mapping out which countries could influence other countries, which person could influence other people," recalls Vincent Garneau, at the time her director of parliamentary affairs. It was "a very Cartesian, very structured approach—how could we use media? How could we use face-to-face time?"

In the year following her cabinet appointment, the *Hill Times* reported, Chrystia personally had eighty-two official communications with her European counterparts, nearly sixty of which took place in person, in countries including Germany, France, the United Kingdom, Austria, Belgium, Switzerland, Slovakia, and Ukraine.

According to Garneau, her journalistic skills—identifying the right person to speak with on a particular matter, making that person feel comfortable—proved "extremely useful" in negotiations. Chrystia made it a point to keep in touch with her European colleagues, exchanging phone numbers and texting or speaking directly over the phone often. The Prime Minister's Office, Garneau says, had "a lot of trust in her and really let her handle it."

One of the biggest obstacles was Germany, where Chancellor Angela Merkel's Christian Democrats were in a coalition government with the centre-left Social Democratic Party (SPD). Many SPD members took issue with the ISDS mechanism, even after Canada and EU negotiators agreed earlier in the year to create a permanent, impartial trade tribunal to settle disputes, and harboured deep reservations about trade agreements in general. Without the support of the SPD— and the trade unions with which the party had close ties—Europe's largest economy would likely be unable to sign on to CETA.

Chrystia had built a good working relationship with Hassan Yussuff, then the president of the Canadian Labour Congress, who connected her with his German counterpart, Reiner Hoffmann, president of the German Confederation of Trade Unions. Yussuff recalls that over a quick visit to Toronto, which included a barbecue in Chrystia's backyard, Chrystia convinced both labour chiefs that she was willing to "forge a new direction" on issues that were important to both the unions and the SPD, such as including a strong labour chapter with enforceable provisions.

In September, she spoke at an SPD conference in Wolfsburg, Germany, where she highlighted Canada's shared values with Europe, reinforcing, Yussuff says, "that Canada was different than the US." At the conference, the party voted in favour of CETA, subject to "formal clarifications" on issues of outstanding concern, such as sanctions for labour and environmental violations.

"We were deep in German territory," says chief of staff Brian Clow. "A lot of them were highly skeptical … but she spoke there and won enough of them over that they came onside."

Yussuff says Chrystia's "direct and personal relationship" with Sigmar Gabriel, the SPD's leader, was instrumental. "She built that relationship on her own; people knew her, and vice versa."

. . .

WITH GERMANY ON BOARD, it looked as though the finish line was in sight. A Canada-EU summit was scheduled for October 27 in Brussels, where Trudeau was expected to join top EU officials for the signing of CETA. Though all EU member countries would still need to ratify the treaty—a process that would take years—the majority of the deal would provisionally come into force after approval by the Canadian and European parliaments.

But a final curveball was waiting for Chrystia and Malmström— this time originating from Wallonia, a tiny, socialist Belgian region of 3.5 million people. On Friday, October 14, at the eleventh hour, its francophone Parliament voted by a large majority to reject CETA, citing the need for stronger safeguards on labour, agricultural, environmental, and consumer standards. Walloon premier Paul Magnette called for the reopening of negotiations, so that "European leaders could hear the legitimate demands which have been forcefully expressed by an organized, transparent civil society."

Under Belgian law, all regional parliaments must approve trade deals before the federal government can sign on. Without Wallonia, Belgium couldn't sign, and without Belgium, Europe couldn't either. "It's hard to overstate what a bad situation that was," says Clow. "We sent our CETA representative, Pierre Pettigrew, who Chrystia appointed, to help with this; he went there, couldn't get them onside."

A couple of days later, Chrystia herself arrived in Namur, Belgium, with Steve Verheul, Canada's chief trade negotiator, to meet with EU officials and Wallonian representatives at the Élysette, which houses the Wallonian government. By Friday, October 21, the talks were dragging on, with the parties no closer to an agreement.

"We were at the table trying to resolve some fairly extreme positions that [the Wallonians] were taking in the context of the negotiations," says Verheul. "We were going on for hours without any real progress. At one point, I did suggest to Chrystia that we take a pause."

During the break, Verheul was frank, telling Chrystia that they were wasting their time and that they risked losing what leverage they did have if they continued to engage. He advised that it was time for a walkout—something dramatic that would send a strong signal.

Chrystia knew that pulling out of the negotiations, especially as a fairly new minister, would draw a lot of attention and would be disruptive to the entire negotiation process. "She and I walked around this courtyard outside the negotiation room for maybe twenty minutes talking about how we do this, what should be said to the press, how do we play it all out," says Verheul. They agreed that she should leave the table not in anger but in sadness—and that that was going to be the way to play it in public as well.

With billions of dollars hanging in the balance, "this was putting her in a bit of a difficult position, because it was going to be a somewhat controversial move to make ... But she decided right away that she thought that was indeed the right thing to do."

Back at the negotiating table, Verheul and Chrystia stated that they didn't think the discussions were productive and that Canada would be walking away.

Outside, speaking to reporters in French and appearing to fight back tears, Chrystia announced that she would be heading home. "It seems evident to me and to Canada that the EU is now not capable of having an international agreement, even with a country that has such European values, like Canada, and even with a country as nice and patient as Canada," she said. "Canada is disappointed, I personally am disappointed. I worked very, very hard, but I think it's impossible ...

The only good thing that I can say is that tomorrow morning I will be home with my three children."

As word of the walkout spread back home, Canadian officials—including Trudeau himself—were taken by surprise. "It was huge news here in Canada—I didn't know about it, the team in Ottawa didn't know about it, and certainly the folks in [the Prime Minister's Office] didn't know about it," says Clow. The PMO was "very good about it," he adds. "It was kind of like, 'Okay, keep us posted.'"

Malmström, too, notes that throughout the negotiations, it was clear that Chrystia was speaking for Trudeau: "She was very much trusted by the prime minister to handle this file, and she could make concessions—she could be brave and say, 'Okay, I'll take that risk, and then I'll anchor it afterwards.'"

There was another risk involved in the gambit: by displaying visible emotion and vulnerability in front of the world's media, Chrystia had left herself open to sexist charges that she was weak and unable to handle the task at hand. In the House of Commons the next week, Conservative MP Gerry Ritz accused Chrystia of having a "meltdown" and said she needed "adult supervision."

"I am all in for Canada when I am at the negotiating table," Chrystia responded. "I was disappointed and sad but also tough and strong. I think those are the qualities that Canadians expect in their minister."

Clow nevertheless thinks the walkout was the right choice: "It was a high-risk gamble, but it worked, and that set the stage for the whole thing to come together."

Part of what Chrystia hoped to convey was that the impasse should be Europe's problem, not Canada's. "That's eventually what happened," says Verheul. "They managed to provide certain assurances to the Wallonians, and the European Commission was able to get things back on track from there."

In an interview with the *Globe*, Chrystia later reflected: "I had all the Europeans calling me up for the next 24 hours going, 'Please don't go home, please, we're so sorry, you're so right, we're going to make it work.' And in the end, they did."

Watching the standoff from afar, Alison Franklin, Chrystia's Harvard roommate, had to laugh. Having witnessed her friend's negotiating chops early on, when dealing with the bunk bed situation, Franklin thought, "She's got this."

On October 30—after a mechanical failure on board Trudeau's government plane forced it to return to Ottawa briefly, in one last Kafkaesque moment, before finally reaching Brussels—the Canadian prime minister sat alongside the presidents of the EU Council and EU Commission and signed the long-awaited 1,600-page CETA deal, seven years in the making.

"Okay, we did it!" Chrystia exclaimed during a photo after the signing, hugging her colleagues.

Her "sister-in-trade" says Chrystia was instrumental in making CETA a reality because she felt so strongly about the Canada-EU partnership and saw real value to the agreement, espousing free trade not for the sake of it but as a means of enriching the middle class: "She's very intelligent, and she knows what she wants, and she argues for it." Malmström credits Chrystia's sense of humour and pragmatism with helping her to keep a level head when negotiations were at their most surreal. "Nothing really surprises her."

Malmström adds, "She managed to connect with people and to listen, to go beyond the disagreement. That's not always easy—the trade world is full of grumpy men. You're always a minority, and you always have to be better prepared."

Verheul would add an extra element to the mix that led to success: Chrystia's staunch belief in Canada's ability to be a major player on the world stage. While most cabinet ministers tend to want to stay within certain parameters, adhering to what is expected of them, Chrystia, he says, "was always prepared to make bold moves."

He adds, "We talked about this on many occasions—Canada has a certain influence in the world, but I think we often underestimate how much influence we do have. And if we do take bold moves, it tends to work out pretty well, most of the time, if it's well thought through. She was entirely supportive of not being too hesitant, in terms of trying to advance the file, and that's rare."

CHRYSTIA'S TIME AS CANADIAN trade minister afforded her ample opportunity to work on her delegating skills—getting away from that go-to impulse, as her sister Natalka put it, to want to do everything herself. Given the priorities on her plate, that just wasn't possible: in addition to CETA and the TPP, Canada's 2006 Softwood Lumber Agreement with the United States had expired, and Trudeau had tasked her with exploring trade relationships with China and India; Canada also signed a trade agreement with Ukraine in July 2016.

Vincent Garneau recalls a management style that was "very inclusive, in terms of really being a leader, rather than a boss." Chrystia, he says, identified and surrounded herself with people she trusted— Steve Verheul being a great example—to "constantly carry the ball" while she worked on other files, with her "intervening at the right moment." She made a deliberate, conscious effort to keep tabs on "who was playing what position at which moment" and to leave different stakeholders with "a little mission, something to do."

Over the course of her career in government, Chrystia would develop something of a reputation for not readily deferring to the public service. When she became trade minister, says one senior government official, the department was keen to present its agenda, which included the rapid ratification of the TPP. Chrystia was quick to assert—maybe too severely, says the official—that she wouldn't be devoting much attention to areas of focus outside of the ones Trudeau had identified as priorities (one associate deputy minister responsible for the Asia Pacific region really wanted her to do a week-long trade mission to South Korea, for example; something Chrystia thought was a waste of time). This ruffled feathers and left some long-time public servants bruised—but, the official argues, it was also necessary to be an effective minister.

Chrystia and her Liberal colleagues failed to make much progress on the TPP, choosing instead to focus on "consultations" that involved a "seemingly never-ending series of meetings with TPP stakeholders and critics," Peter Mazereeuw wrote in the *Hill Times*. They also didn't manage to reach a deal with the United States on softwood lumber before the departure of President Barack Obama.

But at home, Chrystia's work on CETA earned her "incredible respect" across Canada, says Hassan Yussuff: "People, all of a sudden, were taking notice of Chrystia and her success."

It also earned her praise from across the aisle. "I do give Chrystia a lot of credit for maintaining CETA," says former Harper cabinet minister Erin O'Toole. "I thought she did a really good job. I would have liked the investor-state stuff staying, but at the end of the day, the deal was at risk."

However, there would be little time to celebrate. A week after CETA was signed in Brussels, the United States elected former reality TV–star Donald Trump as its president. For all its drama, CETA would end up being the dress rehearsal for a much larger negotiating challenge for Canada—and for Chrystia.

SIXTEEN

Keep Calm and Negotiate NAFTA

I N THE SUMMER OF 2016, almost eight years to the day after ending her campaign against Barack Obama, Hillary Clinton became the first woman to secure the presidential nomination of the Democratic Party—or of any major American political party. Regardless of Chrystia's past feelings about Clinton as an "imperfect standard-bearer" for feminism, she and nearly all of her Canadian government colleagues hoped and expected that Clinton, who had served as Obama's secretary of state, would become the next president of the United States. Clinton's Republican opponent, Donald Trump, had no government experience, was brash and erratic, and was openly disparaging of women, people of colour, and other minorities. National and state election polls consistently pointed to Clinton as the heavy favourite.

But on November 8, in what the *New York Times* called a "stunning repudiation of the establishment," Trump was elected president. Riding a wave of populist discontent sweeping through the country, Trump was a beacon for voters looking for dramatic change—Americans who, experiencing the effects of the glaring income inequality that had been a concern of Chrystia's for a while now—were fed up with their economic circumstances and felt left behind, blaming decades of globalization and multiculturalism.

The astonishment at Trump's victory extended to the upper echelons of the Canadian government. While there had been some conversations around the possibility of Trump being elected, Brian Clow says he has "no problem admitting—because I think the whole world felt this way—we really thought Hillary was going to win. Obviously, that didn't happen, and it really was an earthquake."

Within hours, PMO officials met to begin preparing for what promised to be an unpredictable, protectionist US administration—one that would have a profound effect on Canada's relationship with its closest neighbour and ally. The Trudeau government's most urgent task was to establish some sort of connection to members of Trump's transition team. The problem, said former Conservative prime minister Brian Mulroney in a 2022 interview, was that "the Liberals had put all their eggs in the Hillary basket." As a result, "they had absolutely no communication or contact with anybody of influence in the Republican Party in the United States."

The work Chrystia had put in during her time in the United States—getting access to the country's movers and shakers, first with the *Financial Times* and then with Reuters—would pay off in a way she'd likely never expected. She emailed friends from her New York circle, who connected her to real estate executive Jared Kushner, the husband of Trump's eldest daughter, Ivanka. Chrystia and Kushner met in person on December 7, and Kushner, who had played a key role in managing Trump's campaign and would soon be appointed a senior White House advisor to his father-in-law, then facilitated introductions to other officials.

As Trump had not yet taken office, it was important that these overtures be made as discreetly as possible. Clow, Chrystia, and Katie

Telford flew to New York City for a December 13 meeting with hawk-ish economist Peter Navarro, who would become Trump's top trade advisor, and Jason Greenblatt, the long-time chief legal officer and executive vice-president for the Trump Organization. The Canadians turned down an invitation to Trump Tower on Fifth Avenue—as home to Trump's penthouse apartment and headquarters for the presidential transition, the skyscraper attracted anti-Trump protesters and a police presence for weeks after the election. They opted instead for the conference room of the Chambers boutique hotel across the street. "It was hysteria there; we kind of went through a barricade down the street to this hotel and met the staffers in the basement," says Clow. "At that point we were just trying to meet whoever we could and build relationships ... Truly that all would not have happened without Chrystia's contacts and her network in the United States."

Though Trump, and those in his circle, espoused a world view that was diametrically opposed to her own, Chrystia was nevertheless focused on understanding their perspective. It was how she had been raised; Halyna, Chrystia wrote in the *Financial Times* after her mother's death, "never hated the people whose politics she disagreed with."

Trudeau shared the same mentality, according to Clow. "We obviously disagreed with a lot of what they stood for, but they are at the same time our biggest partner and our best friends as a country, and we've got to work with whoever they elect. And we worked with them," Clow says.

One weekend in early January, Chrystia and Clow were both asked to come to what was then known as Langevin Block (now the Office of the Prime Minister and Privy Council) on Monday, to meet with Trudeau and Michael McNair, the prime minister's head of policy, respectively. They flew from Toronto to Ottawa together and walked into the heritage building on Wellington Street, directly across from

Parliament Hill. They had an inkling that they'd be receiving "major life news," says Clow, and sure enough, they were both told they were going to be promoted.

Clow would be moving to the Prime Minister's Office as director of Canada-US relations and would head up an election-style war room to help coordinate the government's strategy toward the new US administration. As part of Trudeau's first major cabinet shuffle, Chrystia, fresh off the success of the Canada–European Union Comprehensive Economic and Trade Agreement, would be replacing Stéphane Dion as foreign affairs minister. It was the first time the position would be held by a female Liberal MP, and only the third time a woman of any party would occupy the post.

On January 10, 2017, Chrystia was sworn in as Canada's top diplomat, tasked by Trudeau "to restore constructive Canadian leadership in the world and to promote Canada's interests and values." Specifically, Chrystia's mandate letter listed maintaining "constructive relations" with the United States as her top priority. Responsibility for North American trade would also fall under her purview, rather than that of her replacement at international trade, François-Philippe Champagne.

In many ways, it was a job she had been preparing for her whole life, flying the flag of Canada at every opportunity, building a network of well-placed international contacts, and learning more about the world outside her own country's borders by immersing herself in it. Nevertheless, Chrystia would need to summon all her smarts, mettle, and charm as she faced an economic challenge that would eclipse CETA and imperil the future of Canada's prosperity.

IN THE 1980S, CANADIAN prime minister Brian Mulroney and US president Ronald Reagan negotiated a bilateral free trade agreement that came into effect on January 1, 1989. In 1992, Mulroney and George H. W. Bush signed a trilateral accord with Mexican president Carlos Salinas. NAFTA entered into force on January 1, 1994, creating the world's largest free trade bloc. Over the next two decades, the deal would fundamentally reshape North American economic relations, eliminating tariffs on imports and exports between the three countries and deeply integrating their cross-border supply chains and manufacturing industries. A 2016 report from the US Chamber of Commerce noted that trade with Canada and Mexico had nearly quadrupled since 1994, to $1.3 trillion, and that the two countries purchased more than one-third of US merchandise exports.

Though economists disagreed over NAFTA's impact on the economies of its signatories, many argued that the agreement had had a positive effect on wages in all three nations, with millions of jobs supported by the trade it generated. But according to critics, the gains were not evenly distributed.

On September 26, 2016, during the first US presidential debate, Trump called NAFTA "the worst trade deal maybe ever signed anywhere, but certainly ever signed in this country." For Trump, and the more nationalist-minded faction of his advisors—which included Peter Navarro and chief strategist Steve Bannon, the former head of alt-right website Breitbart News—NAFTA was a symbol of all of the downsides of globalization. He argued that the agreement was responsible for the hollowing out of working and middle classes in Midwestern states, as American companies moved their factories— and, along with them, manufacturing jobs—to Mexico, where workers were paid lower, more competitive wages.

On October 19, Trump tweeted: "I will renegotiate NAFTA. If I can't make a great deal, we're going to tear it up. We're going to get this economy running again."

For Canada, which relied on the United States for 70 percent of its trade, an American exit from NAFTA would mean tremendous economic uncertainty, with an inevitable spike in the cost of consumer goods, the disruption of supply chains, and tens of thousands of jobs at risk. In Chrystia's view, withdrawal could also lead to something equally alarming: significant damage to the rules-based international order, the framework of liberal and economic rules and the network of treaties and alliances—the United Nations, Group of Seven (G7), NATO, World Trade Organization, IMF, and others—that had been put in place by Western democracies after the Second World War, designed to secure lasting peace and co-operation.

"I feel very strongly that one of the most pressing challenges today is the threats that the liberal order faces," Chrystia told *The Walrus* magazine. "That order is something we have taken for granted, especially my generation—the postwar peace and prosperity generation. It's like that Joni Mitchell song, 'You don't know what you've got till it's gone.'"

On January 20, 2017, ten days after Chrystia took up her post as Canada's minister of foreign affairs, Trump was sworn in as US president. His inaugural address, on the steps of the US Capitol, featured a marked shift in tone from the soaring rhetoric of the Obama years to something darker and more combative. Citing the "American carnage" that he argued was a reality for many, and lamenting the offshoring of jobs and factories, he promised to put "America first."

"Protection will lead to great prosperity and strength," Trump said. "America will start winning again, winning like never before."

In her effort to contain the threat emanating from beyond Canada's southern border, Chrystia would employ, as she described in a speech at the University of Ottawa, a "whole-of-government, bi-partisan, full-court press to preserve everything good about NAFTA for Canada, and also to find what elements of the deal can be improved." Chrystia would have assistance in this endeavour from across the country, in the form of her government colleagues, opposition and provincial politicians, the business community—and even a former Conservative prime minister.

To help facilitate access to top White House officials, Trudeau reached out to Mulroney, who had known Trump for decades; they both owned homes in Palm Beach, Florida, and their children were friendly. The former prime minister, who believed staunchly that NAFTA should be "treated with care and concern, and shouldn't be the target of abuse by political leaders," was happy to help, consulting with Chrystia a number of times and offering her his advice when asked.

A small army of Canadian officials—MPs, premiers, mayors, consuls general—were recruited for a "maple charm offensive" designed to ensure that their American counterparts understood the mutually beneficial nature of their trade relationship. Over hundreds of trips, the Canadians met with American members of Congress, governors, local politicians, and business and labour leaders, highlighting the fact that Canada was the largest foreign market for American exports and that millions of jobs depended on trade with Canada.

Ministers made it personal: Champagne visited Cincinnati, Ohio, where he'd once studied, reportedly noting in every meeting that a local politician had once called him "a son of Ohio"; Finance Minister Bill Morneau travelled to Gary, Indiana, where he tweeted a photo of himself, wearing an "I *heart* Gary" T-shirt, with the city's mayor; and Transport Minister Marc Garneau went to Florida, where he had worked during his career as an astronaut.

A number of unlikely cross-border friendships were made at the highest levels. Telford spoke often with Kushner, who considered her a "talented operator"; Canadian ambassador to the United States David

MacNaughton got to know Trump's national security advisor, H. R. McMaster, well; and Morneau struck up enough of a rapport with US treasury secretary Steven Mnuchin to receive an invitation to his wedding in Washington. In one of the "most bizarre combinations," says MacNaughton, "Steve Bannon really thought Gerry Butts was great too."

Chrystia also established a close relationship with her Mexican counterparts, foreign minister Luis Videgaray Caso and economy minister Ildefonso Guajardo Villarreal. The three presented a united front, insisting publicly that any changes to NAFTA would be negotiated trilaterally—and that no one would be thrown under the bus. Neither country was shy about signalling that while the outright cancellation of NAFTA would be disastrous, there were areas of the treaty they would like to see modernized for the twenty-first century. As Mulroney noted to a Toronto audience at an event hosted by the Canadian Council for the Americas, when he was negotiating the original Canada-US deal with Reagan in the 1980s, "cellphones didn't exist" and "the internet was in its embryonic infancy."

In their initial conversations, Videgaray remembers being impressed by Chrystia's "well-thought-out, all-hands-on-deck" approach to impending negotiations, as well as her "thorough understanding" of the US political landscape. "Her personality, her wit, her charm is so impressive that sometimes people don't realize what a smart and thoughtful strategist she is," he says. "I think when you combine that kind of strategic mind with the passion with which she pursues her goals and values, you get a very unique kind of leadership."

For the first couple of months after Trump's inauguration, Canada's charm offensive appeared to be warding off the worst of the president's tumultuous impulses. On February 13, Trudeau travelled to Washington for his first face-to-face meeting with Trump. There were

no fireworks—Trudeau even managed to resist the pull of the presi
dent's unusual, jerky handshake—and the trip was largely considered
to be a success. Speaking to reporters during the visit, Trump said
that he merely intended to tweak certain elements of the US's "very
outstanding" trade relationship with Canada, adding: "It's a much
less severe situation than what's taken place on the southern border."

In March, Trudeau sat alongside Ivanka Trump at a Broadway
performance of *Come from Away*, a heartwarming Canadian musical
about how residents of Gander, Newfoundland, came together to help
the thousands of passengers who were diverted to their town after the
September 11 attacks.

The *New York Times* lauded Trudeau's strategy for managing Trump, noting that the Canadian prime minister had "largely
succeeded where even experienced leaders like Angela Merkel of
Germany have fallen short." However, with such a mercurial US
president, harmonious relations were never guaranteed for long.

Trudeau and his team, Guajardo says with a chuckle, "had this
romantic idea" that by deploying Mulroney and charming Ivanka
they'd have "easy lobbying access to the new US president," which
would in turn stave off any major risks to the Canada-US trading relationship. "They thought they were off the hook—little they knew."

In April, Trump suddenly directed Kushner and other officials
to prepare an executive order to withdraw from NAFTA completely,
despite having no alternative plan in place and disregarding the fact
that simply cancelling the deal could have been economically catastrophic, according to Kushner's book, *Breaking History*. The president
reportedly hoped the threat of withdrawal would light a fire under
Congress, which had yet to confirm his nominee for US trade representative, Robert Lighthizer, which in turn was holding up the start
of negotiations.

According to Kushner, Mnuchin, Secretary of Commerce Wilbur Ross, and Secretary of Agriculture Sonny Perdue were all against terminating the agreement. After a flurry of calls to the White House from aggrieved business owners, as well as personal calls from Trudeau and Mexican president Enrique Peña Nieto, Trump walked back his threat, declaring in a late-night statement that it would be his "privilege to bring NAFTA up-to-date through renegotiation."

On May 18, Lighthizer, finally confirmed as the US trade representative, sent a letter notifying Congress of the administration's intent to begin negotiations in mid-August, following the required ninety-day consultation period with lawmakers.

Running for the NDP in Edmonton-Strathcona in 1988, Chrystia's mother, Halyna, had been against the Canada-US Free Trade Agreement negotiated by Mulroney. Almost three decades later, her daughter would lead the charge to save its three-nation successor.

Over the summer, Chrystia convened a thirteen-member NAFTA Council to advise her throughout the negotiations. In keeping with her "Team Canada" strategy, it included former Conservative and NDP politicians, as well as labour and business leaders.

The approach of Canada's negotiating team, Chrystia said days before talks commenced, would be "in keeping with our national character; hard-working, fact-based, cordial ... In all these discussions, we will come to the table with goodwill, and Canada's characteristic ability and willingness to seek compromise and find win-win solutions. But we are committed to a good deal, not just any deal. That will be our bottom line."

ROBERT LIGHTHIZER, A VETERAN Republican lawyer who had worked as deputy US trade representative in the Reagan administration, believed that NAFTA had been a failure for working-class American families. Nevertheless, like Kushner, he recognized how catastrophic a sudden withdrawal would be for the Trump administration, according to his book *No Trade Is Free*. His challenge would be to overhaul NAFTA in a way that would be acceptable to all parties involved: the new president and his voters, Congress, Canada, and Mexico.

Lighthizer—who was known for both his sense of humour and his temper—writes that, contrary to media reports at the time, relations between himself, Chrystia, and Guajardo were professional and friendly. But according to those who participated in the negotiations, things didn't start out that way.

For their first meeting, Guajardo remembers, Chrystia had done "her homework very deeply" and had evidently familiarized herself with the US trade representative's background. (After interviewing Ukrainian prime minister Yulia Tymoshenko in 2008, Chrystia wrote in the *Financial Times* that Tymoshenko opened their conversation with "the practised pol's trick of telling me something nice about myself, thus making me feel good while letting me know she is on top of her game.")

"She knew the stories behind Lighthizer's position during the Reagan [administration], his job as a lawyer, his sports hobbies, his taste for good wine," Guajardo says. But Lighthizer was "extremely rude," which Guajardo puts down to his "very interesting position ... on Canadians and about gender."

Steve Verheul, who once again supported Chrystia as Canada's chief negotiator throughout the talks, says Lighthizer "had a fairly negative view of her coming in, because a minister on our side is different than a more professional, cabinet-level person on the US side." Verheul explains, "He certainly underestimated her. I think he felt that he was going to have free rein in this kind of discussion because he had so much more experience, he was more aggressive, he was on the US side, which, you know, obviously always gives them a sense of superiority. I think he was a bit taken aback by the fact that this woman had the temerity to push back against him and disagree with him."

On August 17, at a hotel in Washington, Chrystia, Guajardo, and Lighthizer began their first formal round of negotiations, joined by about a thousand government officials from their respective countries. It soon became apparent that what Chrystia lacked in negotiating experience she would make up for by arming herself with facts—not unlike the way she had built an airtight case before putting allegations to testy oligarchs in Moscow in the 1990s.

During negotiations, Chrystia surrounded herself with piles of paper, and to the amusement of her Harvard friends who remembered the habit from university, scribbled notes in ink on her hands. She read every briefing book at least three or four times, according to Verheul, eventually coming to understand them even better than he did.

"There are three things you have to know about negotiations: preparation, preparation, preparation," said Mulroney. "You have to be on the tip of your toes at all times, and she was. Moreover, she had a pleasant style about her—she was not aggressive, but she was firm. She was not threatening, but she was resolved. She had a first-class knowledge of everything that was going on."

Mulroney could also tell from conversations with Trudeau that, as during the CETA negotiations, Chrystia very much enjoyed the prime minister's "complete confidence" and that he took his guidance from her.

Occasionally, over a phone call, Mulroney said, Trudeau would ask for his advice: "You know, 'We're up against a major obstacle, and I have to call the president on Tuesday, what do you think I should say?' What should our position be?' And I found that when I would give my opinion to him, he had already touched base with Chrystia."

Mulroney continued: "When I was prime minister, I wouldn't ever consider entering this kind of negotiation without having complete confidence in my negotiator. And I could tell that that was the way Trudeau viewed Chrystia's leadership."

The negotiation process itself started out in a fairly standard way. Over a number of rounds in various North American cities, the three sides made progress on issues over which there wasn't much disagreement, managing to quickly close chapters that were non-controversial.

While there was no set deadline for the completion of the talks, Lighthizer was keen to have them wrapped up by late spring 2018, to give the Republican-controlled Congress enough time to pass a new agreement ahead of the November midterm elections. Delay past that point, he writes in *No Trade Is Free*, meant the Trump administration could be at the mercy of a House of Representatives controlled by the Democrats. It would also have to contend with a new president in Mexico—elections there were scheduled for July 1, with Peña Nieto set to leave office on December 1.

As months went by, however, Lighthizer got the impression that Canada and Mexico failed to share his sense of urgency. In fact, it seemed to Lighthizer that the Canadians were avoiding negotiating with him and his team at all, instead choosing to lobby members of Congress who might then put pressure on the administration to drop its demands.

According to Verheul, Lighthizer grew "increasingly frustrated" as Canada and Mexico failed to make any sort of meaningful concession by the spring, joining forces to reject a number of "unusual and radical positions" that the United States had brought to the table. "We do have a fairly long history of the US not necessarily following the rules in trade agreements," says Verheul, so a key element for the Canadians was the inclusion in any new deal of an effective dispute settlement process, which the United States was trying to reject out of hand. "And we said, if that's something you're not going to talk about, then we're not talking about any other issues."

Verheul characterizes the discussions between the Canadian and US sides as "quite intense," with voices raised at times. "But Chrystia held her own against a very seasoned trade negotiator and did not back down on key positions," he says.

"She never turned aggressive, and she kept her cool," adds Guajardo. "And that really infuriated [Lighthizer]. Things really deteriorated very fast with the Canadians."

(Away from the negotiating table, Chrystia did have to work on not appearing too keen to engage in discussion. Verheul remembers reaching one stalemate with the United States; the Canadians left their counterparts with a proposal and departed the talks on somewhat unfriendly terms. Shortly after the meeting, Chrystia asked Verheul if she could call them back. "I said 'No, you have to wait for them to get back to us, and just have to let that play out,'" he says. "She said, 'It's kind of like dating then, you can't be too eager.' And I said, 'That's exactly it.'")

Though outwardly there were few obvious cracks in the Team Canada approach, behind the scenes, not everyone was as steadfast as Chrystia in wanting to hold out for a good deal, not just any deal. "There were members of the government who thought we should give the US what they wanted very quickly—basically rip off the bandaid," says one Canadian official who worked closely with Chrystia on the NAFTA file.

In particular, there was tension between Chrystia and Morneau around what the endgame should look like. The finance minister, according to his book *Where To from Here*, felt there was great value in his informal, back-channel tête-à-têtes with Mnuchin. After meeting the treasury secretary, says a different senior government official, Morneau would report back to his Canadian colleagues that the two of them had mapped out a path to bring negotiations to a swift conclusion. Chrystia, exasperated, felt he wasn't seeing the bigger picture, and maintained that there could be no shortcuts on the road to a revamped NAFTA that worked for Canada.

Chrystia's slow-burn strategy, according to the second official, was partly a result of something that had occurred even before Trump was sworn in. Ahead of his inauguration, the president-elect's team presented the Canadians with a paper listing the elements of NAFTA they wanted to modify, hoping that the Canadians would speedily agree, which would in turn demonstrate how Trump could get things done. The proposals, however—such as changes to the rules-of-origin requirements that would be detrimental to the Canadian auto sector—were troubling to the Canadians, who were in no hurry to capitulate.

The decision whether to angle for a quick deal or delay rested with Trudeau, and ultimately, the prime minister sided with Chrystia, according to the first official, who puts this down to her ability to build internal coalitions and get others onside. "She spoke with Gerry Butts, she spoke with Katie Telford, she spoke with Ambassador MacNaughton, with Brian Clow. She explained her thoughts, she explained her strategy. She listened to them—and when she listens, it's not just for the sake of listening. She actually incorporates other ideas that people have. If they have concerns, she'll try to find ways to address them or mitigate them ... and really try to make sure that everyone is comfortable with the strategy," the official adds.

"I think that's one of the reasons she had the prime minister's ear, and why he really thought that what she was presenting also had the support of other people in government. And maybe people advocating for other policies did not have as strong support because maybe they didn't do their homework."

BY LIGHTHIZER'S LATE-SPRING DEADLINE, the three parties seemed no closer to an agreement than they had been the previous fall—and things were about to get worse. In May, Ross announced that the Trump administration would be slapping stiff tariffs on steel and aluminum imported from Canada, Mexico, and the European Union, using a section of US trade law that allowed the president to impose duties on countries deemed to be threats to national security. According to Lighthizer, the decision was meant to send an "unmistakable signal that business as usual was over."

Chrystia learned of the decision the morning the tariffs were announced via a call from Lighthizer while waiting for a Porter flight at Billy Bishop Toronto City Airport. In response, she announced that Canada would retaliate by imposing its own dollar-for-dollar tariffs on US products. "I think what is important for Americans to understand is the justification under your rules for the imposition of these tariffs was a national security consideration. So, what you're saying to us and to all of your NATO allies is that we somehow represent a national security threat to the United States," she told CNN's *State of the Union*. "And I would just say to all of Canada's American friends ... Seriously?"

A week later, with a full-blown trade war looming, leaders of the G7 gathered in the picturesque region of Charlevoix, Quebec, on June 8 and 9 for their annual summit. Talks were tense, and the US president—who had already withdrawn his country from major international agreements such as the landmark Paris climate accord, the

Trans-Pacific Partnership, and a deal meant to curtail Iran's nuclear program—appeared to be the odd man out. By the summit's close, Trudeau, as host, nevertheless seemed to have managed to avoid any theatrics, and the seven countries issued their traditional joint communiqué, showing fragile consensus on pressing international issues. Trump left slightly early, boarding Air Force One en route to Singapore for a highly anticipated meeting with North Korean leader Kim Jong Un.

In a late-afternoon press conference in Charlevoix, Trudeau was asked about American tariffs. The prime minister reiterated that Canada would be moving forward with retaliatory measures on July 1, adding that Canadians would "not be pushed around."

This was all too much for Trump, who was watching aboard Air Force One. "Based on Justin's false statements at his news conference, and the fact that Canada is charging massive Tariffs to our US farmers, workers and companies, I have instructed our US Reps not to endorse the Communique as we look at Tariffs on automobiles flooding the US Market!" the president tweeted, slamming Trudeau in a second tweet as "dishonest & weak."

Navarro told Fox News that "there's a special place in hell for any foreign leader that engages in bad faith diplomacy with President Donald J. Trump and then tries to stab him in the back on the way out the door."

To reporters the next day, Chrystia said that "Canada does not believe that ad hominem attacks are a particularly appropriate or useful way to conduct our relations with other countries."

On June 14, after being named Diplomat of the Year by *Foreign Policy* magazine, Chrystia gave a speech in Washington warning of the dangers facing liberal democracies and the international rules-based order that underpinned them. She never named Trump, but the speech was largely viewed as a rebuke of the president's protectionist and inward-looking foreign policy, as well as his habit of playing fast and loose with the truth.

She took direct aim at the administration's decision on tariffs:

For the past 70 years and more, America has been the leader of the free world. We Canadians have been proud to stand at your side and to have your back. As your closest friend, ally, and neighbor, we also understand that many Americans today are no longer certain that the rules-based international order of which you were the principal architect and for which you did write the biggest checks still benefits America.

We see this most plainly in the US administration's tariffs on Canadian steel and aluminum imposed under the 232 national security provision. We share the world's longest undefended border.

Our soldiers have fought and died alongside yours.

The idea that we could pose a national security threat to you is more than absurd, it's hurtful. The 232 tariffs introduced by the US are illegal under World Trade Organization and NAFTA rules. They are protectionism pure and simple. They are not a response to unfair actions by other countries that put American industry at a disadvantage. They are a naked example of the United States putting its thumb on the scale in violation of the very rules it helped to write. Canada has no choice but to retaliate with a measured, perfectly reciprocal, dollar for dollar response. And we will do so.

... You may feel today that your size allows you to go *mano a mano* with your traditional adversaries and be guaranteed to win. But if history tells us one thing, it is that no one nation's preeminence is eternal.

The *Washington Post*'s David Hoffman, Chrystia's friend and colleague from her Moscow reporting days, was in the audience. He says the speech was written by Chrystia personally and was motivated by the lessons they had taken to heart in the 1990s, as they witnessed Russia's failure to fend off crony capitalism and authoritarian rule.

The speech was not well received inside the White House. Neither was Chrystia's appearance on a panel at the Women in the World Summit in Toronto three months later called "Taking on the Tyrant," which featured a video montage with footage of Trump alongside strongmen like Syria's Bashar al-Assad and China's Xi Jinping.

To critics, the decision to give the speech and appear on the panel—sure to provoke the US president, with a $1 trillion trilateral trade accord hanging by a thread—was careless. "That actually hurt our negotiating position," says Erin O'Toole, then the Conservative shadow minister for foreign affairs, "because it was performing for kind of the intellectual class, hammering Trump, which they loved. But how did that help the autoworker in Windsor or in Oshawa?"

O'Toole also took issue with what he considered to be "virtue-signalling" by the Trudeau government. "If there's one criticism I have of Chrystia, it is sometimes she performs and comes up with policy based on the little crucible she comes from, which is media." At the outset of negotiations Chrystia had emphasized Canada's "progressive trade agenda" and announced that her team would be seeking new chapters on gender rights and Indigenous peoples.

"It was hard for me to criticize these things, because I believe in reconciliation, I believe in gender equality," says O'Toole. "But this is a trade agreement ... they really used that negotiation as a way to show how different the Trudeau government was from the Trump administration."

Morneau, too, worried about the tone and substance of Chrystia's address, writing that it "tested" the trust he had built with Mnuchin, who was "obviously irritated" by the speech. "It's not that I or anyone else with Canadian ties disagreed with her perspective. But it's not easy to get what you want from your neighbour if you poke him in the eye while bargaining," he writes. "Minister Freeland's point of view may have been valid, but her timing couldn't have been worse."

Throughout Chrystia's tenure as foreign minister, though, time and time again she would act according to her belief that calling out injustice where she saw it should trump diplomatic niceties, whatever the cost.

On June 29, Trudeau and Trump spoke on the phone. During the call, Trump referred to Chrystia as a "nasty woman," the epithet he had previously reserved for Hillary Clinton during the final 2016 presidential debate. MacNaughton says that he never saw Chrystia react negatively to criticism from the president: "I congratulated her on being—it's kind of a badge of honour—the 'nasty woman.'"

AS THE SUMMER PROGRESSED, while talks between Canada and the United States were at a standstill, negotiations between the United States and Mexico were ramping up. Andrés Manuel López Obrador, a leftist who in the past had strongly criticized NAFTA, had won the Mexican presidential election. He was prepared to support an agreement negotiated by Peña Nieto, but only if it was completed by the December 1 handover date—otherwise, he would insist on starting from scratch. And under US law, Trump was required to notify Congress ninety days before signing a trade deal. This meant, working backwards from the December 1 deadline, talks would need to wrap up by the end of August.

With only a few hours to spare, a bilateral agreement was reached. When the Americans and Mexicans announced the news, they made it clear that Canada was welcome to join—but also that the two countries would move forward either with or without their north-ernmost neighbour. "That really put the cat among the pigeons," says MacNaughton, and as a result the Canadian negotiating team was under a "huge amount of pressure," as commentators complained that Canada had been thrown under the bus after all.

The Mexicans, for their part, felt they had little choice but to cut a deal, given that they were operating under a different timetable. "Chrystia will tell you, I resisted to my last breath," says Guajardo. "In the end, I was forced to join this process—but I kept Chrystia informed of every step we were doing, in order for the Canadians not to be surprised."

According to MacNaughton, though, Chrystia was taken by surprise, "not just by the fact they did a deal but by some of the contents of the deal." MacNaughton remembers a meeting with Guajardo and Videgaray in his office at the Canadian embassy when Chrystia was forceful in her criticism. She never raised her voice, he says, but her Mexican counterparts had no doubt where she stood: "I said to her after, remind me never to do to you what the Mexicans did."

Videgaray says that while it was very clear that Chrystia "would have preferred something different," she was "extremely professional, and the communication never stopped. When she's happy, when she's unhappy, she's always direct."

All the while, the clock was still ticking: under US law, following the announcement of a deal, American negotiators had only thirty days to provide Congress with the full text. If the Canadians were to join the bilateral deal, they would need to do so by midnight on September 30.

In early September, Chrystia, Telford, and Butts flew to Washington to resume talks over outstanding major issues, which included the steel and aluminum tariffs, maintaining the dispute resolution mechanism guaranteed by Chapter 19 of the original NAFTA, protecting Canadian cultural industries, and Canada's tariffs on dairy products.

For three weeks, it seemed to the Americans that the Canadians were still in no rush to make a deal. According to Kushner, Chrystia sat back and allowed Lighthizer to spar with her trade officials on technical details, while refusing to commit to any significant changes. "Following this theatre, she would walk to the steps of the [US Trade Representative] building and hold an outdoor press conference, uttering platitudes like, 'I get paid in Canadian dollars, not US dollars,'" Kushner writes. (On one occasion, she also handed out fruit-flavoured popsicles to reporters waiting in the sweltering Washington heat.)

On September 18, she arrived in Washington wearing a white T-shirt given to her as a Christmas gift by her children. Written in black text on the front was the message: "Mama ≠ Chopped Liver." On the back: "Keep Calm and Negotiate NAFTA."

A week later, during a press conference on the sidelines of the UN General Assembly in New York, Trump criticized Canadians officials, making a not-so-veiled reference to Chrystia: "We're unhappy with the negotiations and the negotiating style of Canada. We don't like their representative very much."

The next day, according to the *Washington Post*, in another apparent reference to Chrystia, Trump said at a private event for campaign donors at the Trump International Hotel in DC that Canada's negotiator "hates America."

Nevertheless, away from the cameras and crowds, things were finally starting to move. Telford reached out to Kushner with an offer on dairy market access that, for the first time, communicated to the US side that the Canadians were in closing mode.

The final sprint to a deal took place over several days leading up to the September 30 deadline—a Sunday. The furious back-and-forth was all done by conference call, with Chrystia, Verheul, Telford, Butts, MacNaughton, and others huddled around a speakerphone in Telford's office at 80 Wellington.

On Saturday, the Americans agreed to leave Chapter 19 intact. "That was where I started to realize that, okay, I think we're going to be able to get to a place," Trudeau later told reporters.

On Sunday afternoon, in the White House residence, Trump informed Kushner and Lighthizer that he'd be requiring one more tweak: he wanted the agreement to be called U-S-M-C-A, like the United States Marine Corps. Just before midnight, both sides announced that they had reached a deal.

AS DETAILS OF THE new pact emerged, there was criticism from skeptics—Canadian dairy farmers declared themselves "deeply disappointed" that Canada had given, in their view, too much ground on dairy market access, and Conservative leader Andrew Scheer tweeted: "Would I have signed this deal? I would have signed a better one."

But the overwhelming sense from the Canadian public and political class was that the agreement was good enough. Canadians had narrowly avoided economic disaster and could collectively exhale.

"I think it was a massive success, largely because it represented so little change from the original NAFTA agreement," says Brett House, then Scotiabank's deputy chief economist, adding that the "most important thing Canada and Mexico were negotiating for was maintaining the status quo, and they disproportionately managed to do that in the face of rhetoric from the US that contemplated entirely ripping up that status quo. Sometimes no change is the biggest thing you can achieve, and I think that's largely what we got."

Even after the fact, MacNaughton marvels at the scale of what Chrystia and the entire negotiating team had to deal with. "I never fully appreciated the complexity and the nuance of these trade deals—you get one clause wrong and all of a sudden you wipe out an industry or something," he says. "I didn't know there was a sugar beet business in southern Alberta, and I didn't realize that there was a factory being built in Kingston to manufacture infant formula. Had we not been on top of a couple of things, both of those would have been gone."

Clow says the responsibility of defending Canadian interests and preserving the majority of the trilateral deal weighed heavily on Chrystia throughout negotiations. "I'm not trying to be generous when I say this, but I honestly believe it could not have happened as well as it did without her," he adds.

Chrystia's sparring partners also emerged from the fog of negotiations with a deep respect for her. Guajardo and Videgaray both speak of her in the warmest terms and regard her as a straight shooter who can be relied upon to keep her word.

In the end, according to several officials closely involved in the talks, she even won over Lighthizer, who during the White House USMCA signing ceremony referred to Chrystia as his "good friend." One senior US official characterizes their relationship as "constructive and warm," adding that the US negotiating team appreciated her ability to compartmentalize—she never held the fact that they were working for Trump against them—and to work with people with whom she didn't see eye to eye.

After the deal was inked, Chrystia invited Lighthizer and his deputy, C. J. Mahoney, to dinner at her house. MacNaughton brought a 1992 bottle of Château Margaux from his wine collection, in honour of the original NAFTA's signature date, and Chrystia prepared a repast of Alberta beef.

Her performance as Canada's lead negotiator also further cemented her relationship with Trudeau, who came to realize that the renegotiation of NAFTA would be "one of the historical highlights of his government's achievements," said Mulroney. "The importance of that was not lost on him, believe me."

Afterwards, Chrystia maintained that her faith in the ability of the three countries to reach a reasonable outcome never wavered; she told journalist Aaron Wherry that it would be hard for someone to look at the numbers and facts and view the Canada-US trade relationship as anything other than both vital and balanced.

At an Ottawa press conference on October 1, Trudeau thanked Chrystia for her "tireless, relentless efforts" over the previous nineteen months—and gave a nod to Graham, Natalka, Halyna, and Ivan, who, he said, knew she was doing "extraordinarily important work." He continued: "We owe you all a debt of gratitude. No minister in a generation has been given a more difficult task than this one. And you delivered."

SEVENTEEN

Moving the Dial

S HORTLY AFTER WINNING THE 2015 federal election, Justin Trudeau told his supporters that Canada was back. The implication was that the country had lost its way under Stephen Harper, who had strayed from Canada's traditional liberal internationalist roots to espouse a more aggressive, neoconservative foreign policy—one that critics alleged had alienated Canada from its international allies and led to a loss of influence on the world stage.

More so than his recent Liberal predecessors, Harper viewed international politics as a zero-sum game between friends and foes, with democratic leaders on one side and authoritarian despots on the other. He made it clear that Canada, in his opinion, should not just "go along" to "get along," and should double down on its commitment to the rule of law and human rights.

In practice, this translated into foreign policy decisions that Harper's opponents slammed as isolationist. Over the course of nearly a decade, his Conservative government withdrew from the Kyoto environmental accord, arguing for a new agreement that included major emitters such as China and India; distanced Canada from its tradition of peacekeeping and moved away from the importance placed by successive governments on multilateral institutions such as the United Nations; advocated for military interventions such as the bombing of Islamic State militants in Iraq; and opposed the Iran nuclear deal and shut Canada's embassy in Tehran, arguing that the government of Iran posed the "most significant threat to global peace and security in the world today."

On the first day of the 2014 Group of Twenty (G20) summit in Australia, Harper was approached by Vladimir Putin, hand extended. According to Harper's spokesperson, the prime minister told the Russian leader: "I guess I'll shake your hand but I have only one thing to say to you: You need to get out of Ukraine."

When, for the first time since the creation of the United Nations in the 1940s, Canada failed to win a seat on the organization's Security Council—reportedly at least partly a result of the government's shift toward stronger support for Israel—it was widely regarded by opposition politicians and the media as an embarrassing rebuke of Canada's retreat from its global responsibilities.

Though experts disagree on how much Harper's foreign policy truly deviated from that of his predecessors, Trudeau came to government promising to return Canada to the more "constructive" role of a "fair-minded and determined peace builder," as his new foreign minister, Stéphane Dion, put it. (The concept of the more conventional "honest broker," Dion said, was too often confused with a lack of strong moral convictions.)

On March 29, 2016, Dion gave a speech at the University of Ottawa laying out his guiding principle of "responsible conviction," a twist on the thinking of German sociologist Max Weber, arguing that Canadians must engage with government leaders with whom they did not agree. "We take no more joy than our conservative friends in keeping open channels with authoritarian regimes. Of course, we would like it if the world were made up of nothing but exemplary democracies. But our world is highly imperfect, and to improve it we must engage in it with our eyes open, not withdraw from it," Dion said. "It is often a mistake to sever all ties with a regime that we dislike. On the contrary, we must speak to such regimes frankly, and clearly express our convictions, with a view to effecting positive change."

Jocelyn Coulon, who at the time was a policy advisor to Dion and helped write the speech, argues that Canada must "trade with dictatorships," as it has done for all of its recent diplomatic history. "Do you think that when Pierre Elliott Trudeau recognized China, he did not know that Mao Zedong was a psychopath who had killed millions of people?" Coulon asks. "But he thought that we are in a world that's imperfect, and we have to communicate, exchange, try to have good relations with everyone."

As his most prominent example of re-engagement, Dion argued for restoring relations with Russia, despite its incursions into Ukraine, declaring that "Canada must stop being essentially the only one practising an empty chair policy with Russia, because by doing so, we are only punishing ourselves."

Though the purpose of Dion's speech was purportedly to lay out the Trudeau government's vision for its foreign policy, debate continued behind the scenes in the prime minister's circle on whether Dion's "responsible conviction" route was the right one to take, according to a government official who worked closely with Chrystia when she was minister of international trade. "Stéphane Dion wanted to engage more with Russia, with Iran, and that was part of the [2015 election] platform. Chrystia was not in agreement," the official says.

It's hard to imagine Chrystia taking issue with the core of both Harper's and Dion's views on foreign policy, each of which involved championing human rights and democratic values around the world. But unlike Harper, she was of the opinion that Canada should act, when possible, in concert with its like-minded allies; and unlike Dion, she felt that Canada shouldn't hesitate to talk tough when necessary.

"The notion that the objective of foreign policy is to be friends with everyone is to misread very much the situation in the world today, where some very big principles and issues are at stake," she would later tell the *Globe and Mail*.

Bob Rae, currently Canada's ambassador to the United Nations, says Chrystia wouldn't disagree that running Canada's foreign policy involves talking to and dealing with "people we don't like." But she believes strongly that the value proposition for Canada is being a country that "speaks the truth to every issue that it sees," whether that be internally or internationally.

"I think that there's a growing school of people who actually get that, and understand that it's important to be clear about who you are and also who they are," says Rae. "Because if you fail to understand the nature of those regimes and what they will do, you fail to understand how they will behave in the world. So yeah, you have to talk to those people and have relationships with them, professionally, but you don't have to go out of your way to cater to them."

Following Trump's election victory, according to Coulon's book *Canada Is Not Back*, the prime minister didn't think Dion had the profile or personality required for dealing with the new administration. The two men never developed a close or trusting relationship; Coulon writes that over the fourteen months Dion was foreign minister, he did not once meet with Trudeau in private to discuss Canada's foreign policy.

When, in January 2017, Trudeau replaced Dion with Chrystia, Trudeau still wasn't fully committed to either of their world views.

But eventually, the government official says, Chrystia was able to get the prime minister onside. Over her tenure, the official believes, "Trudeau's foreign policy [was] actually mostly Chrystia Freeland's foreign policy."

THREE DECADES EARLIER, CHRYSTIA'S friends at Harvard felt it wasn't a stretch to joke about her one day becoming Canada's foreign minister. And indeed, at the beginning of 2017, there she was, Canada's top diplomat, charged with leading the country's relations with the rest of the world.

"I don't think she enjoyed opposition; I don't think opposition is what she was made out for," says Rae, reflecting on the early years of Chrystia's political trajectory. But at Global Affairs Canada, as Trudeau had renamed the foreign affairs department in 2015, she found herself at the heart of government—and at the heart of decision making. "I think she felt that she was dealing at a substantive level with issues that she knew how to deal with. She was very, very happy to do that."

While her international trade duties had kept her exceptionally busy, it's difficult to overstate how much bigger the foreign affairs file would be. In addition to Chrystia's nearly all-encompassing top priority—the Canada-US relationship, in particular the NAFTA negotiations—she was responsible for everything else that fell under the foreign affairs rubric. The job involved a dizzying amount of travel, whether to meet with international counterparts or to attend conferences and summits hosted by the G7, G20, NATO, and others.

At Global Affairs Canada, says Vincent Garneau, who became her director of parliamentary affairs and senior advisor for Canada-US relations, "you can have a surprise at any given time—in the middle of the night, on Christmas Day, on weekends ... It's really a portfolio that never stops; you're always on."

In her nearly three years in the post, Chrystia would become Trudeau's most high-profile cabinet minister, but she never lost the air of informality that set her apart from many of her colleagues. Peter Boehm, at the time Canada's deputy minister of international development, remembers first getting to know Chrystia at the May 2017 G7 summit in Taormina, Italy. In a meeting with their foreign counterparts, the arm of her glasses broke. "She wasn't fazed—someone gave her a paper clip and a rubber band, and she reattached it and continued with her program as if nothing had happened," says Boehm, who joked that he'd have a roll of duct tape on hand for next time.

She continued to personally respond to correspondence, firing off emails at lightning pace. "She is remarkable in how much she does herself; I used to actually criticize her for it," said the late former Canadian foreign minister Bill Graham in 2022. While his inclination was to contact Jeremy Broadhurst, then Chrystia's chief of staff, when he wanted to get in touch with her, she insisted that he email her directly, and she would reply that same day.

Chrystia jogged and cycled regularly and frequently took public transportation, never with any form of security detail. Following the Taormina summit, in June, Chrystia and Graham took the kids to visit Don in Alberta, borrowing his old car to go camping in the Rockies. "In any Third World country, the minister of foreign affairs wouldn't go tent camping with a thirty-one-year-old car," Don said to his daughter, according to Jason McBride's 2017 *Toronto Life* profile. "They'd have four Mercedes and six bodyguards."

"That's why they're Third World countries," Chrystia replied.

At her home in Toronto's Summerhill neighbourhood, she continued to host a coterie of international figures: a former chairman of the

US Federal Reserve, the former prime minister of Australia, a delegation of Ukrainian diplomats, her G7 foreign minister counterparts (she served waffles). Dominic Barton, the former global managing director of consulting firm McKinsey & Company, remembers one gathering where Chrystia cooked dinner with the assistance of the late Ian Shugart, then Canada's deputy minister of foreign affairs, who was "kind of like the sous-chef, running around."

Chrystia's aunts maintained their rotating shifts, though Natalka, Halyna, and Ivan were given an increasing amount of independence, as Chrystia and her sister Natalka had been given as children. The kids featured in various magazine profiles of their mother, always doing something impressive: reading the biographies of every US president, running marathons, practising violin, speaking fluent Ukrainian.

"The Freeland-Bowley kids like to joke that their mother is the only tiger mom in the world who's literally never around," writes Leah McLaren in her *Chatelaine* feature.

Despite their jam-packed schedules, Chrystia and Graham managed to carve out some time for themselves. "On weekends, when Freeland's home, the family's Saturday routine is an over-achiever's reverie," writes McBride. "She and Bowley dispatch the kids by cab to a Ukrainian school in Etobicoke for four hours. While they study, their parents go for a long run—Freeland had completed two half-marathons and was training for a third when we met—and then they grab brunch at Rose and Sons on Dupont and subway home."

In what little downtime she did have, Chrystia would read cheesy science fiction novels to unwind. While she and Graham also enjoyed the Danish political drama *Borgen*, as in high school, Chrystia remained happily ignorant of popular trends.

"Her knowledge of pop culture was firmly rooted in mom territory," says Adam Austen, her press secretary at the time. He remembers being surprised when, at a meeting in the Philippines, Chrystia correctly identified the song being played by a string quartet in the building's lobby as the 2017 megahit "Despacito."

While she managed to make time for family, there were inevitably some tasks that had to give, starting with housework. Journalists frequently described Chrystia's home in much the same way McBride does in *Toronto Life*: "Despite the postal code, the house is surprisingly modest. In the cramped living room, every surface was covered in books, board games and homework ... Paintings by Ukrainian artists, all from Freeland's late mother's collection, hung askew on the walls, and while the windows had rods and hooks, they had no curtains. Housekeeping seemed an afterthought. It was a humblebrag of a home, really, projecting, intentionally or not, a cabinet-ministers-are-just-like-us vibe."

Chrystia's sister Natalka laughs at the notion that the messiness could be staged. "I don't know how to convey this enough that people would believe it ... that is one hundred percent what her house looks like every day," says Natalka. "She literally is just very unpretentious in those ways."

Along with Chrystia's heightened public profile came commentary from armchair stylists and journalists who questioned why she appeared to wear a similar style of red dress over and over. "And I was like, 'Literally, that was what was clean,'" says Natalka. "With her household and her wardrobe and her travel, it's just like any other middle-class Canadian or American that you would know."

She adds that, like their mother, Chrystia has two modes of dress: her work clothes and tatty loungewear. One time, she recalls, Chrystia forgot to put out the trash in time and frantically raced down the street in her sweats, yelling out to get the attention of the garbage-truck driver. "[Chrystia] looks around and all their neighbours are at their windows going, 'There she is, our minister of foreign affairs!'"

Throughout her ministerial career, staff would sometimes try to convince Chrystia to put more thought into her image, like Amanda Alvaro had attempted on the campaign trail. "Whenever we'd go to events, I'd be like, 'Let's make you Christine Lagarde! Let's get you a scarf!'" says Ben Bergen of Chrystia's time as trade minister, referring to the then–managing director of the IMF, who is known for her sleek, elegant style.

But for Chrystia, time spent thinking about her appearance was time wasted. "If she could just be a brain in liquid, that would be her ideal situation. I think she hates the fact that she has a body, and that she doubly hates that as a woman she has to look a certain way," Bergen says. "That for her is the greatest offence of all time."

Part of the answer, then, to how she was able to devote such tremendous energy to being Canada's foreign minister and also a mother of three was by "systematically siphoning off certain areas that she's just not going to be bothered about," says Natalka. "She does have a very strict division between the things that are important, which she works on insanely hard, and then the things that aren't important, which she won't even pay lip service to."

ON TOP OF LEADING Canada's NAFTA negotiations, the issues Chrystia cared most about as foreign minister fell into three broad baskets: one, advancing Canada's newly introduced feminist foreign policy, designed to empower and uphold the rights of women and girls around the world; two, encouraging opportunities for diplomatic engagement by hosting conferences and meetings in Canada; and three, championing human rights and reinforcing the significance of international institutions and organizations.

Once in her new role, Chrystia decided that it would be beneficial and important to explain her foreign policy outlook to Canadians, says Garneau. As trade minister, she had made it clear to her staff that she didn't want to give speeches for the sake of it; if she was going to give an address, she wanted to present a concrete argument or lay out a particular position.

On a flight from Alaska to Seattle after a May 2017 meeting of the Arctic Council, Chrystia drafted a rough outline of her remarks on her BlackBerry. Over the next few weeks, she drew inspiration from various sources, speaking with Global Affairs Canada officials and academics. She read old addresses by former Canadian prime ministers Lester B. Pearson and Louis St-Laurent and former governor general Vincent Massey that touched on both Canada's relationship with the United States and the creation of the current rules-based international order. At a dinner in Taormina, when Peter Boehm mentioned he had written his doctoral thesis on Canada's contribution to shaping the postwar international system in the 1940s, she requested he send it over for her to read. Boehm figured she wasn't serious—"I mean, I'm used to dealing with ministers," he says—until she phoned him with a follow-up request.

On June 17, Chrystia rose in the House of Commons and spoke for almost forty minutes, laying out her belief in Canada as an "essential country" and the role it must play in defending the rules-based international order. She spoke of her grandfather, Wilbur Freeland, who'd left northern Alberta for war-ravaged Europe in the 1940s, along with so many Canadians who risked and gave their lives to preserve peace. In their memory, she argued, Canadians must "use the multilateral structures they created as the foundation for global accords and institutions fit for the new realities of this century." The challenge was all the more urgent, Chrystia told Parliament, because of the many

American voters who in 2016 had "cast their ballots, animated in part by a desire to shrug off the burden of world leadership."

She continued: "The fact that our friend and ally has come to question the very worth of its mantle of global leadership, puts into sharper focus the need for the rest of us to set our own clear and sovereign course. For Canada that course must be the renewal, indeed the strengthening, of the postwar multilateral order."

Though couched in gentle terms (she made sure to profoundly thank "the indispensable" nation for its "seven-decades-long contribution to our shared peace and prosperity"), it was a defiant rhetorical break with the Trump administration, echoing German chancellor Angela Merkel, who had the month before told an audience in Munich that "the times when [Europe] could completely rely on others are, to an extent, over."

The speech didn't contain many specific action items outside of the shoring up of international institutions and trade, though it did argue for the principled use of force—which hadn't yet obviously been presented as a policy by the Trudeau government—against the threats facing the liberal democratic world, citing "dictatorship in North Korea, crimes against humanity in Syria, the monstrous extremists of Daesh [Islamic State], and Russian military adventurism and expansionism."

But it was largely praised in the Canadian media for its articulation of the role that Chrystia saw for Canada in a world no longer led by the United States. It also made headlines abroad—the *New York Times* called it "the latest evidence of how Canada sees itself in a new light these days," describing her language as a "marked shift in tone for the Trudeau government."

Experts have long debated how much one individual can determine the course of a country's foreign policy—and also how much a middle power like Canada can contribute to world affairs. But over the course of Chrystia's time as minister, she made it a point to harness what foreign policy muscle Canada does have in ways she believed were appropriate.

She wasn't on the job long before discovering that adhering to her principles would come with a personal cost. The Kremlin, too, had noticed the shift in tone coming from Canada under its new foreign minister. In March, stories about Chrystia's grandfather, Michael Chomiak, and his role as editor-in-chief for the pro-Nazi *Krakivski Visti* newspaper in occupied Poland during the Second World War appeared in online blogs with links to Russia. When asked about the articles, Chrystia dismissed them as the sort of propaganda that had been used by Russia in disinformation campaigns aimed at influencing elections in the United States and Europe.

"I don't think it's a secret. American officials have publicly said, and even Angela Merkel has publicly said, that there were efforts on the Russian side to destabilize Western democracies, and I think it shouldn't come as a surprise if these same efforts were used against Canada," she told reporters. "I think that Canadians and indeed other Western countries should be prepared for similar efforts to be directed at them."

It wasn't a direct or satisfying answer to the questions raised by the articles about Michael's wartime activities. As Canadian journalists uncovered more details about *Krakivski Visti*, columnists debated whether Michael had been a Nazi collaborator—something an official in Chrystia's office, according to the *Globe and Mail*'s Robert Fife, denied.

On March 7, under the headline "Freeland knew her grandfather was editor of Nazi newspaper," Fife reported that Chrystia had helped edit a 1996 article in the *Journal of Ukrainian Studies* written by historian John-Paul Himka, her uncle by marriage, that mentioned Michael's position as editor-in-chief of *Krakivski Visti*."

Fife wrote that Himka said in an interview that "he never knew that Mr. Chomiak had worked for the Nazis until after his father-in-law passed away and he discovered copies of *Krakivski Visti* in his personal papers." But according to Himka's wife, Chrystia Chomiak, Michael's work was never a secret among his relatives: "We knew that he was the editor, of course ... Did he talk about the newspaper? No. But we had bound copies of it." Nobody ever actually went through it while he was alive, she says, but they knew its "basic outline." In accordance with Michael's wishes, after his death in 1984, his copies of *Krakivski Visti* and his personal papers were given to the Provincial Archives of Alberta.

Months later, McBride asked Chrystia about her grandfather for his *Toronto Life* profile: "Her normally chipper demeanour cracked. 'I have been very clear about this,' she said, frostily. 'The research into my grandfather's activities during the war has been entirely done by my own family, and published by my own family, and that's research I have personally supported.' She wouldn't provide any specific evidence she had about Russian involvement, but she did offer this: 'I may be privy to some information that is not publicly available.'"

It's hard to gauge what was behind Chrystia's choice of communications strategy; given her deep understanding of both Ukrainian history and the way journalistic news cycles work—as well as the importance she places on facts and truth—it's perhaps puzzling that she would, with vague responses, leave herself open to headlines like the one in the *Globe*, implying that she had something to hide.

One possibility is that her loyalty to and admiration for her beloved grandfather led to a certain defensiveness. John Lloyd, her *Financial Times* mentor, says when the stories came out, "obviously that hurt her, because she was very close to her family."

According to another former *Financial Times* colleague, her unwillingness to comment on Michael stems from a personality quirk: "There is an information-hoarding-ness about Chrystia. It might be more a function of being a woman making her way up the greasy pole, but it's definitely counterproductive, because it raises more questions; it implies there's something being concealed. It's better just to be frank."

At any rate, the Kremlin's attempts to use kompromat to undercut Chrystia's willingness to swing Canada's foreign policy from the brief desired détente of Dion back to a hard line on Russia were unsuccessful. One of the most obvious examples of this was Canada's passing of the Justice for Victims of Corrupt Foreign Officials Act, also known as the Sergei Magnitsky Law, later that year.

Magnitsky legislation, adopted by the United States, the United Kingdom, and a number of other countries, was the initiative of Bill Browder, an American-born British financier who was once the largest foreign investor in Russia. In the 1990s, Chrystia impressed him with her readiness to report on the oligarchs' corrupt business dealings.

In 2008, Magnitsky, as Browder's lawyer, investigated Russian government officials who had fraudulently seized companies belonging to Browder's asset management firm, Hermitage Capital Management, uncovering an alleged $230 million tax scam in the process. As a result, Magnitsky was arrested, imprisoned, and beaten, ultimately dying in jail after being denied medical treatment.

Determined to hold those responsible for Magnitsky's death accountable, Browder embarked on a global campaign to persuade governments to adopt legislation that would impose visa bans on and freeze the assets of officials who engaged in corruption and human rights abuses.

In 2010, Browder had met with former Canadian minister of justice and attorney general Irwin Cotler, who agreed to take on the effort in the Canadian Parliament. In a 2012 Centre Block press conference, Cotler was joined in his campaign by Kremlin critic Vladimir Kara-Murza and Boris Nemtsov, then a Russian opposition leader; Chrystia had gotten to know Nemtsov well during her Moscow years, when he was a young regional governor who admired Margaret Thatcher and enjoyed *The Economist* magazine.

In a *National Post* op-ed, Kara-Murza and Nemtsov argued: "It is time for personal responsibility for those who continue to violate the rights and freedoms—and plunder the resources—of Russian citizens. Targeted sanctions will end impunity for crooks and abusers, and will introduce a measure of accountability otherwise unachievable in today's Russia. The idea that not even the Kremlin's protection and oil money can guarantee access to the West and its financial system will send a chill down the backs of Mr. Putin's autocratic enablers."

The two men were themselves examples of the high stakes—and risk—involved in confronting Putin. Like Magnitsky, Nemtsov would pay for his outspokenness with his life. Late one evening in 2015, while walking near the Kremlin, he was shot and killed, just hours after giving an interview in which he called Putin a "pathological liar." And in 2023, after publicly denouncing Russia's war in Ukraine, Kara-Murza was convicted of treason and sentenced to twenty-five years in prison (he was later released in a prisoner swap).

Cotler was able to get a unanimous resolution adopted to recommend Magnitsky legislation, and in 2016 Conservative Raynell Andreychuk introduced a Magnitsky bill in the Senate. However, with the election of the Trudeau government, efforts stalled.

As foreign minister, Browder told the CBC, Dion "just outright vetoed" the legislation. "He said, 'I want to have better relations with Russia, I don't think this is important, I don't want to do it.'" Browder added: "It made no sense to me why this man would basically try to deny justice for Sergei Magnitsky, so that he could get an invitation to a conference ... that's effectively the trade he was doing."

The tipping point, Cotler says, was when Chrystia became foreign minister and "acted immediately" to ensure the legislation was adopted—not without some threats, he adds, from Putin's Russia.

Internally, too, there was pushback, according to Andriy Shevchenko, then Ukraine's ambassador to Canada, who believes Dion was convinced by Global Affairs Canada officials that Canada could not afford another escalation with Russia. Chrystia, by contrast, met with key department officials and, having heard them out, said: "Listen guys, I respectfully disagree. We are going to pass the Magnitsky law and this is why.'"

"Without her leadership, it wouldn't have happened," Cotler says. "If you had had another foreign minister, they wouldn't have known who Nemtsov was. She knew Nemtsov, and so the assassination had an impact for her."

Shevchenko agrees: "I think it was a very strong example of how one person can change the tides." Through sheer force of personal will, he says, Chrystia shifted Canada's "intellectual foundation" from its traditional honest broker reputation to "passionate actor, passionate player, passionate contributor."

DURING CHRYSTIA'S TENURE AT Global Affairs Canada, she strove to nudge the needle in favour of democracy and away from authoritarianism in several other international points of conflict.

One instance was the ongoing political and economic crisis in Venezuela, where President Nicolás Maduro's United Socialist Party had increasingly gained control over the country's key institutions. In March 2017, the pro-Maduro Supreme Court suspended the legislative powers of the country's opposition-led National Assembly, leaving the United Socialist Party in charge of the three branches of the Venezuelan government. Protests erupted in the streets, with the opposition calling the ruling a coup.

On March 31, Chrystia's office issued a statement calling on the Venezuelan government to restore democracy—one of the first foreign ministers, says Ben Rowswell, then Canada's ambassador to Venezuela, to call out Maduro's power grab. "I'm watching this literally from my window—hundreds of thousands of people calling for democracy, and these black-clad riot police coming forward, and tear gas flying," Rowswell remembers. "The traditional diplomatic response is silence, or, if forced to speak, neutrality, or, if forced to say something more significant, vagueness. But [Chrystia] said clearly: there is no democracy anymore."

When there's a contest between two competing narratives, he says, "what the international community says can totally tip the balance one way or the other, because it conveys legitimacy on one side or the other." Chrystia's statement "did shift the tone of the international community's treatment of Venezuela, particularly its neighbours'. The Latin Americans began calling for the release of political prisoners and for a resumption of the constitution and for the organization of free and fair elections."

Rowswell continues, "In the information age, communications is power. There's a lot of hesitation about us using our power. Whereas I think Chrystia wields power, and she's conscious that she's wielding it, and she knows what she's wielding it for."

For Chrystia, that power involved more than just words. In August, under her direction, Canada founded the Lima Group, aimed at bringing together Latin American and Caribbean countries with the goal of peacefully ending the crisis in Venezuela. According to Irwin Cotler, who as part of an Organization of American States panel determined Maduro's government had committed crimes against humanity, Chrystia played a central role in Canada's referral of Venezuela to the International Criminal Court.

She also spearheaded Canada's response in a number of other areas where human rights were being trampled upon, and where she believed Canada could make an impact.

In the winter of 2017, pro-Kremlin Chechen leader Ramzan Kadyrov launched a brutal, targeted pogrom against sexual minorities in Chechnya, with more than a hundred gay men reportedly rounded up, beaten, and tortured. Working with Rainbow Railroad, a Toronto-based charity, Chrystia, LGBTQ2 Special Advisor Randy Boissonnault, and Minister of Immigration Ahmed Hussen were able to help secretly move many other gay Chechens into safe houses in Moscow and Saint Petersburg. At Chrystia's direction, dozens were eventually airlifted to safety in Canada.

In July 2018—while facing a stalemate in NAFTA negotiations and dealing with the fallout of the US's steel and aluminum tariffs—she supported another secret rescue mission, this time to evacuate members of the Syria Civil Defence, better known as the White Helmets, a volunteer organization that had saved the lives of thousands of Syrians caught up in the bombing campaigns of the Assad regime and its allies.

Robin Wettlaufer, then Canada's Istanbul-based special envoy to Syria, had received worrisome text messages from contacts in southern Syria, warning that government forces were rapidly advancing on rebel-held territory. Wettlaufer was chilled by what she heard from Raed Saleh, the head of the White Helmets, who she says is normally very measured. "He was just like, 'They're going to take the south, they're moving fast, and they're going to kill us.'"

Knowing that the Assad regime wouldn't care about a statement of condemnation by the international community—that in fact, in some ways, officials took a certain pleasure at thumbing their noses at the rules-based order—Wettlaufer proposed to a group of her Western counterparts that they try to provide safe haven to a small number of White Helmets, perhaps leadership figures or those who were most visible in the press and therefore most vulnerable to attack.

When Germany agreed to take in five, Wettlaufer shared her idea with colleagues in Ottawa. "It was a very difficult internal discussion, because this is not something we do," she says—under Canada's immigration laws, members of the White Helmets wouldn't be considered traditional convention refugees, according to the United Nations Convention relating to the Status of Refugees.

It was only when the proposal hit Chrystia's desk that the wheels of the plan were truly set in motion. According to Wettlaufer, Chrystia not only personally mobilized the Canadian government, but also convinced her counterparts that they had a moral obligation to help the White Helmets. In a meeting with other foreign ministers at the July NATO summit in Brussels, she "basically slammed her hand on the table and said, 'Look, we've supported these guys throughout the war, they've saved more than a hundred thousand lives, many of their own have been killed, and we owe this to them.' And I have to say, in my career, I have not seen a minister do something that bold."

In the end, 422 people—98 White Helmets and their families—escaped Syria via the Israeli-occupied Golan Heights, arriving safely in Jordan.

Wettlaufer thinks that Donald Trump likely ultimately convinced Israeli prime minister Benjamin Netanyahu to provide the White Helmets with safe passage, but that "the Americans probably wouldn't have done that if it weren't for Chrystia Freeland making the point to her counterparts."

She adds, "You don't often see [that kind of action] in a minister who hasn't seen all the plans fleshed out—how would this work?
Who's going to pay for it? What are the modalities? What are the
risks, and who are we going to piss off, and all that. She just knew it
was the right thing to do."

AS WHEN SHE WAS minister of international trade, as foreign minister,
it was clear Chrystia's style of doing politics involved taking action
she believed was warranted without looking for approval or permis-
sion. Sometimes, her strong convictions around human rights and
democracy had unpredictable consequences—and created issues for
the Canadian government.

On July 31, 2018, as part of Saudi Arabia's ongoing crackdown
on civilians speaking out about human rights abuses in the country, news broke that activist Samar Badawi—the sister of imprisoned
dissident blogger Raif Badawi, whose wife had fled to Canada—had
been arrested.

On August 2, Chrystia tweeted: "Very alarmed to learn that Samar
Badawi, Raif Badawi's sister, has been imprisoned in Saudi Arabia.
Canada stands together with the Badawi family in this difficult time,
and we continue to strongly call for the release of both Raif and Samar
Badawi."

Just as her walkout during the Canada-EU trade negotiations had
been done without prior warning to the Prime Minister's Office, the
tweet was not sanctioned by the PMO, according to a senior government official who says that, with the benefit of hindsight, Canada
should have been even harsher with the authoritarian monarchy. But
that just wasn't the PMO's view of Saudi Arabia at the time, particularly
given the $15 billion arms contract with the Kingdom that Canada had

negotiated under Harper and approved under Trudeau.

After two similar tweets were sent from the accounts of Global Affairs Canada and Canada's embassy in Saudi Arabia, the reaction from the Saudi government was swift and fierce: it announced it was expelling Canada's ambassador, severing trade ties, ceasing flights to Canada, and recalling roughly fifteen thousand Saudi exchange students living in Canada.

For those who argue that diplomacy involves engaging with countries whose values are at odds with one's own, Chrystia's tweet was more of a blunder than a principled stand. "I hate aspects of that regime, but you also have to have realpolitik," says Erin O'Toole, noting that Canada and Saudi Arabia have "huge trade linkages" and were working together in areas of Middle Eastern policy, such as the fight against Islamic State militants.

"Something this complicated is not meant for Twitter diplomacy … With her approach, you're going to get many occasions where she gets it completely right based on her gut, like with Russia." But others, he says, call for "more nuance, because she's not representing Chrystia Freeland's interests on the world stage, it's Canada's interests. And sometimes they're not going to completely align with [her] moral framework."

Dennis Horak was the Canadian ambassador to Saudi Arabia at the time. He was on holiday in Canada when the tweets were posted and was not consulted about the language they contained. When his vacation was over, he was not allowed back into the Kingdom. Like O'Toole, he believes that sometimes Canada should hold its nose and engage with unsavoury regimes, and that diplomacy shouldn't be conducted via social media.

"Engagement gives you access, and access gives you opportunity for influence. Standing on the sidelines and yelling—or tweeting—has zero impact," Horak says. "This reliance on tweets and social media is a trend which I think is not productive to achieving our moral or commercial goals. It's not a productive way to work. What you're doing is preaching to the choir. What's the point—to get a lot of likes? You've done nothing to change anything in a substantial way; in fact, you may actually undercut your ability to make a difference on the ground for the people we profess to care about. And in some cases, we're hurting them."

Others would disagree. Ben Rowswell says Twitter can be a powerful tool, and that Chrystia sharing her message via the social media platform was "normal diplomatic practice" and "exactly the right thing for her to do." He says, "When you have a human rights activist who has been speaking truth to power, year after year after year, being thrown in jail, being tortured, coming back and continuing to advocate—to have a foreign government say 'I hear you' is unbelievably powerful. It basically makes the difference between those activists continuing to do what they do, or giving up and giving in."

And, he argues, while Chrystia's decision to make a more public issue of human rights abuses in Saudi Arabia broke with what was diplomatic consensus at the time, her stance became diplomatic consensus two months later with the murder of Saudi journalist and regime critic Jamal Khashoggi, who walked into the Saudi consulate in Istanbul one morning to obtain papers he needed to remarry and never walked out.

Irwin Cotler notes that at the time of the spat, not one of Canada's Western allies publicly came to its defence. But according to a government official, after news of Khashoggi, there were European diplomats who apologized to Chrystia for not speaking up.

"There was a straight line from the silence of the democracies to the brutal murder of Khashoggi," says Cotler. Chrystia "understood instinctively that we're living in a world where we have a resurgent global authoritarianism, a backsliding of democracies, assaults on human rights, and therefore one has to stand up."

"She didn't need to wait for a prominent *Washington Post* columnist to be dismembered in the consulate of another country in order to know that that was what was happening," Rowswell adds.

In a 2019 interview with the *Globe and Mail*, Chrystia's response to criticism of the Saudi incident was simple: "I think we need to be honest with ourselves and honest with Canadians that standing up on these issues will not always be without a cost. And that's okay."

WHILE CHRYSTIA'S PERFORMANCE AS foreign minister was generally applauded, critics argued she should have spent more effort on improving Canada's relations with India, China, and African countries. They also contended that, similarly to when she was trade minister, she failed to capitalize on the resources available to her via her ministry. Some public servants at Global Affairs Canada considered her to be dismissive and unwilling to take advice, and regarded her as a one-woman show.

"She was famously inaccessible as minister," says Rowswell, who attempted several times to speak directly with her as ambassador to Venezuela and was unsuccessful in doing so. Dennis Horak, too, was unable to meet with her during the Saudi crisis.

"I certainly have heard no end of situations where someone absolutely critical in the foreign service who really knows something and who's *the* authority—Chrystia would just go off and do something and not consult that person. That seems to be an MO for her," says Rowswell. "The critical version of this would be that she has this incredible institution at her beck and call and she doesn't bother to use it, which is not efficient. It's probably not sustainable, because any one person is going to make mistakes at some point."

In a 2017 interview with the *Globe*, Chrystia was frank when asked about morale at Global Affairs Canada headquarters on Sussex Drive. "My job is to represent Canadians in the world," she said. "My job is not to represent the Pearson Building in the world." She has spoken of her desire to hear directly from "the people who are at the coal face," telling Bloomberg in 2021 that the "system really doesn't want politicians to do that, it's just not designed for politicians to be picking up the phone all the time. But that's what I believe in doing."

Ultimately, says Rowswell, there was an upside to Chrystia going against the grain of a foreign service establishment that tends to produce outcomes that are safe but not always the best policy direction for Canada. "There are risks when an individual minister will break from that and make their own decisions. Often, those will be decisions that are worse than what the collective decision-making process would produce—Chrystia's were invariably better," he says. With countries that are not only non-democratic but also actively undermining the rules-based order, her "Cold War mentality ... is absolutely necessary for our times."

Chrystia's relationships were more positive with colleagues in cabinet and in the Liberal caucus, though there were fellow politicians who felt she perhaps didn't view them as equals. "She doesn't suffer fools," says one senior government official. "There can be a lot of annoying people in politics, and she does not like dealing with those people—she doesn't hide it very well."

By the end of Chrystia's time as foreign minister, there was no doubt that she was the Trudeau government's top performer. Her reputation had also caught the attention of international allies. In 2018, she was the first Canadian to receive Germany's Eric M. Warburg

Award, which honours "great accomplishments in transatlantic relations" (previous recipients included Angela Merkel and George H. W. Bush). In a warm, glowing tribute, foreign minister Heiko Maas called her "a real influencer" who had "made Canadian foreign policy into a 'brand' that clearly and recognisably goes beyond the usual diplomatic chitchat."

He added: "You are also an activist in the best sense of the word. You are both principled and realistic—not an easy combination these days."

THOUGH THE JURY IS still out on the impact that countries and individuals, rather than social movements or economic forces, can make in the world, in Chrystia's case, her friends and allies believe she was able to decisively move the dial. "Individuals matter, and she matters, as an individual. I think she's a good demonstration of the fact that if you put the right people in the right place, it makes all the difference," said Bill Graham.

Whether it was pushing through Magnitsky legislation, rescuing the White Helmets, or addressing human rights abuses in Venezuela, Chechnya, and Saudi Arabia, Canada was a major player in the international arena when she was foreign minister, says Cotler: "There's just no doubt."

EIGHTEEN

Minister of Everything

FOUR YEARS AFTER JUSTIN TRUDEAU'S Liberal party swept to power promising transparency, inclusivity, and "sunny ways," it was time for Canadians to return to the polls. On October 21, 2019, the Liberals were re-elected, but the party that in 2015 had surged from behind to win a majority did not fare as well this time out. The Liberals secured only enough seats to form a minority government, losing the popular vote to the Conservative party, led by Andrew Scheer.

By the end of the Liberals' first term, it was fair to say that some of the shine had worn off the prime minister. His public image had been tarnished by a series of missteps and controversies. He'd been found to be in violation of federal ethics laws over his family's late-2016 holiday on a private Caribbean island owned by the Aga Khan, the billionaire philanthropist and spiritual leader of Ismaili Muslims whose foundation receives money from the Canadian government. In 2018, during a widely panned visit to India, Trudeau was criticized for his Bollywood-like attire and slammed for the inclusion of Jaspal Atwal, a businessman who had been convicted of attempting to murder an Indian cabinet minister, on the guest list for a dinner reception. And then there was the blackface scandal. During the election campaign, *TIME* magazine published a 2001 photo of Trudeau at an Arabian Nights–themed gala at West Point Grey Academy, where he was working as a teacher at the time. He was dressed as Aladdin, wearing a turban and blackface—dark makeup widely considered to be a racist caricature of people of colour. Other photos and a video of Trudeau wearing blackface soon emerged, and the prime minister told reporters he couldn't definitively say there weren't more photos out there. It was a humiliating bombshell that made headlines in the international press.

None of these incidents, however, was as damaging as what would become known as the SNC-Lavalin affair. On February 7, 2019, the *Globe and Mail* reported that Trudeau and his staff had inappropriately pressured former justice minister and attorney general Jody Wilson-Raybould to defer the criminal prosecution of Quebec-based engineering giant SNC-Lavalin, which was facing fraud and corruption charges related to nearly $48 million in payments made to the Libyan government. Testifying before the House of Commons justice committee later that month, Wilson-Raybould said she'd experienced "veiled threats" and "a consistent and sustained effort" by senior government officials seeking to convince her to interfere in an independent criminal prosecution.

Ultimately, both Wilson-Raybould and her close friend Treasury Board president Jane Philpott—two women Trudeau had formerly held up as star ministers in his gender-equal cabinet—resigned their posts, saying they had lost confidence in the government. It wasn't a good look for a prime minister who regularly touted his feminist bona fides—and it put some cabinet members in a difficult position with constituents looking for explanations.

Chrystia, for her part, chose not to wade into the murky waters. As deputy editor of the *Financial Times* a decade and a half earlier, she had not had a critical word to say against her boss, Andrew Gowers, even after it became clear that the newspaper was struggling under his leadership and that his days as editor-in-chief were numbered. Now, Chrystia afforded the same loyalty to Trudeau, expressing in interview after interview her absolute confidence in the prime minister. The day after Wilson-Raybould's testimony, Chrystia told CBC *Ottawa Morning* that while she believed Wilson-Raybould had spoken "her truth," she was "very clearly of the view that the prime minister would never apply improper pressure." She also emphasized her belief that while differing opinions in caucus and cabinet are important contributors to the prime minister's decision-making process, Trudeau should ultimately have the last word—and suggested that government officials should "play as a united team" in public.

Chrystia's robust defence of her boss failed to convince many pundits of Trudeau's trustworthiness—in an opinion piece for CBC News, for example, Robyn Urback called it "obsequious blather." But those who know Chrystia say it's unlikely she would suffer a "fake feminist," and indeed, from his first attempts to convince her to join Team Trudeau, the prime minister had shown unequivocal support for her as a mother. "I really appreciate that, and my kids really appreciate it," she told reporters in the wake of the SNC-Lavalin news. If Chrystia had doubts about the man she worked alongside every day, she was keeping them to herself.

THOUGH THE LIBERAL PARTY had managed to hold on to power in 2019, there was no question that the results of the federal election showed a country split along regional lines. The Conservative party struggled to make significant inroads in much of eastern Canada, while the Bloc Québécois surged to success in Quebec, regaining official party status in the House of Commons. The Liberal party performed well in Ontario, but the Conservatives swept the Prairies—not one Liberal MP was elected in Alberta or Saskatchewan, where frustration with the federal government's energy policies had been mounting. Unlike after the Liberals' resounding victory in 2015, Trudeau would now have to contend with governing from a slightly weakened position—and it wasn't going to be easy.

After the election, separatist voices began calling for the independence of Canada's four westernmost provinces, a so-called Wexit. Faced with this new challenge, Trudeau called on his most trusted minister to deal with the managing of regional tensions and the maintaining of national unity. On November 21, when Trudeau unveiled his new cabinet, Chrystia was named minister of intergovernmental affairs—one of the government's trickiest files.

In a CBC interview after her swearing-in, she reiterated that she would describe herself as a "grateful daughter of Alberta." With her Prairie roots and propensity for coalition building, it was clear she was Trudeau's best hope for bridging the growing divide between the federal government and the provinces' mostly Conservative premiers.

While on the surface, it seemed the role would require a marked shift in focus from the international arena, where she had so obviously thrived, Chrystia saw national unity as another tool in Canada's arsenal when it came to addressing the urgent issues facing the world's liberal democracies, like climate change and middle-class prosperity. "There are only 37 million Canadians ... we have to be united in how we confront those big challenges," she told CTV *Power Play*'s Don Martin, adding that while she didn't expect everyone to be on the same page, she believed it was possible to find a way to work together.

The intergovernmental affairs brief would have been enough to keep a minister's hands full, but in a nod to just how much he had come to rely on Chrystia, Trudeau also appointed her his deputy prime minister. It was the first time since 2006 that a leader had chosen to fill the position. In the past, the duties associated with the posting had varied, depending on the prime minister. While some former deputy prime ministers played a more ceremonial role, it was clear Trudeau saw Chrystia in much the same way as former prime minister Brian Mulroney had viewed his deputy, Albertan cabinet minister Donald Mazankowski: as the "chief operating officer" of the government.

Chrystia's mandate letter listed an eye-popping number of tasks: on top of her intergovernmental affairs responsibilities, she was expected to see the new NAFTA agreement through to legislation and continue to oversee the Canada-US file; work with her ministerial colleagues on strengthening medicare, transitioning to a green economy, introducing a national ban on assault rifles, and laying the groundwork for a national child-care system; and sit on various cabinet committees.

"Are you not taking on too much?" Martin asked. "Your kids are going to ask for ID when you walk in the door."

"I like working hard," she replied, joking that her children had seen quite a bit of her during the election campaign and wouldn't mind a break from her cooking. Plus, she added, she hadn't taken on the job to be a "spokesmodel."

From a rookie political candidate in 2013, uncertain whether she'd even win her party's nomination, Chrystia had risen to the number-two position in government and become Trudeau's indispensable right-hand woman.

Shortly after the appointment, Trudeau and Chrystia began to meet every week at 80 Wellington to go over agenda items. At first, their interactions were a bit awkward. Conversation could be stilted, with neither quite sure where to start. The staff who accompanied Trudeau—a self-proclaimed introvert—and Chrystia to these weekly "bilats," as they referred to them, felt almost as if they were parents bringing two teenagers on a date, prompting them to ask each other about their weekends to get the discussion going. A senior government official speculates that Chrystia had so much on her mind—how to make the most of her time with the prime minister, whether to bring up certain issues, what approach to take—that when it came time to meet, general pleasantries fell by the wayside in the interests of efficiency.

But before long, the two became much more at ease with each other. "The prime minister and I felt like we came up with a successful way of working together on a really difficult negotiation known as NAFTA and we're going to take that approach and bring it to bear on our big national challenges," Chrystia told CBC Radio's *The House*.

OF COURSE, IN POLITICS, as in life, the best-laid plans are at the mercy of the unexpected. In December 2019, shortly after Chrystia's swearing-in, reports began to surface of dozens of people in Wuhan, China, being treated for a mysterious pneumonia-like illness. The number of cases soon climbed to the hundreds, and on January 23, 2020, Chinese authorities sealed off the city of eleven million people, ordering a strict lockdown for residents and cancelling flights and train travel in an effort to contain the outbreak.

But it was too late. Cases of what the World Health Organization (WHO) referred to as a "novel coronavirus"—COVID-19—had already spread to other countries in Asia and Europe, and to the United States. On January 25, a Toronto man in his fifties who had returned from Wuhan with a fever and a cough and had been placed under isolation at Sunnybrook Hospital became the first person to test positive for the virus in Canada. Within days, cases were identified in British Columbia and in Quebec. By March 11, 2020—with more than 118,000 cases in 114 countries, and nearly 4,300 dead—the WHO declared that the world was facing an unprecedented pandemic.

"We cannot say this loudly enough, or clearly enough, or often enough: all countries can still change the course of this pandemic," WHO director-general Tedros Adhanom Ghebreyesus told reporters at a briefing. "If countries detect, test, treat, isolate, trace, and mobilize their people in the response, those with a handful of cases can prevent those cases becoming clusters, and those clusters becoming community transmission."

Ghebreyesus continued: "This is not just a public health crisis, it is a crisis that will touch every sector—so every sector and every individual must be involved in the fight. I have said from the beginning that countries must take a whole-of-government, whole-of-society approach, built around a comprehensive strategy to prevent infections, save lives, and minimize impact."

As chair of the government's newly created cabinet committee on COVID-19, Chrystia became the point person for the government's response to the pandemic. As the virus threatened countries with economic disaster, pushed health-care systems to their extreme limits, and upended the lives of billions of people around the globe, she let people know that she'd be relying on the same consensus-building approach that she'd used so often in her life and political career. "This is a whole-of-government, indeed a whole-of-country, effort," she told reporters at a press conference after her appointment was announced.

By mid-March, businesses and schools across Canada had shut their doors as people were instructed to stay home to save lives. Chrystia's experience of the lockdown would differ from that of most Canadians. When so many were forced to stay home from work, she—along with tireless first responders and medical staff from coast to coast to coast—worked harder, maybe, than she ever had in her life, she would later tell *Toronto Life*'s Sarah Fulford. Far from being cooped up with her family, she continued travelling back and forth between Toronto and Ottawa, replacing her usual Porter Airline flights with long drives along the Trans-Canada Highway. (As when she was foreign minister, something had to give: "I think I have the messiest house in Canada, possibly in the world. That is the aspect of my domestic life which has gone completely to pieces," she later told the IMF's managing director, Kristalina Georgieva.)

On March 12, after Trudeau's then-wife, Sophie Grégoire Trudeau, tested positive for the virus, the prime minister entered self-isolation at his residence at Rideau Cottage. As head of the cabinet committee, Chrystia was very comfortable stepping into the role of conductor, according to various government officials. Perhaps it felt similar to when she'd been left to direct the *Globe and Mail* newsroom coverage during the September 11 terrorist attacks almost two decades earlier, when her boss, Richard Addis, was stranded overseas.

During these chaotic and stressful days, she hearkened back to the lesson she had learned as UK news editor at the *Financial Times* in the late 1990s, trying to make sure a paper got published every twenty-four hours: that being in charge meant recognizing perfection is the enemy of the good. "I think it's very easy, when you're in a tough situation, to think that the safest thing is to do nothing," she later said in an interview with Sharon Hodgson, dean of Western University's Ivey Business School. "But there are a lot of situations in life where the choice not to act, which seems to be the neutral, safe one, is actually the most dangerous one."

This thinking seems to have guided her approach when it came to the shutting down of the Canada-US border to non-essential traffic. According to a government official, cabinet ministers had been informally weighing the pros and cons of the measure, with some in favour and others of the opinion that it was too drastic.

During a mid-March phone call with US vice-president Mike Pence, Chrystia raised the issue of the border in order to take Pence's temperature on the idea, regardless of whether or not a decision had been taken in government. They agreed that closing the border was a good option and that they would recommend that course of action to their respective leaders. After they hung up, Chrystia called Bill Blair, then–minister of public safety and emergency preparedness, to keep him in the loop.

The following day, Trudeau and Trump had a follow-up call, and on March 20, Trudeau announced that both countries had agreed to temporarily restrict all non-essential travel across the border.

On Canada's larger COVID-19 strategy, Chrystia was "extremely involved in speaking to her fellow ministers," the official says, "in constant discussion" with Anita Anand, then–minister of public services and procurement, and Jean-Yves Duclos, then–president of the Treasury Board. She also worked closely with provincial premiers, building an unlikely friendship with Ontario leader Doug Ford, whom she called her "therapist."

In cabinet meetings, "she is a stellar performer," says Peter Boehm, who has attended many such gatherings under various governments. "She doesn't dominate. When she feels it's her turn, or the PM turns to her, she is focused, prepared, and sees the complete picture."

Chrystia had come to believe that the most important quality in leadership was seeking out and considering a wide range of views— though she hadn't always felt that way, as she would readily admit. "That is definitely an evolution for me. I can be impatient, and I can want to get things done," she said in the interview with Hodgson. "Taking the time to really listen carefully, before really crystalizing your own point of view—that is something I think I have learned to do over time, and, people close to me would say, I am still learning to do."

Once she was sure of a course of action, she would direct her colleagues in much the same way as she had during the CETA and NAFTA negotiations, giving them a clear mission and trusting them to deliver.

BY THE END OF MARCH, despite measures to limit its spread, COVID-19 had taken hold in communities around the country, tearing through long-term care homes and threatening to overwhelm hospitals. Health-care professionals warned of a dire shortage of the personal protective equipment (PPE) necessary to keep front-line workers safe, and pleaded with the government to do more to procure surgical masks, N95 respirators, gowns, gloves, and face shields.

Internationally, the competition for PPE manufactured in China was intensifying as countries, Canada included, raced to build up their own supply networks. Dominic Barton, then Canada's ambassador to China and formerly of McKinsey & Company, didn't realize the gravity of the situation until Chrystia called him up one day in early March.

"She said 'Dom'—she never called me 'ambassador,' which I loved—'we've got a massive problem right now. We don't have PPE, there's no supply chain. Your job is to build the supply chain, and it's going to save Canadians,'" Barton recalls. "She fired me up—she said, 'This is going to be the biggest management challenge you've ever dealt with, anything you did at McKinsey is chicken shit compared to this.'"

One of the items Canada desperately needed was reagent, a substance used in COVID-19 testing kits. "I said, 'Well, I don't even know what reagent is.' And she goes, 'Dom, you get it here by Friday, or people will die, you understand me?' And then she hung up the phone."

Over the next few days, Barton completely reorganized Canada's missions in China and put a team of twenty-five together to map out potential PPE suppliers, staying in close contact with Chrystia and Anand. ("During COVID, Anita and Chrystia were the duo that got shit done," says Maryam Monsef, who was Canada's minister for women and gender equality at the time.) One of the impediments to getting the medical supplies off the ground at Shanghai's chaotic airport was that governments would swoop in with cash and take one another's purchases right off the tarmac.

The maximum amount of money available to the embassy was $10,000, and any payments to vendors' accounts took several days to arrive via wire transfer from Canada. Chrystia, according to Barton, said, "Leave it with me." Soon, the embassy managed to get $225 million in its account—more than four times the allowance of all of Canada's diplomatic missions around the world combined—to process same-day payments to secure PPE.

A week after Chrystia and Barton spoke, an Air Canada flight carrying the required reagent landed in Canada. In mid-April, planes began arriving with millions of masks and thousands of kilograms of reagent, as well as other critical emergency supplies. Over the next six months, Barton's team would facilitate over 151 federally chartered cargo flights for Public Services and Procurement Canada.

"Chrystia's the one who grabbed me by the collar and said, 'Get it done,'" Barton says. "I've never been tasked as directly, bluntly, but also inspiringly. She energized the whole place—it was like plugging my phone into the wall, I'd call her up and get another blast."

EVEN BEFORE COVID-19 HIT, Chrystia was being referred to in the media as Trudeau's "minister of everything." It's an honorific traditionally associated with C. D. Howe, who ran the William Lyon Mackenzie King government's industrial war effort in the 1940s and was also in charge of transitioning the Canadian economy to peacetime after the Second World War. The pandemic highlighted Chrystia's ability to operate in the same kind of high-stakes and chaotic atmosphere—and underlined the fact that the prime minister's trust in her was warranted. So it was not a shock to anyone that when Trudeau found himself embroiled in yet another ethics controversy, he turned to Chrystia as part of the solution.

In the summer of 2020, as part of its COVID-19 relief efforts, the government awarded a sole-source contract to WE Charity, a non-profit focused on international development and programming for young people, to administer a $900 million student grant program. The opposition quickly drew attention to the Trudeau family's close connections to the charity, noting that the prime minister's mother and brother had made many paid appearances at WE events over the years.

The connections didn't stop there. On July 10, the website Canadaland reported that two of Finance Minister Bill Morneau's immediate family members were also involved with WE, one as a paid employee of the charity. Later that month, Morneau told the House of Commons finance committee that he had written a cheque to repay WE Charity for over $41,000 in costs it had covered for the minister and his family during trips to Ecuador and Kenya in 2017.

The problem was clear: neither Trudeau nor Morneau had recused themselves from cabinet discussion around the awarding of the student grants contract to WE. On behalf of the opposition, Pierre Poilievre, then the Conservative finance critic, called on Morneau to resign, saying he had lost the "moral authority" to hold his position.

In the wake of the revelations, articles began to appear in various outlets quoting anonymous sources who described a fraying relationship between Trudeau and Morneau; they were reportedly at odds over how to revive an economy suffering from the effects of the pandemic, with Morneau wanting to take a more conservative approach. On August 17, Morneau announced he would be resigning both his ministerial post and his seat in the House of Commons in order to put his name forward as a candidate for secretary-general of the Organisation for Economic Co-operation and Development.

Citing the historic economic and public health crisis facing the country, Morneau said it was the right time for a new finance minister: "I think that it's really important for someone to want to be in this political role for the next period of time, and I think that period of time will be very challenging."

At this critical juncture in the life of his Liberal government, Trudeau called on Chrystia. The next day, in addition to maintaining her deputy prime minister title, she was named Canada's finance minister—the first woman to ever hold the role. She had achieved what her sister Natalka describes as a "huge" life goal. It was the post Chrystia had wanted when she first entered politics, and she had "worked her way toward it."

In a small, pared-down ceremony at Rideau Hall, Chrystia was sworn in, tasked with shepherding Canada's economy through its greatest crisis since the Second World War. Her family looked on proudly from chairs spaced six feet apart, Graham's eyes crinkling above his face mask. After taking the oath of office, she gave Trudeau a socially distant elbow bump.

"It was a pretty big moment for all of us, for women everywhere," says Monsef.

While she would prefer not to be lauded as the first woman to hold the position and simply judged on the merits of her performance,

Chrystia recognized that it was "unfortunately" still true that "gender matters and that it makes a difference," as she later acknowledged in remarks before presenting US treasury secretary Janet Yellen with the 2023 Atlantic Council Global Citizen Award.

At a press conference after her swearing-in ceremony, Chrystia was asked by the *Toronto Star*'s Tonda MacCharles to reflect on her historic appointment. "I am conscious of the fact that I am Canada's first woman finance minister," she said. "It's about time that we broke that glass ceiling, and I'd like to say to all the Canadian women across our amazing country who are out there breaking glass ceilings: 'Keep going, we are a hundred percent with you.'"

She noted her pride in the government's feminist agenda, and also the sharp drop in the participation of women in the workforce since the pandemic: "Certainly I'm glad that I'll have an opportunity to bring my experience as a woman, as a mother, to this really important challenge our country is facing."

As at other points in her life—while breaking stories about Russia's oligarchs or in various senior editor roles at major media outlets— Chrystia would be faced with comments from armchair pundits questioning her credentials and whether she was fit for the job at hand. "I'm on vacation but can't stop watching the train wreck taking place in slow motion in Ottawa," tweeted the *National Post*'s John Ivison. "Trudeau has now removed the only person in Cabinet with business experience and handed the task of economic recovery to a journalist. As a journalist, I find that concerning."

For the most part, though, Chrystia's appointment was met with approval. While providing coverage of the swearing-in ceremony, CBC parliamentary bureau chief Rob Russo said what many were thinking: "In some ways, I wonder if we're seeing the beginning of the beknighting of Chrystia Freeland as [Trudeau's] unofficial preferred candidate to succeed him at some point. She's done everything else—what is there left for her to do?"

CHRYSTIA HAD NO TIME to pay much mind to either the criticism or the growing speculation about her political future, turning her focus instead to the monumental twin tasks of reopening Canada's economy—which had never been done before, because the economy had never been shut down before—and reorienting it toward a more fiscally sustainable path. In tackling the latter, Chrystia would be dealing with the political reality that cabinet ministers, including the prime minister, had gotten used to spending magnitudes of money that in the past no one would ever contemplate spending. As the immediate danger of the pandemic subsided, there would need to be less emphasis on protecting and taking care of people and more on investing in the economy to expand the growth prospects of the country.

For the government's first pandemic budget, "one of the things that the prime minister really wanted was something that would stimulate growth and create jobs—that was really the overarching theme," says Vincent Garneau, then Chrystia's director of policy.

For Chrystia, that "something" quickly became a Canada-wide early learning and child-care system. The idea wasn't new; in 1970, a full five decades earlier, a report by Canada's Royal Commission on the Status of Women had recommended universal, government-funded child care as a necessary measure for gender equality.

The Liberals had promised to create a national child-care program in their 1993, 1997, 2000, and 2004 election campaigns. In 2005, Paul Martin's government managed to sign deals for such a program with every province—but when Stephen Harper defeated Martin at the polls in early 2006, the Conservatives abandoned the agreements, opting instead to provide parents with direct subsidies.

During the Trudeau government's first term, neither the Prime Minister's Office nor public servants were enthusiastic about once again taking on the child-care challenge, according to someone who was following the debate closely at the time. "The bureaucracy was trying to block child care as a federal initiative for constitutional reasons, in terms of jurisdiction, and for cost reasons," they say, adding that there was also resistance to the idea in Trudeau's inner circle. "The men in the PMO over and over and over again said, 'This isn't a vote-getter.'"

But when the pandemic hit, they got it: "Suddenly, you're in an economic situation where if you don't have it, you've got this massive chokehold on recovery, not just during COVID but for the next ten, twenty years."

With talk of a "she-cession," as women disproportionally left the labour force to care for children out of school, Chrystia saw child care as the best way to get women back to work, and as a significant driver of long-term economic growth. "She really was the one that [advocated for] this idea of the child-care system—she was not asked to do it by the prime minister," says Garneau. Though it may have ruffled some feathers with cabinet colleagues whose responsibilities included child care and federal-provincial relations, she stepped in to personally oversee the implementation of the initiative.

Chrystia worked closely with her deputy, Michael Sabia, who also had a mother who had been deeply involved in the feminist power circles of Canada in the 1970s and knew how important child care was to the pursuit of equality. "They had a real alignment of purpose, and machinery of government, and political will. And they got it— barely—over the line. About ten days before the budget, we didn't even know if we had it. There was still that much antipathy at the PMO, because it wasn't a vote-getter. And it was very expensive," says the source who was closely following the debate.

On April 19, Chrystia tabled the Liberal government's first budget in more than two years. In a near-empty House of Commons, she announced that the government would be allocating $30 billion over the next five years, and $8.3 billion each year after that, to create a universal, affordable, and accessible child-care system that would eventually cost parents an average of $10 a day, modelled off Quebec's system of subsidized spaces. The federal government, acording to the budget, would share the costs of the program fifty-fifty with the provinces and territories.

The opposition scoffed at Chrystia's pledge to get it done—then–Conservative leader Erin O'Toole questioned whether the provinces would agree to a deal, and NDP leader Jagmeet Singh noted that the Liberals had been promising a child-care program for decades: "If they had any intention of doing it, it would already be done."

But for Chrystia, this was a personal ambition—and an intergenerational one. As a young mother in law school, Halyna's child-care solution involved bringing her infant daughter to class. Later, she fought for and got a town-run daycare in Peace River.

"That's what it takes to get half the population to contribute," says Chrystia's sister Natalka. "[Chrystia] had a lot of family support—she first had my mom, and then after my mom died, she had this rotating cast of my aunts coming through and basically taking care of her kids full-time. I think it's great that she had that, and I think it's also great that society [does] things for women who don't, because not everybody has aunts."

In her conversation with the IMF's Georgieva, Chrystia recalled advice that Halyna had offered her when she was trying to balance her demanding job at the *Financial Times* with being the mother of two small children. "I was just so tired, and I was worried I wasn't doing a good job with my children, and I wasn't doing a good job at work," Chrystia recalled. In tears, she turned to Halyna and asked if she should keep going—or if she should just quit. "And she said to me, 'Right now, when your children are young, it just seems impossible, and it seems as if it will never end. But you'll blink your eye, and your children will be in school, and you'll be past this really hard time. But if you drop out now, it will be almost impossible to recover.'"

Chrystia continued: "And so for anyone who is listening who is a mother of young children, let me pass on that advice from my mother, and just say, hang in there. I know it's really hard, I know, certainly speaking for Canada, we don't offer you all the support that we should. We're trying to get better, but really, hang in there. You can do it."

Within a year of the 2021 budget, the federal government had reached an agreement on child-care funding with every province and territory.

"If you'd asked me in January 2021 whether she would get all provinces on [board], I'd say there's no fucking chance [Conservative Alberta premier] Jason Kenney is going to sign a deal with the federal government for frickin' state-run child care," says economist Kevin Milligan, who has advised the Liberals on various policies. But, he says, Chrystia's experience with dealing with the premiers during the pandemic "led her to believe that she could get this done across all the provinces. And she did."

Convincing the premiers to sign on wasn't the only challenge; the actual rollout of the program over the next few years would be uneven across Canada's provinces, with some parents seeing substantial savings in tuition but others unable to find affordable spots for their children. According to figures obtained by Radio-Canada, with two out of five years to go ahead of the March 2026 deadline, 97,000 of a projected 250,000 new child-care spaces had been created. "I would suggest Rome was not built overnight, and this is a process. Hard things are hard, and this is one of those things," Minister of Families Jenna Sudds told CBC News.

Alison Franklin, Chrystia's Harvard roommate, remembers her friend's complete certainty, buoyed by Halyna's example, that she would be able to have both a meaningful career and a family of her own. She's not surprised Chrystia would champion a policy designed to assist other women to do the same.

"There could have been someone who wanted to do that because they were a working mom and understood how hard it was, and there could have been a finance minister who could do the numbers," says Franklin, but it took someone who was both of those things to finally get done what the party had been trying to do for years.

"She's effortlessly brilliant in some ways, with people, with languages, all this stuff. But she also really does the work," Franklin adds. "That's what we saw in college, and that's how she got the Rhodes, and that's what she's doing now. Because you can't stand up to [the opposition] if you don't also say, 'Here's why what you're saying isn't true, that's bad for the people of Canada, that's an over-simplification,' or whatever."

AS FINANCE MINISTER, Chrystia would have no shortage of challenges to tackle: a ballooning deficit, post-pandemic inflation, a cost-of-living crisis, a housing shortage with home ownership becoming increasingly out of reach, the balancing of Canada's energy and climate policies, and more.

And then there was the snark that Chrystia had warned about in her 2014 *Politico* essay. A society that constantly pointed toward how "vile, venal, stupid and hypocritical" politicians are and that denigrated the role of government, she wrote, would lead to people disengaging from the democratic system entirely. (Trudeau didn't help this cause when, in the summer of 2021, he called a snap election that was widely viewed as unnecessary during the pandemic. The decision was roundly criticized; the election cost hundreds of millions of dollars and resulted in an unchanged political landscape, with the Liberals securing another minority government.)

As the pandemic subsided, it left in its wake a country that, in many ways, felt more divided than ever before. In an October 2021 column, the *Globe and Mail*'s Gary Mason wrote that politics had become a thankless, dangerous profession, with elected officials more and more the target of anger and abuse. "I think the biggest thing was as a cabinet minister I constantly felt on edge," former environment minister Catherine McKenna—nicknamed "climate Barbie" by far-right website Rebel News—told Mason. "It was the constant threats, people verbally accosting my staff and defacing my constituency office and sending me smashed up Barbie dolls."

"Every day it seems there is another report of a politician being screamed at or threatened in a public place. It happened to Conservative MP Michelle Rempel Garner when she and her husband were out for dinner during the election campaign. A man came up and started yelling at her. The same thing happened recently to Vancouver Mayor Kennedy Stewart. He and his wife were at a downtown liquor store when a man in his 50s approached the mayor and started screaming at him, daring him to step outside and fight," Mason wrote.

In January 2022, a group of anti-government protesters calling itself the Freedom Convoy occupied the streets in front of Parliament Hill, demanding an end to COVID-19 restrictions and mandatory vaccinations, and bringing downtown Ottawa to a standstill. After the government invoked the Emergencies Act and took action to freeze the bank accounts of key individuals involved in the blockades, Chrystia, as finance minister, was the target of misogynist and threatening comments on social media.

The abuse wasn't just online; in August, while waiting for an elevator in the reception area of an office building in Grande Prairie, Alberta, she was approached aggressively by a large man wearing jeans and a tank top. In a clip that went viral, the man could be heard yelling profanities at Chrystia, calling her a "traitor" and demanding she leave the province.

More than ever, it seemed Chrystia's philosophy of assuming positive intent in others was being tested. In November, she was accused of being out of touch after telling Mercedes Stephenson of Global News that her family had cut its Disney+ subscription to save money. It was perhaps ironic that Chrystia, whose frugality has been noted by university friends and political colleagues alike, would misread the prevailing public sentiment of the time, coming off as "smug," "elitist," "clueless," and "entitled" instead of relatable to families struggling to make ends meet, according to emails sent to her office and obtained by the Canadian Press.

But as she would with the chatter over her next moves, Chrystia likely chose to tune these things out as best as possible; in public, she maintained her upbeat and optimistic tone, confident that Canada's economy would "come roaring back" post-pandemic. According to those who worked closest with her, her role in helping that to happen weighed heavily on her mind.

Over nearly a decade in power, the Trudeau government has suffered from the perception that fiscal issues are not a top priority, which has made Chrystia's task harder. While not all of her government colleagues would assign the same level of importance to getting the country on a sustainable path, says one advisor, she takes the fiscal stewardship side of her job very seriously.

She hasn't been alone in this, the advisor notes; she has had allies around the table who were sympathetic to her view that the fiscal house needed to be managed. Over time, this group of allies came to include the prime minister, who has stepped in and defended her—with his colleagues and with his own office—when he has had to.

Opinions on how the economy is performing under the Trudeau government vary wildly, depending on who is doing the assessing. After each of Chrystia's budgets, pundits slammed the Liberals as fiscally irresponsible, pointing to ballooning spending and slow growth. Others don't see cause for alarm, noting that Canada has the lowest deficit of all G7 countries. In addition, its "debt-to-GDP ratio is amongst the lowest of the industrialized world," says economist Brett House. "So despite the fact that we had a couple of years of blow-out budget deficits, we are still blessed with one of the best public balance sheets in the world. There is no question that we're even close to looking at some sort of financial crisis, funding crisis, [or] credit rating downgrade."

Economist Jim Stanford says that, without the benefit of hindsight, it's impossible to put Chrystia on a historical spectrum in terms of her performance as finance minister, given the "absolutely unprecedented circumstances that she was thrown into the middle of." But he gives her credit for the way she confronted the economic devastation wrought by COVID-19.

In a way, he says, Chrystia came into the role at the worst moment—no vaccines had been rolled out yet, and while Bill Morneau had quickly introduced the Canada Emergency Response Benefit and other income support measures, "a million questions" remained about "what comes next, and how long those supports would last, and how would fiscal policy be normalized without throwing the whole economy into another tizzy, which would have been an enormous risk."

Stanford concludes: "I think that she has handled it successfully and cautiously, but with an emphasis on the right things ... We have to be concerned first and foremost with the well-being of Canadians, not with any arbitrary fiscal targets, or inflation targets, or any other traditional rules. This is something we've never experienced before, and our policy response to it has to be flexible and innovative, and I think she has done that."

A Woman of Substance

O N OCTOBER 11, 2022, eight months after Russia's invasion of Ukraine, Chrystia Freeland stood before an audience gathered in the headquarters of the venerable Brookings Institution, just east of Dupont Circle in Washington, DC. Never one to give a speech just for the sake of it, Canada's deputy prime minister may have been addressing the crowd in front of her, but her message was designed to reach far beyond the think tank's walls, to the international finance ministers, politicians, business titans, and academics gathered in the US capital for the annual meetings of the IMF, and also to those in her own government circles back home in Ottawa.

"When Vladimir Putin·ordered his tanks across the Ukrainian border in the early hours of February 24, he brought a brutal end to a three-decade-long era in geopolitics," Chrystia declared. The fall of the Berlin Wall on November 9, 1989, and the subsequent collapse of the Soviet Union, she reminded her listeners, had ushered in a thirty-three-year "sunny season in human history."

She had personally witnessed its beginnings as a reporter on the ground in Kyiv in the early 1990s, experiencing first-hand the joy and optimism of Ukrainian citizens who had taken their future into their own hands by voting unequivocally for independence. She shared the prevailing wisdom of the time, best characterized by Francis Fukuyama's "end of history" theory, that with the fall of communist governments in eastern Europe, "the contest between competing forms of human, social, and political organization was over, and that capitalist democracy had emerged as the single best way for people to live."

The economic corollary to that theory, she added, was the widespread belief that "as countries became richer—and as they built their increasing prosperity on trade with one another—war would become an anachronism." But ultimately, that's not how events had unfolded. History had not ended, and authoritarian regimes, far from being on the decline, were making a comeback. The war in Ukraine had thrown into stark relief the glaring truth: the "end of history" period was over. It would now be up to the world's democracies to decide what paradigm would replace it.

In order to build a system "in which all liberal democracies can not just survive, but thrive," Chrystia proposed three pillars. First, democracies must strengthen their economic ties through a trade practice US treasury secretary Janet Yellen called "friendshoring," to better safeguard their supply chains. Second, they should extend a welcoming hand to the "in-between" countries of Latin America, Asia, Africa, and the Middle East, to encourage them to side with the West over "more hostile economies" and see the value in the liberal order. Third, they must view their economic relations with the world's strongmen through a more critical lens, avoiding "strategic vulnerabilities" like those experienced after Putin's invasion by European countries, which were highly dependent on Russian energy resources.

Crucially, Chrystia emphasized, going forward, Western countries would need to be willing to "spend some domestic political capital in the name of economic security for our democratic partners." Like the European companies that honoured their contractual duties to send vaccines to non-European countries during the COVID-19 pandemic, "Canada must, and will, show similar generosity in fast-tracking, for example, the energy and mining projects our allies need to heat their homes and to manufacture electric vehicles."

As journalist Paul Wells wrote in his Substack newsletter, the speech was "impossible to reconcile with anything Steven Guilbeault, the environment minister, has been saying all year on the question of Canadian energy exports to Europe." But, he added, "this may not be a problem so much as a process. Sometimes when Freeland gets out over the government's skis, the government catches up."

In the media, commentators would refer to Chrystia's vision as "the Freeland doctrine." It was a natural extension of the world view she'd espoused as foreign minister, rooted in the practical attitude friends had noticed as far back as Harvard. As Lucan Way puts it: "She's profoundly a pragmatic centrist—like, hardcore." Though she acknowledged the need to co-operate with authoritarian countries on global challenges like climate change, she insisted that Western politicians should make no bones about the despotic nature of their rulers.

As Wells noted, not everyone would agree with her stance, including some in her own government. Years after her tenure at Global Affairs Canada, critics argue that, far from being "back," Canada's standing in the world has continued to slide under the Trudeau government, as the country finds itself at loggerheads with major powers like Russia, China, Saudi Arabia, and India.

In an October 30, 2023, speech to the Economic Club of Canada in Toronto, Foreign Minister Mélanie Joly seemed to break with

Chrystia's more Manichaean foreign policy views. "We must resist the temptation to divide the world into rigid ideological camps. For the world cannot be reduced to democracies versus autocracies. To the North versus the South. The East versus West. Forcing the majority of the world to fit into any one category would be naive, short-sighted, and counterproductive," she said.

"We are not naive about what engagement will accomplish. But if we refuse to engage, we create additional incentives for those whose actions we strongly oppose to join together. As respect for the rules diminishes, empty chairs serves [*sic*] no one. Let me be clear: I am a door opener, I'm not a door closer. Therefore, with rare exceptions, Canada will engage."

But in Chrystia's view, resisting temptation is a luxury no longer available to the leaders of the rules-based international order: the world has already fractured into duelling ideological camps, whether Western politicians like it or not. This state of play requires a doubling down on democracy, and the stakes are too high for Canada to be anything other than firmly rooted in the Western alliance.

As the Trudeau government's second-in-command, Chrystia has had a significant influence on the direction of Canada's relations with both its friends and its foes—though of course she does not have the ultimate say. The "Freeland doctrine" gives a good indication of how she would govern, if given the opportunity.

AFTER NEARLY A DECADE in government, Justin Trudeau's Liberal party is in an increasingly precarious position. In March 2022, the Liberals and New Democrats reached a supply and confidence agreement, intended to keep the minority government in power until June 2025—but on September 4, 2024, NDP leader Jagmeet Singh announced he would be terminating the agreement. The Conservative party, led by firebrand Pierre Poilievre, is consistently polling well ahead of the Liberals, and Trudeau has faced a barrage of questions about whether he is the right person to lead the party into the next federal election, scheduled for no later than October 2025.

Despite the odds against him—in the last century, no prime minister has won four consecutive terms in office—Trudeau has maintained that he will run again, determined to protect his political legacy. But his assertions have yet to quell the chatter around who might replace him, whether in advance of the next election or following a Liberal loss at the ballot box. Chrystia's isn't the only name that has been tossed around by pundits and pols as a potential contender for the Liberal leadership—Mark Carney, Mélanie Joly, Anita Anand, and François-Philippe Champagne have all been mentioned as possible challengers. But given her position as Trudeau's number two, Chrystia would be his most obvious successor. It would be another historic first, in the trailblazing vein of her mother—the Liberal party has never been led by a woman.

If Chrystia has any such ambitions, she is keeping them close to the vest, taking care to shut down any hint of leadership speculation, even among friends and family. This reservedness is not at all surprising, given the importance Chrystia places on loyalty. Her sister Natalka calls it one of her "institutional strengths," noting that she doesn't think "it would even occur to her to try to push her agenda over Justin Trudeau's."

Many people, including Natalka, have asked Chrystia what her plans would be if Trudeau decided to retire from politics. It's a question she refuses to answer, even to her sister.

As Liberal leader, Trudeau personally convinced Chrystia to put everything on the line for the chance to serve her country, and as prime minister, he has been responsible more than anyone else for her remarkable rise. "You dance with the one who brought you, and he brought her, so she'll dance with him," says Ben Bergen, Chrystia's former executive assistant.

The big question, should Chrystia decide she has designs on the top job, is whether there's a clear path for her in terms of the Liberal party leadership, absent Trudeau. Given how closely her record is linked to the prime minister's—on many policy issues, their views are virtually indistinguishable—would her status as Trudeau's "right-hand woman" put her at risk of going down with a sinking ship?

Should Trudeau lose in 2025 and step aside, some also question whether Chrystia would want to throw her hat into the ring to lead a party that is not in power. Being at the centre of it all is what she craves, and it would be hard to scratch that itch as—in the best case scenario—leader of the Official Opposition.

For a few months in 2022 and 2023, rumours swirled in the press about Chrystia being a contender in the race for the next secretary-general of NATO. While nothing ultimately came of the rumours, they speak to the heightened expectations around her next move, and the sort of prominent positions in the international arena that she could credibly occupy.

But given her ever-present drive and deep commitment to liberalism, people who know Chrystia well say that it's hard to see her leaving Canada. In the United Sates, for example, says Lucan Way, she'd be "one of hundreds of thousands of highly talented, charismatic individuals. I am sure she could be a successful executive of a media company or something like that. But in Canada she has become a leader of the free world; a major actor on the world stage in the battle against Russian autocracy. Only in Canada can she plausibly be government leader and a global force for democracy. I just cannot imagine her giving that up—even after an electoral defeat."

Making predictions in politics is a mug's game, so only time will tell where Chrystia will land next. But these are interesting questions for a woman who has accomplished so much and is, by all indications, not ready to stop.

WHATEVER THE FUTURE HOLDS, Chrystia has been a rare example in politics of how to effectively move the needle in an arena where doing so is notoriously difficult.

She, and so many of her generation, grew up in a world where the pre-eminence of liberal democracy as a political system wasn't in question. But the viability of that system is now up for debate, in part because of issues of uneven growth and distribution, but also because people are becoming increasingly disillusioned with their government representatives and skeptical of their ability to deliver on their promises. In this environment, it's important that politicians are perceived to be able to step up and get things done.

Chrystia's record has been praised not only by many of her government colleagues and international counterparts, but also by those across the aisle. "I would think she's got to be pretty proud of her own work to date," says former Conservative party leader Erin O'Toole. "I've had some quibbles here and there, but I think she's in it for the right reasons, and she has shown a real ability to represent the country."

Though she might wish there were no need to view her accomplishments through a gender lens, Chrystia has also been a model for how to succeed as a woman—and a mother—in politics. More than any other MP or cabinet minister, she draws power players into her orbit, hosting them at home and unapologetically involving her children in dinner table discussions.

That's not to say balancing her "two true loves," as she put it in that column for the *Financial Times* years ago, has been easy, and she couldn't have done it alone. She has gotten to where she is by standing on the shoulders of the women who've come before her, chief among them Halyna, who, one imagines, would be not at all surprised by her daughter's achievements. To pursue her dreams, Chrystia has leaned heavily on her Ukrainian village, as well as the steadfast support of her husband, Graham—by all accounts a wise choice.

"They have a very egalitarian marriage; each of them makes a lot of space for the other person to pursue what is important to them," says Natalka. "I think that was challenging—there are forms of journalism you can't do when your wife is the deputy PM. And yet I think they've always made sure to make his career also something that's viable for their marriage."

From her father, Don, Chrystia learned that making a mark sometimes requires going against the grain and doing things your own way—a philosophy that has served her well in government, as she did her best to stay true to her moral compass. And of course, in different ways, both sides of her family instilled in her how lucky she is to be Canadian.

As one American former colleague notes, her journey from a tiny town in northern Alberta to the number-two position in Justin Trudeau's government is a "Chrystia story, but also a Canada story." As Chrystia kept in mind when making the decision to leave journalism, Canada has given her so much, from scholarships to the freedoms that go along with its system of government to the core liberal values she holds so dear.

As the country's deputy prime minister, Chrystia has made clear her belief in its ability to make a difference in an uncertain and unpredictable world. It's something she discussed many times with former prime minister Brian Mulroney before he passed away in 2024.

"She can't delude herself—we're not the United States, we don't have that [kind of] power," Mulroney said in 2022. But, as he found when rallying countries to end apartheid in South Africa, negotiating a major environmental treaty with the United States to reduce acid rain, and being the first Western country to recognize a newly independent Ukraine, "we have enormous influence in the world."

What Chrystia does next is anyone's guess, but there's little doubt that it will be something worth watching. "We're dealing with a woman of substance here," Mulroney said. "She's going to be a big player, no matter what."

Acknowledgements

In 2020, when Chrystia Freeland was named Canada's first female finance minister, I was on maternity leave with my first child. Over countless long stroller walks, I found myself wondering how a woman manages to rise to such a position of power while also raising a family. A few years later, pregnant with child number two and hard at work on this manuscript, I found myself wondering how anyone ever manages to complete a book. It turns out that the answers to those two questions are the same: it takes a village. And so, I'd like to take this opportunity to thank mine.

To Som Tsoi, my former manager at the Centre for International Governance Innovation, who, unprompted, said aloud what I had only been thinking in my head: that a book on Chrystia Freeland would be a project worth pursuing, and that I should be the one to put it together. Thank you for always encouraging me to trust my gut and to dream big.

To Marilyn Biderman and Rob Firing at the Transatlantic Agency, thank you for your unbridled enthusiasm from day one, and for expertly guiding me through this entire process. I'm lucky to have you both in my court.

To Linda Pruessen, working with you on this manuscript was an absolute delight, thank you for taking such care with it, and for your myriad improvements.

I've been in such great, steady hands with everyone at House of Anansi, particularly Michelle MacAleese, Karen Brochu, Shivaun Hearne, Jenny McWha, and Melissa Shirley. Thank you for your professionalism and support, and for sharing my belief that we need more stories about Canadian women in public life. Thank you, also, to copyeditor Tilman Lewis, proofreader Allegra Robinson, and indexer Siusan Moffat.

To everyone who agreed to be interviewed for this book, thank you for taking the time to answer my questions so thoroughly and thoughtfully, and for trusting me with your recollections and insight. I simply wouldn't have been able to tell the story of Chrystia's life without you. Thank you also to the Ontario Arts Council and the Access Copyright Foundation for the generous grants that allowed me to conduct key interviews in person, in Edmonton, Ottawa, and New York City.

To Robert Bothwell, thank you for your wise counsel and friendship over two decades. You have a remarkable ability to ignite a spark in those who are lucky enough to be your students—it's one that propels me in my career to this day. You have always made me feel as though I have something to say, whether in TRIN419 or with this book.

To Arne Kislenko, another top-notch professor I've had the good fortune of being taught by; thank you for casting a discerning eye over—and improving substantially—an early draft of the history of the Chomiak family.

To my friends and family, thank you for cheering me on and for being such excellent sounding boards over these past few years—and throughout my life.

To my dad, Dino, thank you for your unwavering encouragement throughout this project, for the kitchen chats that helped me work through my material, and for always checking in—no challenge seems insurmountable when I have you to talk things over with. To my mom, Nota (my original editor): From Roméo Dallaire to Samantha Power, you were the first to introduce me to the power of non-fiction works to move and inspire. I truly would not have been able to write my own without the top-notch babysitting services you have so adoringly provided over the last four years. Thank you both for a lifetime of love and constant championing.

Finally, to my husband, Mike: Despite having just strung tens of thousands of words together for this book, I struggle to find the right ones to adequately describe just how much your steadfast love and support has meant to me over the years. In writing Chrystia's story, it became clear to me that her choice of partner was instrumental to her success—I don't think it's hyperbole to say that you have been my wisest choice. You pull out all the stops every single day to ensure I'm able to pursue work that is meaningful to me, all while keeping me laughing (and fed!). Thank you for tolerating my kvetching and soothing my anxieties. I am eternally grateful for our partnership and for the life we have built together.

And to my little sunshines, Ava and Nate: You have already taught me so much. May you continue to greet the world with joy, curiosity, and Chrystia-level confidence.

Notes

Unless otherwise noted, all the quoted material that appears in this book has been taken from over 130 interviews conducted by the author with Chrystia's relatives, friends, and colleagues between 2021 and 2024.

INTRODUCTION

In a televised pre-dawn address: "Address by the President of the Russian Federation," February 24, 2022, en.kremlin.ru/events/president/news/67843.

Canadian prime minister Justin Trudeau made his way to a wood podium: "PM Trudeau Announces Additional Sanctions in Response to Russian Invasion of Ukraine," CPAC, February 24, 2022, youtube.com/watch?v=DyNeZquKrxI.

"Today, we woke up to a changed world": "PM Trudeau Announces Additional Sanctions in Response to Russian Invasion of Ukraine," CPAC, February 24, 2022, youtube.com/watch?v=DyNeZquKrxI.

"The verses were illegal": Chrystia Freeland, "The Quiet Revolutionaries," *Financial Times*, December 3, 2004.

As a politician, she subscribes to the theory: Chrystia Freeland, "Character, Collaboration and Canada. A Conversation with Deputy Prime Minister Chrystia Freeland," interview with Sarah Hodgson, Ivey's Ian O. Ihnatowycz Institute for Leadership, September 29, 2020, ivey.uwo.ca/leadership/news/2020/09/character-collaboration-and-canada-a-conversation-with-deputy-prime-minister-chrystia-freeland/.

CHAPTER ONE

"the great life-sustaining article of wheat": J. H. Ward, *The Contributor: Representing the Young Men's and Young Ladies' Mutual Improvement Associations of the Latter-Day Saints (1879–1895)* 5, no. 9 (June 1884): 331.

From his Indigenous interpreter, Mackenzie learned that: Blanche Black, "Peace River Legend Handed down from Indians," *Peace River Record-Gazette*, May 30, 1973.

"twenty million acre hothouse of fertility": "Peace River Country Is a Twenty Million Acre Hothouse of Fertility," *Peace River Record*, June 1, 1928.

"The Peace River country is on every man's tongue": "The Third Chapter," *Maclean's*, May 1, 1914.

By 1913, Edmonton, which had grown from a small frontier town: "The Growth of Edmonton," *The Scotsman*, January 15, 1913.

Given Wilbur's track record of wanderlust, wrote Beulah: Beulah Baldwin, *The Long Trail: The Story of a Pioneer Family* (NeWest Press, 1992).

On the hills of Misery Mountain: John Freeland Obituary, Legacy Remembers, March 18, 2011, legacy.com/us/obituaries/legacyremembers/john-freeland-obituary?id=44832765.

Helen started a market vegetable garden: Helen Bell Freeland (Caulfield) Obituary, *Peace River Record-Gazette*, September 21, 2012, prrecordgazette.remembering.ca/obituary/helen-freeland-1070884436.

the Kremlin under Vladimir Putin has disputed this narrative: Anaïs Marin, "The Peoples of Ukraine, Belarus and Russia Are One Nation," in *Myths and*

Misconceptions in the Debate on Russia, Chatham House Report, updated July 2, 2021, chathamhouse.org/2021/05/myths-and-misconceptions-debate-russia/myth-11-peoples-ukraine-belarus-and-russia-are-one.

In the early twentieth century: Philippe Sands, "Before the Nazis: A Ukrainian City's Contested Past," *New York Review of Books*, May 30, 2012, nybooks.com/online/2012/05/30/nazis-lviv-contested-past/.

As part of the limited freedoms bestowed on Ukrainians: "The Ukrainian Central Committee," Lviv Interactive, lia.lvivcenter.org/en/themes/reherit/uck/.

a German military unit made up of Ukrainian volunteers: "Commemorating Poles Murdered in Huta Pieniacka," Institute of National Remembrance, March 1, 2021, ipn.gov.pl/en/news/7133,Commemorating-Poles-murdered-in-Huta-Pieniacka.html.

the German press chief in Kraków: John-Paul Himka, "'Krakivs'ki visti': An Overview," *Harvard Ukrainian Studies* 22 (1998): 251–61, jstor.org/stable/41036740.

According to a letter he wrote: Ernest Gyidel, "The Ukrainian Legal Press of the General Government: The Case of Krakivski Visti, 1940–1944" (PhD diss., University of Alberta, 2019).

as they systematically exterminated: "Poles: Victims of the Nazi Era, 1933–1945," *A Teacher's Guide to the Holocaust*, Florida Center for Instructional Technology, College of Education, University of South Florida, fcit.usf.edu/holocaust/people/USHMMPOL.HTM.

"Their ranks included, among others": Adina Hoffman, "How a Million Refugees Became Postwar Pawns of the Allies," review of *The Last Million* by David Nasaw, *New York Times*, September 15, 2020.

CHAPTER TWO

At home, Michael and Alexandra spoke: Chrystia Freeland, "My Ukraine," Brookings, May 12, 2015, csweb.brookings.edu/content/research/essays/2015/myukraine.html.

Nevertheless, growing up, the Chomiak children: Chrystia Freeland, "The Richness of Her Life," *Financial Times*, July 13, 2007

"atheist by intellectual conviction": Freeland, "Richness."

tongue-in-cheek list of "the many good things": Helene [Halyna] Chomiak, "Thanksgiving: Let Us Give Thanks," *The Gateway*, October 7, 1966, archive .org/details/GAT_1966100701.

in an old house on the outskirts of campus: Myrna Kostash, "Not a White-Bread Childhood," *Alberta Views*, April 1, 2021.

Michael, for his part, was deeply unhappy: Ernest Gyidel, "The Ukrainian Legal Press of the General Government: The Case of Krakivski Visti, 1940–1944" (PhD diss., University of Alberta, 2019).

During an entrance interview: Chrystia Freeland, "Mothers Have Their Day," *Financial Times*, May 12, 2007.

By the end of their freshman year: "The Challengers: Halyna Freeland," *Alberta Women*, October–December 1982.

"I ... was told I was a dirty disgusting person": "The Challengers: Halyna Freeland."

She also lobbied for the university to accept: Chrystia Chomiak, "Interview with Chrystia Chomiak Part 1 for the Local Narratives Project," interview with Kalyna Somchynsky, MacEwan University, May 30, 2022, youtube.com/ watch?v=782bBsrMIoE.

Years later, while giving a lecture: "2012–13 Merv Leitch Q.C. Memorial Lecture feat. Chrystia Freeland at UAlberta Faculty of Law," Faculty of Law, University of Alberta, March 19, 2013, youtube.com/watch?v=ymOS3ZjWgqo.

They acquired a plot of land: Myrna Kostash, "To Keep Quebec in Canada: How Far Are Canadians Prepared to Go?," *Chatelaine*, October 1977.

"It is hard to overstate just how out of sync": Freeland, "Richness of Her Life."

The dozen or so lawyers in the area: Kostash, "To Keep Quebec in Canada."

"I remember how hard that was for my mother": Heather Scoffield, "Chrystia Freeland's Personal Story Shaped Canada's First Feminist Budget," *Toronto Star*, April 25, 2021, thestar.com/politics/political-opinion/chrystia-freeland-s-personal-story-shaped-canada-s-first-feminist-budget/article_389c7ec2-b219-55a4-9856-845f55c25ee2.html.

In 1977, *Chatelaine* sent writer Myrna Kostash: Kostash, "To Keep Quebec in Canada."

CHAPTER THREE

She has described her childhood: Linda Diebel, "How Chrystia Freeland Became Justin Trudeau's First Star," *Toronto Star*, November 29, 2015, thestar.com/news/insight/how-chrystia-freeland-became-justin-trudeau-s-first-star/article_addef1be-c916-56b9-ac7b-041ace9fff35.html.

"One of my earliest memories": Leah McLaren, "Chrystia Freeland's Dilemma," *Chatelaine*, April 12, 2019, chatelaine.com/living/politics/chrystia-freeland/.

Don was fined $500: "Lawyer Fined; Resisted Arrest," *Peace River Record-Gazette*, February 13, 1985.

expressed interest in becoming a lawyer: "Keeping the Law in the Family," *Peace River Record-Gazette*, December 29, 1971.

Of all her contributions to the legal field: Halyna Chomiak Freeland Obituary, Legacy Remembers, July 12–13, 2007, legacy.com/obituaries/edmontonjournal/obituary.aspx?pid=90579918.

"I was taught at the kitchen table": Chrystia Freeland, "My Country and My People," *Blacklock's Reporter*, December 12, 2014, blacklocks.ca/guest_commentary/my-country-my-people-2/.

"You can do anything to me": Chrystia Freeland, "The Quiet Revolutionaries," *Financial Times*, December 3, 2004.

an interview given by twelve-year-old Natalka: Myrna Kostash, "Sisters: The Unbreakable Bond," *Chatelaine*, April 1983.

CHAPTER FOUR

Over forty thousand alumni: Elizabeth Kastor, "Harvard's 350th: Pomp and a 600-Foot Rainbow," *Washington Post*, September 4, 1986.

as if the "center of the universe had briefly lodged itself" in Harvard Square: Kastor, "Harvard's 350th."

The dinner was cancelled: Sabrina A. Mohamed and Alyza J. Sebenius, "Harvard Turns 350," *Harvard Crimson*, May 23, 2012, thecrimson.com/article/2012/5/23/350-Anniversary-Celebration/.

Before Chrystia departed for Harvard: Jessica Demello, "Chrystia Freeland at Teatro; Reuters Chief Lauds Canadian Caution," *National Post*, March 27, 2010.

In Edmonton, she had developed an interest: CIUS Newsletter, Canadian Institute of Ukrainian Studies, vol. 10, November 1986.

"Whatever I wear, wherever I go": Chrystia Freeland, "Dominique Strauss-Kahn and a Rush to Judgment," *Globe and Mail*, May 19, 2011.

"a pair of wire-rimmed glasses": Elaine Ellis, "Let's Go Keeps Its Editor Going," *South Florida Sun Sentinel*, February 7, 1988.

"It made me a lot more self-confident": Ellis, "Let's Go."

CHAPTER FIVE

Despite her grandparents' convictions: Chrystia Freeland, "The Quiet Revolutionaries," *Financial Times*, December 3, 2004.

At first, Soviet officials welcomed her: Don Retson, "Student 'Glasnost' Chilly," *Edmonton Journal*, May 20, 1989.

They were dealt with swiftly: Chrystia Freeland, "Popular Movement Radicalizing Ukraine," *Student*, March–April 1989, susk.ca/wp-content/uploads/2021/01/STUDENT-1989-March-April.pdf.

Despite freezing temperatures: David Marples, "Mass Meeting in Kiev Focuses on Ecological Issues, Political Situation," *Ukrainian Weekly*, December 4, 1988, archive.ukrweekly.com/print-media/1988/The_Ukrainian_Weekly_1988-49 .pdf.

That fall, some of his amateur photography: Efrem Lukatsky, "About the KGB and Canada's Foreign Affairs Minister" [in Ukrainian], *Censor.NET*, January 24, 2017, censor.net/ru/blogs/1104232/o_kgb_i_ministre_inostrannyh_del_kanady.

whose choir was that year the first to begin: "Homin," Kharkiv Human Rights Protection Group, November 11, 2006, museum.khpg.org/en/1163155684.

Chrystia was profoundly moved: Coilin O'Connor and Oleksandra Vagner, "The Kyiv Photographer Who Captured the 'Gloomy Dignity' of Soviet Life," RadioFreeEurope/RadioLiberty, September 30, 2020, rferl.org/a/ukraine-photographer-oleksandr-ranchukov-soviet-streets-ussr/30864692.html.

After waiting for three hours: Lukatsky, "About the KGB."

her first byline in a major international newspaper: Krystia [Chrystia] Freeland, "Ukrainian Party Chief under Fire," *The Independent*, February 10, 1989.

"I saw how important Bill was": Linda Diebel, "How Chrystia Freeland became Justin Trudeau's First Star," *Toronto Star*, November 29, 2015, thestar.com/news/insight/how-chrystia-freeland-became-justin-trudeau-s-first-star/article_addef1be-c916-56b9-ac7b-041ace9fff35.html.

"turned into an impressive manifestation of Ukrainian national assertiveness": Bohdan Nahaylo, "Ukrainian Language Society Conference Reveals Defiance," *Ukrainian Weekly*, February 19, 1989, ukrweekly.com/archive/1989/The_Ukrainian_Weekly_1989-08.pdf.

Customs officials pulled her aside: M. Derimov, "Caught Red-Handed," *Pravda Ukrainy*, April 30, 1989.

On campus, following the delivery of her speech: Retson, "Student 'Glasnost' Chilly."

News of Chrystia's adventures: Don Retson, "City Woman in USSR Tells KGB to Get Lost," *Edmonton Journal*, April 28, 1989.

In Kyiv, too, Chrystia made headlines: Derimov, "Caught Red-Handed."

a top-secret report on Chrystia—code-named "Frida": Stroĭ, "Emissarskaia missiia byla prervana," *Sbornik KGB SSSR*, no. 144 (June 1990)ı 31 34.

On her last night in Kyiv: Retson, "Student 'Glasnost' Chilly."

When *Pravda Ukrainy* published its accusations: Chrystia Freeland, "Ukraine Facing Real Challenge," *Edmonton Journal*, September 20, 1989.

In a 2013 interview with Little PINK Book: Chrystia Freeland, "The Accidental Journalist," interview by Rebecca Wetherbee, Little PINK Book, May 20, 2013, littlepinkbook.com/chrystia-freeland-u-s-managing-editor-financial-times/.

She befriended, for instance, economics professor Larry Summers: Chrystia Freeland, "Crisis Manager," *Financial Times*, July 11, 2009.

"I was in complete shock": Marina Jimenez, "Albertan Wins Rhodes Prize; Scholarship a Ticket to Oxford for Feisty Chrystia Freeland," *Edmonton Journal*, December 12, 1990.

CHAPTER SIX

In January 1990, hundreds of thousands of people: "Ukraine Marks Unity Day, Commemorates 'Human Chain,'" RadioFreeEurope/RadioLiberty, January 23, 2010, rferl.org/a/Ukraine_Marks_Unity_Day_Commemorates_Human_Chain/1937542.html.

David Kynaston writes in a brief history of the *FT*: David Kynaston, "A Brief History of the Financial Times," *Financial Times Historical Archive*, Cengage Learning, 2010, gale.com/binaries/content/assets/gale-us-en/primary-sources/intl-gps/intl-gps-essays/full-ghn-contextual-essays/ghn_essay_ftha_kynaston1_website.pdf.

In Kyiv, Chrystia obtained one of the first press cards: "Chrystia Freeland: Interview with *The Buzz*," *The Buzz*, Stanford School of Humanities and Sciences, May 9, 2014, ethicsinsociety.stanford.edu/news/chrystia-freeland-interview-buzz.

a lecture in Edmonton in 2000: Marco Levytsky, "Shevchenko Lecture Focuses on Ukrainians and the Media," *Ukrainian Weekly*, April 23, 2000.

In 1992, after Chrystia wrote articles: Chrystia Freeland, "The Rough Etiquette of Russian Deal-Making," *Financial Times*, April 16/17, 1994.

At the time, Balls was a London-based *FT* journalist: Ed Balls, "Ed Balls' Fantasy Dinner: Steak Teppanyaki with Gordon Brown, Janet Yellen and Chrystia Freeland," *Financial Times*, August 27, 2021.

On May 30, 1991, for her first *FT* story: Chrystia Freeland, "New Soviet Union Runs the Risk of Losing Its Head in the Ukraine," *Financial Times*, May 30, 1991.

Khmara stood up and walked out of the courtroom: Marta Dyczok and John Rettie, "Police Commandos Seize Ukraine MP," *The Guardian*, July 20, 1991.

"I guess they expected us to jump": Marta Dyczok, "The Collapse of the Soviet Union and the Birth of an Independent Ukraine, 1988–1991," Hewko/Sievers Oral History Files, Ukrainian Catholic University in Lviv, created by Margarita Hewko and Sara Sievers; produced by John Hewko, Margarita Hewko, and Sara Sievers; directed by Margarita Hewko, vimeo.com/19652547.

Inside, the coal miners ripped the bathroom door: Chrystyna Lapychak, "Khmara Re-arrested in Kiev," *Ukrainian Weekly*, July 28, 1991, ukrweekly.com/archive/pdf3/1991/The_Ukrainian_Weekly_1991-30.pdf.

Two years later, Canada's diplomatic representative in Kyiv: Edward Greenspon, "Quebec Fears Felt in Ukraine," *Globe and Mail*, September 5, 1991.

She was embarrassed and angered: Chrystia Freeland, "Shunning a Resurgent Ukraine Ottawa Is Missing a Unique Opportunity for Fear of Supporting a 'Separatist' State," *Toronto Star*, July 8, 1991.

"Kyiv came up on the chopping block": Nestor Gayowsky, "Ukraine, Canada and a Satellite Phone: How History Happened in 1991," interview by Marta Dyczok, Hromadske Radio, February 12, 2016, hromadske.radio/en/podcasts/ukraine-calling/ukraine-canada-a-satellite-phone-how-history-happened-in-1991.

a personal essay called "My Ukraine": Chrystia Freeland, "My Ukraine," Brookings, May 12, 2015, csweb.brookings.edu/content/research/essays/2015/myukraine.html.

He warned against "suicide nationalism": George H. W. Bush, "Remarks to the Supreme Soviet of the Republic of the Ukraine in Kiev, Soviet Union," George H. W. Bush Presidential Library and Museum, August 1, 1991, bush41library.tamu.edu/archives/public-papers/3267.

For Chrystia, this was a moment: Linda Diebel, "How Chrystia Freeland Became Justin Trudeau's First Star," *Toronto Star*, November 29, 2015, thestar.com/news/insight/how-chrystia-freeland-became-justin-trudeau-s-first-star/article_addef1be-c916-56b9-ac7b-041ace9fff35.html.

"It was thrilling and rewarding": Chrystia Freeland, "The Accidental Journalist," interview by Rebecca Wetherbee, Little PINK Book, May 20, 2013, littlepinkbook.com/chrystia-freeland-u-s-managing-editor-financial-times/.

The day before the referendum: David Staples, "A Dash for Freedom; In Edmonton: A Special Prayer for the Homeland," *Edmonton Journal*, November 30, 1991.

"The experts, including the CIA": Chrystia Freeland, "Finding a Place in a Rebalanced Global Economy: The New Foreign Policy Challenge," O. D. Skelton Memorial Lecture, March 2011, international.gc.ca/gac-amc/programs-programmes/od_skelton/chrystia_freeland_lecture-conference.aspx.

"I am leaving my post with apprehension": Mikhail Gorbachev, speech, December 25, 1991, publicpurpose.com/lib-gorb911225.htm.

"When I was 25, I was married with two small children": Liane Faulder, "Halyna's Life Took an Astounding Turn during Ukraine Visit," *Edmonton Journal*, August 17, 1992.

In a 2012 interview with *The Walrus*: John Lorinc, "Embedded with the .01 Percent," *The Walrus*, November 26, 2012, thewalrus.ca/embedded-with-the-01-percent/.

CHAPTER SEVEN

Through her Rhodes Scholarship: "7 Awarded Rhodes Scholarships," *Waterloo Region Record*, January 2, 1991.

"once-in-a-lifetime moment": Chrystia Freeland, "My Oxford," interview with John Garth, *Oxford Today* 23, no. 2 (2011).

"make Russia rich again": Chrystia Freeland, "Blood, Sweat and Tears—for Others," *Financial Times*, December 9, 1993.

Nemtsov, who had a photograph of himself: Chrystia Freeland, "Russian Prophecy of Doom," *Financial Times*, December 8, 1993.

She opened with a description of the in-flight antics: Chrystia Freeland, "The Rough Etiquette of Russian Deal-Making," *Financial Times*, April 16/17, 1994.

Chrystia reviewed *Comrade Criminal*: Chrystia Freeland, "Cowboys in the Wild, Wild East," review of *Comrade Criminal* by Stephen Handelman, *Financial Times*, October 13, 1994.

While covering the first years: Email from John Thornhill to author, September 12, 2022.

As she recounts in the prologue: Chrystia Freeland, *Sale of the Century: Russia's Wild Ride from Communism to Capitalism* (Crown, 2000).

"Soviet shortage has been replaced by capitalist excess": Chrystia Freeland, "Moscow as a Business Centre," *Financial Times*, September 17, 1997.

The president expected to be able: "Chechnya Profile—Timeline," BBC News, January 17, 2018, bbc.com/news/world-europe-18190473.

"As I watched Russia's jostling progress": Freeland, *Sale of the Century*, 8.

The small team that Chrystia headed up: Email from John Thornhill to author, September 12, 2022.

Built by German prisoners of war: Dan Shea, "'Sad Sam' Building Loses Lustre," *Moscow Times*, September 19, 2006, https://www.themoscowtimes.com/2006/09/19/sad-sam-building-loses-lustre-a202360.

a casual Italian restaurant whose owners: Chrystia Freeland, "Comforts for the Well-Heeled," *Financial Times*, April 11, 1996.

Moscow, she wrote in an *FT* article about their trip: Chrystia Freeland, "Big Thaw in the Great White North," *Financial Times*, February 1, 1997.

"When I started visiting": Graham Bowley, "The Dis-United Kingdom," *Montreal Gazette*, August 31, 2008.

"Russian soldiers, many of them alleged to be drugged": Chrystia Freeland, "Samashki: A Symbol of Unbroken Spirit," *Financial Times*, August 26, 1996.

she lauded the bravery of the Chechen fighters: Chrystia Freeland, "A City Rises from the Rubble," *Financial Times*, August 24, 1996.

In the mid-1990s, the oligarchs were eager: Email from John Thornhill to author, September 12, 2022.

Chrystia would eventually become known: Author interview with Edward Lucas, October 13, 2021.

the dress code of Russian women: Chrystia Freeland, "Giving Oprah a Run for Her Money," *Financial Times*, July 1, 1998.

subject to "a barrage of sexual innuendo": Freeland, *Sale of the Century*, 247.

secretaries "without sexual complexes": Chrystia Freeland, "The Diva from Central Planning," *Financial Times*, March 7, 1998.

"skies of Fabergé-egg blue": Chrystia Freeland, "Cold Hearts, Warm Milk in Moscow," *Financial Times*, December 17, 1997.

"Do I really need to remember this one's name?": Freeland, *Sale of the Century*, 330.

"ultimate political cypher": Freeland, *Sale of the Century*, 354.

"the young reformers and Western businessmen": Freeland, *Sale of the Century*, 332.

"The biggest danger is that Putin": Freeland, *Sale of the Century*, 332–33.

"At the beginning of the 1990s, the question": Freeland, *Sale of the Century*, 341–42.

In a prescient warning, she noted: Freeland, *Sale of the Century*, 344–45.

CHAPTER EIGHT

Though she would later wish: Chrystia Freeland, "The Accidental Journalist," interview by Rebecca Wetherbee Little PINK Book, May 20, 2013, littlepinkbook .com/chrystia-freeland-u-s-managing-editor-financial-times/.

Chrystia oversaw a staff of about seventy: "Senior Financial Times Journalist Named Globe Deputy Editor," *Globe and Mail*, July 15, 1999.

"'You're an editor now'": Chrystia Freeland, "Chrystia Freeland Is Trying to Supercharge Canada's Growth," interview with Stephanie Flanders, Bloomberg News, May 28, 2021, bnnbloomberg.ca/chrystia-freeland-is-trying-to-supercharge-canada-s-growth-1.1609653.

"After our first raptures": Graham Bowley, "The Big Question of Frosties vs Borscht: Chy tato paiats?," *Financial Times*, October 25, 2003.

Ahead of the celebration: Author interview with Adele Boucher, May 18, 2022.

Halyna had sourced the crowns: Bronwen Jervis, "The List: 10 Things Newly Minted MP Chrystia Freeland Can't Live Without," *Toronto Life*, February 4, 2014, torontolife.com/city/chrystia-freeland-the-list/.

"When I arrived from London, which is the greatest newspaper city": Chris Cobb, *Ego and Ink: The Inside Story of Canada's National Newspaper War* (Toronto: McLelland and Stewart, 2004), 26.

"I always wanted to come back to Canada": "Senior Financial Times Journalist."

In the *Star*, Richard Gwyn wrote: Richard Gwyn, "Don't say 'Newfie'—It Really Is Offensive," *Toronto Star*, August 15, 1999.

"She's the sort of Canadian the New Globe likes": Anthony Wilson-Smith, "The Globe, By Jove!," *Maclean's*, July 26, 1999.

"chipmunk on helium": Cobb, *Ego and Ink*, 178.

While the *Frank* coverage bothered Chrystia: Cobb, *Ego and Ink*, 189.

"at the time a repository": Leah McLaren, "Chrystia Freeland's Dilemma," *Chatelaine*, April 12, 2019, chatelaine.com/living/politics/chrystia-freeland/

Robert Kaplan called it "one of the finest works of journalism": Robert Kaplan, "Who Lost Russia?," *New York Times*, October 8, 2000.

"one of the ornate, high-ceilinged rooms of the Kremlin": Geoffrey York and Chrystia Freeland, "Vladimir Putin's Secret Dream," *Globe and Mail*, December 14, 2000.

At one point, he even rubbed: Adam Radwanski, "Meet Chrystia Freeland, the Woman Defining Canada's Foreign Role," *Globe and Mail*, August 12, 2017.

In February 2001, in a maternity ward: Bowley, "Big Question."

Addis covered them up with wrapping paper: Email from Richard Addis to author, November 16, 2021.

Addis remembers the baby being sick: Email from Richard Addis to author, November 16, 2021.

"I had a big job": Cobb, *Ego and Ink*, 188.

years later, as Canada's foreign minister: McLaren, "Chrystia Freeland's Dilemma."

CHAPTER NINE

FT.com was operating at break-even: John Cassy, "Family Fortunes: Let's Not Do Lunch," *The Guardian*, January 6, 2003.

"Is *The Financial Times* manoeuvring": Martin Waller, City Diary, *The Times*, May 21, 2003.

When Queen Elizabeth II hosted: Robert Jobson, "All the Queen's Women: 180 Attend Special Lunch at the Palace," *Evening Standard*, March 11, 2004.

"Gowers and Freeland agree to everything": Roy Greenslade, "'We Have Sailed through the Perfect Storm,'" *The Guardian*, December 6, 2004.

"At first, I only slightly resisted." Graham Bowley, "The Big Question of Frosties vs Borscht: Chy tato paiats?," *Financial Times*, October 25, 2003.

"On the editorial floor lunches": Cassy, "Family Fortunes."

Over the previous three years: Alan Ruddock, "Alan Ruddock on the Press: Why the City Fell Out of Love with the FT," *The Guardian*, August 22, 2005.

To keep herself grounded: Chrystia Freeland, "Winners of God's Lottery," *Financial Times*, October 6, 2007.

"feminist fatwa": Chrystia Freeland, "Playing by the Boys' Rules," *Financial Times*, September 29, 2007.

"Begging powerful and imperious people": Chrystia Freeland, "Nursery Tales," *Financial Times*, March 25, 2007.

"To get a sense of how deeply": Chrystia Freeland, "The Nice Squad," *Financial Times*, March 15, 2008.

The columns, which Chrystia often finished: Chrystia Freeland, "Face-to-Face Beats Cyberspace," *Financial Times*, September 22, 2007.

"imperfect standard-bearer for the cause": Chrystia Freeland, "Clinton's Real Lesson for Women," *Financial Times*, June 4, 2008.

When it came to feminist icons: Chrystia Freeland, "Tears for Ballot Box Fears," *Financial Times*, January 12, 2008.

Palin was a "genuinely self-made woman": Chrystia Freeland, "Sarah Palin Is a True Feminist Role Model," *Financial Times*, September 3, 2008.

"two true loves—for work and for family": Chrystia Freeland, "Fathers Have Their Day," *Financial Times*, June 16, 2007.

Tempted to attend a lecture by her parent-teacher association: Chrystia Freeland, "The New Model Americans," *Financial Times*, January 20, 2007.

"As we take our Hallmark-sanctioned annual moment": Chrystia Freeland, "Mothers Have Their Day," *Financial Times*, May 12, 2007.

"On her deathbed, my mother": Chrystia Freeland, "The Richness of Her Life," *Financial Times*, July 13, 2007.

"balancing kids and career is a high-wire act": Chrystia Freeland, "The Personal Is Political, but Don't Forget the Kids," *Financial Times*, August 9, 2008.

In 2009, while researching the book: Graham Bowley, "A Taste of Danger, on and off K2: Journey to the Mountain Where Dozens Have Died Crosses Taliban Territory," *International Herald Tribune*, June 29, 2009.

"I was convinced that the crisis": Chrystia Freeland, "Questions for Chrystia Freeland," interview with Karen Christensen, *Rotman Management Magazine*, fall 2013, rotman.utoronto.ca/Connect/Rotman-MAG/IdeaExchange/Chrystia-Freeland.

In his book *The Powerful and the Damned*: Lionel Barber, *The Powerful and the Damned: Private Diaries in Turbulent Times* (W. H. Allen, 2021).

CHAPTER TEN

"world's leading source of intelligent information": "Thomson Completes Acquisition of Reuters; Thomson Reuters Shares Begin Trading Today," Thomson Reuters, April 17, 2008, ir.thomsonreuters.com/news-releases/news-release-details/thomson-completes-acquisition-reuters-thomson-reuters-shares.

"advanced discussions" to leave: Paul Sonne, "FT's US Editor in Talks to Join Thomson Reuters," *Wall Street Journal*, February 28, 2010, wsj.com/articles/SB10001424052748704089904575094161774937630.

"Reuters was never the type of media outlet": Joe Pompeo, "Reuters Adds Some Star Power, Moves Away from the Old 'Wire Mentality,'" *Business Insider*, September 23, 2010, businessinsider.com/the-new-name-recognition-of-reuters-2010-9.

in a 2011 profile, *New York Magazine*: Gabriel Sherman, "83 Minutes with Chrystia Freeland," *New York Magazine*, October 14, 2011, nymag.com/news/intelligencer/encounter/chrystia-freeland-2011-10/.

played a "voice-of-God" role: Chrystia Freeland, welcoming remarks, Centre for International Governance Innovation, October 13, 2011, youtube.com/watch?v=lwpqewOxclk,

in a September 18 email to staff, Rashbass announced: "Reuters News Cancels Its Next Website Project," Reuters, September 18, 2013, reuters.com/article/idUSL2N0HE1BJ/.

"I don't understand what they were thinking": Matthew Zeitlin, "How Chrystia Freeland Hastened Reuters Next's Demise," BuzzFeedNews, September 25, 2013, buzzfeednews.com/article/matthewzeitlin/how-chrystia-freeland-hastened-reuters-nexts-demise.

CHAPTER ELEVEN

Her columns from the time: Chrystia Freeland, "Economic Worries and the Global Elite," Reuters, May 28, 2014, reuters.com/article/idUS171268157520130617.

"the best prosperity-creating system humanity has come up with": Chrystia Freeland, "Retooling Capitalism for the Social Good," Reuters, November 5, 2015, reuters.com/article/idUS183792016320130719.

Through my work as a business journalist: Chrystia Freeland, "The Rise of the New Global Elite," *The Atlantic*, January/February 2011, theatlantic.com/magazine/archive/2011/01/the-rise-of-the-new-global-elite/308343/.

"a rising concern since the collapse of communism": Chrystia Freeland, "Finding a Place in a Rebalanced Global Economy: The New Foreign Policy Challenge," O. D. Skelton Memorial Lecture, March 2011, youtube.com/watch?v=Kb3a4NUOS9k.

Don Freeland had finished up his harvesting responsibilities: Jason McBride, "The Negotiator," *Toronto Life*, November 21, 2017, torontolife.com/city/the-negotiator/.

it would become his "campaign bible": Linda Diebel, "How Chrystia Freeland Became Justin Trudeau's First Star," *Toronto Star*, November 29, 2015, thestar.com/news/insight/how-chrystia-freeland-became-justin-trudeau-s-first-star/article_addef1be-c916-56b9-ac7b-041ace9fff35.html.

But despite having a good chat: McBride, "The Negotiator."

Chrystia met the new leader for a casual breakfast: Diebel, "How Chrystia Freeland Became Justin Trudeau's First Star."

"Freeland eventually confided in Trudeau": McBride, "The Negotiator."

"I grew up in Alberta": Chrystia Freeland, "Chrystia Freeland, Minister of Everything, Has Big Plans for Canada's Economic Future," interview with Trevor Cole, *Globe and Mail*, February 23, 2022.

In an interview with Ezra Klein: Ezra Klein, "Why Is Chrystia Freeland Leaving Journalism to Run for Office?," *Washington Post*, August 16, 2013.

CHAPTER TWELVE

Toronto Centre was a "world-class case study": Jonathan Kay, "The Battle for Canada's Income-Inequality Epicentre," *National Post*, August 7, 2013.

Chrystia laid out her motivations for running: Chrystia Freeland, "The Path Leading to Middle-Class Prosperity," *Globe and Mail*, July 29, 2013.

"I'm not Keynes or Teddy Roosevelt or FDR": Ezra Klein, "Why Is Chrystia Freeland Leaving Journalism to Run for Office?," *Washington Post*, August 16, 2013.

"very consequential moment": Maria Babbage, "NDP, Liberals to Choose Candidates for Toronto Byelection, Set Stage for 2015," Canadian Press, September 14, 2013.

"The Toronto Centre contest, which really isn't one": Warren Kinsella, "A Tale of Two Trudeaus—One We Like and One We Don't," *Toronto Sun*, August 25, 2013.

"How much faith should anyone place": John Ivison, "Trudeau Liberals Still Seeing Stars; Smitherman Pushed Aside for Top Journalist," *National Post*, July 31, 2013.

Chrystia herself maintained that Trudeau had made it clear: Susan Delacourt, "Picking the Political Future for the City's Core," *Toronto Star*, September 15, 2013.

By the cut-off date of August 20: Delacourt, "Picking the Political Future."

having collected five hundred of the thirteen hundred ballots: Tanya Mok, "Journalists Face off for Rae's Seat," *National Post*, September 16, 2013.

Chrystia, frequently in a bright red: Bronwen Jervis, "The List: 10 Things Newly Minted MP Chrystia Freeland Can't Live Without," *Toronto Life*, February 4, 2014, torontolife.com/city/chrystia-freeland-the-list/.

ready to talk about "big ideas": Delacourt, "Picking the Political Future."

"If you are a professional critic": Chrystia Freeland, "How I Gave Up on Snark to Become a Canadian Politician," *Politico Magazine*, January 14, 2014, politico .com/magazine/story/2014/01/chrystia-freeland-politician-journalist-102053/.

Trudeau's "more sunny, float-above-fray approach": Joan Bryden, "Byelections Measure Impact of Senate Scandal, Battle for Opposition Supremacy," Canadian Press, November 24, 2013.

McQuaig, for example, called for a hike: Scott Stinson, "Loss of Toronto Centre Riding in Byelection Would Be Significant Blow to Liberals," *National Post*, November 22, 2013, nationalpost.com/opinion/scott-stinson-loss-of-toronto-centre-riding-in-byelection-would-be-significant-blow-to-liberals.

Chrystia's day "included the obligatory early-morning transit stop meet-and-greet": Anne Kingston, "The Liberals Hold Toronto Centre in By-election," *Maclean's*, November 25, 2013, macleans.ca/uncategorized/scenes-from-the-toronto-centre-by-election/.

"We were so excited that she won": "Political Achievement in Toronto Delights Earl Shilton Relatives," *Hinckley Times*, December 28, 2013, hinckleytimes.net/ news/local-news/political-achievement-toronto-delights-earl-6442122.

In the end, the Liberals took 49 percent: Éric Grenier, "By-election's Winners: Liberals. Losers: Robocall Polls," *Globe and Mail*, November 26, 2013.

CHAPTER THIRTEEN

Through her reporting, she had come to believe: Chrystia Freeland, "Technology, Trade and Fewer Jobs," *New York Times*, February 14, 2013.

In February 2014, with more than a hundred people dead: "Ukraine's Struggle for Independence in Russia's Shadow," Council on Foreign Relations, cfr.org/timeline/ukraines-struggle-independence-russias-shadow.

"everyone in that part of the world is watching Ukraine": Debates of January 27, 2014, openparliament.ca/debates/2014/1/27/chrystia-freeland-1/.

"For my mother, it was a personal decision": Leah McLaren, "Chrystia Freeland's Dilemma," *Chatelaine*, April 12, 2019, chatelaine.com/living/politics/chrystia-freeland/.

Beginning with her time in opposition: Email from Lucan Way to author, June 23, 2022.

"Put your 'big girl' voice on": Ryan Maloney, "Chrystia Freeland Heckled in House, Commentator Tells Her to Use 'Big Girl Voice,'" video, *Huffington Post Canada*, February 4, 2014, huffpost.com/archive/ca/entry/chrystia-freeland-heckled-in-house-commentator-tells-her-to-use_n_4726222.

Susan Delacourt called it a "disgusting little episode": Press Gallery, *Power Play with Don Martin*, CTV Television, February 5, 2014.

"Can we all agree that commenting": Michelle Rempel Garner (@MichelleRempel), Twitter, February 4, 2014, twitter.com/MichelleRempel/status/430795005079601152.

"We applaud Canadian MP Chrystia Freeland for leaning in": Joshi Herrmann, "Why Facebook Queen Sheryl Sandberg Is a Wonder Woman," *The Standard*, March 10, 2014, standard.co.uk/lifestyle/london-life/why-facebook-queen-sheryl-sandberg-is-a-wonder-woman-9125611.html.

Millar apologized for his tweet: Matthew Millar, "I'm Sorry for My Inappropriate Tweet to MP Chrystia Freeland," *Vancouver Observer*, February 5, 2014.

"Don't let the Conservatives shout us down": Chrystia Freeland, "This Is My 'Big Girl' Voice," Liberal Party of Canada, February 17, 2014, liberal.ca/this-is-my-big-girl-voice/.

Chrystia had called Putin the "ultimate political cypher": Chrystia Freeland, *Sale of the Century: Russia's Wild Ride from Communism to Capitalism* (Crown, 2000), 344–45.

"The capital was, almost literally, grievously wounded": Chrystia Freeland, "My Ukraine," Brookings, May 12, 2015, csweb.brookings.edu/content/research/essays/2015/myukraine.html.

"It's really important for me right now as a Canadian MP": Terry Glavin, "Courage and Conviction in Foreign Policy," *Ottawa Citizen*, March 6, 2014.

"It will embolden dictators and discourage democrats": Chrystia Freeland, "We Must Stop Pussyfooting around Putin's Regime," *Financial Times*, March 16, 2014.

"I think of myself as a Russophile": Freeland, "My Ukraine."

CHAPTER FOURTEEN

For all of 2014, the Liberal party: Éric Grenier, "Trudeau's Liberals Led in 2014, but What Does 2015 Hold?," CBC News, December 30, 2014, cbc.ca/news/politics/trudeau-s-liberals-led-in-2014-but-what-does-2015-hold-1.2877711.

Despite her misgivings, Chrystia donned: Laura Ryckewaert, "Knock Knock: Candidates Discuss Their Door Game," *Hill Times*, September 19, 2015, hilltimes.com/2015/09/18/knock-knock-candidates-discuss-their-door-game-2/33462.

Ahead of the first televised leaders' debate: "Trudeau Will Win Debate Points 'If He Comes on Stage with His Pants On': Tory Spokesman," Canadian Press, August 5, 2015, cbc.ca/news/politics/trudeau-will-win-debate-points-if-he-comes-on-stage-with-his-pants-on-tory-spokesman-1.3180169.

"Was he convincing? Not always": David Parkinson, "Trudeau Emerges as Leader with New Economic Vision for Canada," *Globe and Mail*, September 17, 2015.

"Sunny ways, my friends. Sunny ways": "Justin Trudeau's 'Sunny Ways' a Nod to Sir Wilfrid Laurier," CBC News, October 20, 2015, cbc.ca/news/canada/nova-scotia/ns-prof-trudeau-sunny-ways-1.3280693.

Trudeau delivered a message to Canada's allies abroad: "'We're Back,' Justin
Trudeau Says in Message to Canada's Allies Abroad," Canadian Press, October
20, 2015, nationalpost.com/news/politics/were-back-justin-trudeau-says-in-
message-to-canadas-allies-abroad.

where her ministerial office would eventually employ: Peter Mazereeuw, "'I
Think 2017 Will Be Her True Test as a Minister,' Freeland Moves into the
Spotlight," *Hill Times*, January 9, 2017, hilltimes.com/story/2017/01/09/freeland-
spotlight-2017/223182/.

A year after the Trudeau government's swearing-in: Peter Mazereeuw, "Trudeau
Cabinet Ministers Expensed $1,304 per Month for Second Residence in Ottawa,"
Hill Times, December 21, 2016, hilltimes.com/story/2016/12/21/ministers-
housing-expenses-13-per-cent-harper-cabinet/223176/.

she would request a francophone driver: Author interview with Natalka Freeland,
July 25, 2022.

and sit up front in the car's passenger seat: Author interview with Larissa Balvatska,
September 19, 2022.

John Turner, for example, who argued during the 1988 federal election: "CBC
Archives: Betting On Free Trade 1988," CBC, September 17, 2008, youtube.com/
watch?v=gyYjRmM7RDY.

Chrystia's mandate letter from the prime minister: "Minister of International Trade
Mandate Letter," Office of the Prime Minister, November 12, 2015, pm.gc.ca/
en/mandate-letters/2015/11/12/archived-minister-international-trade-mandate-
letter.

"This is a true, high-level, 21st-century trade agreement": Andy Blatchford, "Legal
Review of 'Gold-Plated' Canada-EU Trade Deal Complete: Feds," Canadian
Press, February 29, 2016.

a case of "dotting the i's and crossing the t's": Thomas Walkom, "CETA Critics
Force Europe, Canada to Revise Trade Pact," *Toronto Star*, March 2, 2016.

in 2022 a tribunal ordered the Italian government: Arthur Neslen, "Oil Firm Rockhopper Wins £210M Payout after Being Banned from Drilling," *The Guardian*, August 24, 2022, theguardian.com/business/2022/aug/24/oil-firm-rockhopper-wins-210m-payout-after-being-banned-from-drilling.

European Union officials quietly approached: Janyce McGregor, "EU Quietly Asks Canada to Rework Trade Deal's Thorny Investment Clause," CBC News, January 21, 2016, cbc.ca/news/politics/canada-europe-trade-isds-ceta-1.3412943.

a "lesser prize" for Canadian businesses: Campbell Clark, "With Brexit Leaving CETA on Shaky Ground, Trudeau Can Only Sit and Wait," *Globe and Mail*, June 24, 2016.

"We believe the right choice": Cecilia Malmström and Chrystia Freeland, "For Canada and Europe, Now Is the Time for Bridges, Not Walls," *Globe and Mail*, July 8, 2016.

In the year following her cabinet appointment: Mazereeuw, "'I Think 2017 Will Be Her True Test.'"

so that "European leaders could hear the legitimate demands": Maïa de La Baume, "Walloon Parliament Rejects CETA Deal," *Politico*, October 14, 2016, politico.eu/article/walloon-parliament-rejects-ceta-deal/.

In the House of Commons the next week: Aaron Wherry, "'The Tactic Has Paid Off': Freeland's Dramatic Walk Out May Have Saved CETA," CBC News, October 28, 2016, cbc.ca/news/politics/wherry-freeland-ceta-1.3824374.

"I had all the Europeans calling me up": Adrian Morrow and Robert Fife, "Freeland Talks Tough on Trade with Trump Team," *Globe and Mail*, February 8, 2017.

"consultations" that involved a "seemingly never-ending series of meetings": Mazereeuw, "'I Think 2017 Will Be Her True Test.'"

CHAPTER SIXTEEN

a "stunning repudiation of the establishment": Matt Flegenheimer and Michael Barbaro, "Donald Trump Is Elected President in Stunning Repudiation of the Establishment," *New York Times*, November 9, 2016.

Halyna, Chrystia wrote in the *Financial Times*: Chrystia Freeland, "The Richness of Her Life," *Financial Times*, July 13, 2007

Chrystia was sworn in as Canada's top diplomat: "Archived—Minister of Foreign Affairs Mandate Letter," Office of the Prime Minister, February 1, 2017, pm.gc .ca/en/mandate-letters/2017/02/01/archived-minister-foreign-affairs-mandate-letter.

A 2016 report from the US Chamber of Commerce: "The Facts on NAFTA," US Chamber of Commerce, December 16, 2016, uschamber.com/assets/archived/ images/the_facts_on_nafta_-_2017.pdf.

Trump called NAFTA "the worst trade deal": Patrick Gillespie, "Trump Hammers America's 'Worst Trade Deal,'" CNN, September 27, 2016, money.cnn .com/2016/09/27/news/economy/donald-trump-nafta-hillary-clinton-debate/.

Trump tweeted: "I will renegotiate NAFTA": Donald Trump (@ realDonaldTrump), Twitter, October 19, 2016, twitter.com/realDonaldTrump/ status/788919099275390976.

"I feel very strongly that one of the most pressing challenges today": Simon Lewsen, "Chrystia Freeland Wants to Fix the Twenty-First Century," *The Walrus*, February 14, 2018, thewalrus.ca/chrystia-freeland-wants-to-fix-the-twenty-first-century/.

"Protection will lead to great prosperity and strength": "The Inaugural Address: Remarks of President Donald J. Trump—as Prepared for Delivery," The White House, January 20, 2017, trumpwhitehouse.archives.gov/briefings-statements/ the-inaugural-address/.

a "whole-of-government, bi-partisan, full-court press": "Address by Foreign Affairs Minister on the Modernization of the North American Free Trade Agreement (NAFTA)," Global Affairs Canada, August 14, 2017, canada.ca/en/global-affairs/news/2017/08/address_by_ foreignaffairsministeronthemodernizationofthenorthame.html.

"a son of Ohio": "Canadian Officials in US Hammering Home Importance of NAFTA," *Automotive News Canada* [Reuters], June 29, 2017, canada.autonews.com/

article/20170629/CANADA/170629735/canadian-officials-in-u-s-hammering-home-importance-of-nafta.

Kushner, who considered her a "talented operator": Jared Kushner, *Breaking History: A White House Memoir* (HarperCollins, 2023), 67.

As Mulroney noted to a Toronto audience: Catherine Tsalikis, "No One under the Bus: What We Know about NAFTA Re-negotiations So Far," OpenCanada, February 23, 2017, opencanada.org/no-one-under-bus-what-we-know-about-nafta-re-negotiations-so-far/.

Trump said that he merely intended to tweak certain elements: Kathleen Harris, "Trudeau, Trump Find Common Ground on Economy and Security, but Remain at Odds over Immigration," CBC News, February 13, 2017, cbc.ca/news/politics/washington-trudeau-trump-meeting-1.3979743.

The *New York Times* lauded Trudeau's strategy: Max Fisher, "Canada's Trump Strategy: Go Around Him," *New York Times*, June 22, 2017.

In April, Trump suddenly directed Kushner: Kushner, *Breaking History*, 158.

Trump walked back his threat: Mark Landler and Binyamin Appelbaum, "Trump Tells Foreign Leaders That NAFTA Can Stay for Now," *New York Times*, April 26, 2017.

Running for the NDP in Edmonton-Strathcona: "Chrystia Freeland's Vision for a New NAFTA," prepared remarks for speech at University of Ottawa, *Maclean's*, August 14, 2017, macleans.ca/politics/chrystia-freelands-vision-for-a-new-nafta/.

The approach of Canada's negotiating team, Chrystia said: "Address by Foreign Affairs Minister on the Modernization of NAFTA."

Robert Lighthizer, a veteran Republican lawyer: Robert Lighthizer, *No Trade Is Free: Changing Course, Taking on China, and Helping America's Workers* (Broadside, 2023), 232.

he recognized how catastrophic a sudden withdrawal: Lighthizer, *No Trade Is Free*, 217.

"the practised pol's trick of telling me something nice": Chrystia Freeland, "'No One Will Destroy Us,'" *Financial Times*, August 16, 2008.

As months went by, however, it seemed to Lighthizer: Lighthizer, *No Trade Is Free*, 234.

The finance minister, according to his book: Bill Morneau and John Lawrence Reynolds, *Where To from Here: A Path to Canadian Prosperity* (ECW Press, 2023), 379.

the decision was meant to send an "unmistakable signal": Alexander Panetta and Katie Simpson, "Canada Is Already Preparing for Trump's Potential Tariff Threats," CBC News, March 24, 2024, cbc.ca/news/world/trump-tariff-canadian-diplomatic-deployment-1.7153227.

"I think what is important for Americans to understand": Adam Frisk, "'Seriously?': Chrystia Freeland on U.S. Tariffs, Trump's Claim Canada Is Security Threat," Global News, June 4, 2018, globalnews.ca/news/4250691/tariffs-chrystia-freeland-donald-trump-security-threat-seriously/.

Canadians would "not be pushed around": "Trudeau: Canadians Will Not Be Pushed Around," CNN, June 9, 2018, youtube.com/watch?v=uiVaZSi6MkM.

"Based on Justin's false statements": Donald Trump (@realDonaldTrump), Twitter, June 9, 2018, twitter.com/realDonaldTrump/status/1005586152076689408.

a second tweet as "dishonest & weak": Donald Trump (@realDonaldTrump), Twitter, June 9, 2018, twitter.com/realDonaldTrump/status/1005586562959093760.

"there's a special place in hell": Gregg Re, "There's a 'Special Place in Hell' for Trudeau after His G7 'Stunt,' Top WH Trade Adviser Peter Navarro Says," Fox News, June 10, 2018, foxnews.com/politics/theres-a-special-place-in-hell-for-trudeau-after-his-g7-stunt-top-wh-trade-adviser-peter-navarro-says.

"Canada does not believe that ad hominem attacks": Josh Dehaas, "Freeland Calls 'ad Hominem Attacks' from U.S. Inappropriate," CTV News, June 10, 2018, ctvnews.ca/politics/freeland-calls-ad-hominem-attacks-from-u-s-inappropriate-1.3967509.

By this point, Canada and the United States: Lighthizer, *No Trade Is Free*, 237.

"For the past 70 years and more, America has been": Chrystia Freeland, "2018 Diplomat of the Year Chrystia Freeland: Read the Transcript," *Foreign Policy*, June 14, 2018, foreignpolicy.com/2018/06/14/2018-diplomat-of-the-year-chrystia-freeland-read-the-transcript/.

Morneau, too, worried about the tone and substance: Morneau and Reynolds, *Where To from Here*, 384–85.

"Following this theatre, she would walk to the steps": Alexander Panetta, "Jared Kushner Memoir Chronicles Frustrations of Negotiating Trade Deal with Canada," CBC News, August 20, 2022, cbc.ca/news/world/kushner-book-usmca-cusma-1.6556647.

a not-so-veiled reference to Chrystia: Peter Zimonjic, "Trump Says He Rejected Meeting with Justin Trudeau," CBC News, September 26, 2018, cbc.ca/news/politics/trump-rejects-trudeau-meeting-1.4840015.

Canada's negotiator "hates America": Josh Rogin, "Days before Trade Deal, Trump Said Canada's Foreign Minister 'Hates America,'" *Washington Post*, October 2, 2018.

"That was where I started to realize": Katie Simpson and John Paul Tasker, "'Yay!': How the Canadians Won the Argument That Opened the Door to a NAFTA Deal," CBC News, October 1, 2018, cbc.ca/news/politics/tasker-nafta-tick-tock-nafta-1.4845904.

On Sunday afternoon, in the White House residence: Kushner, *Breaking History*, 196.

Andrew Scheer tweeted: "Would I have signed this deal?": "Andrew Scheer on New NAFTA Deal: 'I Would Have Signed a Better One' Than Trudeau," Canadian Press, October 14, 2018, ctvnews.ca/politics/andrew-scheer-on-new-nafta-deal-i-would-have-signed-a-better-one-than-trudeau-1.4133581.

she even won over Lighthizer: "Ambassador Lighthizer Delivers Remarks at USMCA Signing," US Embassy & Consulates in Canada, January 29, 2020, ca.usembassy.gov/ambassador-lighthizer-delivers-remarks-at-usmca-signing/.

Afterwards, Chrystia maintained that her faith: Aaron Wherry, *Promise and Peril: Justin Trudeau in Power* (HarperCollins, 2019), 254.

Trudeau thanked Chrystia for her "tireless, relentless efforts": "Prime Minister Trudeau and Minister Freeland Speaking Notes for the United States–Mexico–Canada Agreement Press Conference," Government of Canada, October 1, 2018, pm.gc.ca/en/news/speeches/2018/10/01/prime-minister-trudeau-and-minister-freeland-speaking-notes-united-states.

CHAPTER SEVENTEEN

Canada, in his opinion, should not just "go along" to "get along": Laura Payton, "Harper Speech Fires Up Convention Crowd," June 10, 2011, cbc.ca/news/politics/harper-speech-fires-up-convention-crowd-1.976268.

Iran posed the "most significant threat to global peace": Laura Payton, "Canada Closes Embassy in Iran, Expels Iranian Diplomats," CBC News, September 7, 2019, cbc.ca/news/politics/canada-closes-embassy-in-iran-expels-iranian-diplomats-1.1166509.

"I guess I'll shake your hand": "Stephen Harper at G20 Tells Vladimir Putin to 'Get Out of Ukraine,'" Canadian Press, November 15, 2014, cbc.ca/news/world/stephen-harper-at-g20-tells-vladimir-putin-to-get-out-of-ukraine-1.2836382.

the more "constructive" role of a "fair-minded and determined peace builder": "Stéphane Dion: On 'Responsible Conviction' and Liberal Foreign Policy," remarks at opening of Canada in Global Affairs, New Challenges, New Ways, March 29, 2016, macleans.ca/politics/ottawa/stephane-dion-how-ethics-inspires-liberal-foreign-policy/.

"We take no more joy than our conservative friends": "Stéphane Dion: On 'Responsible Conviction.'"

"The notion that the objective of foreign policy is to be friends with everyone": Mark MacKinnon, Adrian Morrow, Nathan VanderKlippe, Geoffrey York, and Michelle Carbert, "For Chrystia Freeland, the Political Is Personal," *Globe and Mail*, October 3, 2019.

Following Trump's election victory: Jocelyn Coulon, *Canada Is Not Back: How Justin Trudeau Is in over His Head on Foreign Policy*, trans. George Tombs (Lorimer, 2019), 177.

Coulon writes that over the fourteen months Dion was foreign minister: Coulon, *Canada Is Not Back*, 67.

"In any Third World country": Jason McBride, "The Negotiator," *Toronto Life*, November 21, 2017, torontolife.com/city/the-negotiator/.

"The Freeland-Bowley kids like to joke": Leah McLaren, "Chrystia Freeland's Dilemma," *Chatelaine*, April 12, 2019, chatelaine.com/living/politics/chrystia-freeland/.

the issues Chrystia cared most about as foreign minister: Author interview with Laurence Deschamps-Laporte, August 30, 2022.

On a flight from Alaska to Seattle: McBride, "The Negotiator."

Canadians must "use the multilateral structures they created": "Address by Minister Freeland on Canada's Foreign Policy Priorities," Global Affairs Canada, June 6, 2017, canada.ca/en/global-affairs/news/2017/06/address_by_ministerfreelandoncanadasforeignpolicypriorities.html.

"the times when [Europe] could completely rely on others": Eli Watkins, "While Campaigning, Merkel Says Europeans Can't 'Completely' Rely on US, Others," CNN, May 29, 2017, cnn.com/2017/05/28/politics/angela-merkel-donald-trump-g7/index.html.

the *New York Times* called it "the latest evidence of how Canada sees itself": Ian Austen, "A Canadian Minister's Speech Shows a Growing Divide with the US," *New York Times*, June 12, 2017.

"I don't think it's a secret": Robert Fife, "Freeland Warns Canadians to Beware of Russian Disinformation," *Globe and Mail*, March 6, 2017.

"Her normally chipper demeanour cracked": McBride, "The Negotiator."

"It is time for personal responsibility for those who continue to violate": Boris Nemtsov and Vladimir Kara-Murza, "Standing up for Freedom in Russia,"

National Post, December 11, 2012, nationalpost.com/opinion/boris-nemtsov-vladimir-kara-murza-standing-up for freedom-in-russia.

Browder told the CBC, Dion "just outright vetoed" the legislation: "Investor Bill Browder Talks about Canada-Russia Relations," CBC News (n.d., *circa* 2017) cbc.ca/player/play/855061059992.

In the winter of 2017: Andrew Kramer, "'They Starve You. They Shock You': Inside the Anti-Gay Pogrom in Chechnya," *New York Times*, April 21, 2017.

Chrystia tweeted: "Very alarmed to learn that Samar Badawi": Chrystia Freeland (@cafreeland), Twitter, August 2, 2018, twitter.com/cafreeland/status/1025030172624515072.

Chrystia's response to criticism of the Saudi incident: MacKinnon et al., "For Chrystia Freeland."

Chrystia was frank when asked about morale at Global Affairs Canada: Adam Radwanski, "Meet Chrystia Freeland, the Woman Defining Canada's Foreign Role," *Globe and Mail*, August 12, 2017.

to hear directly from "the people who are at the coal face": Chrystia Freeland, "Chrystia Freeland Is Trying to Supercharge Canada's Growth," interview with Stephanie Flanders, Bloomberg News, May 28, 2021, bnnbloomberg.ca/chrystia-freeland-is-trying-to-supercharge-canada-s-growth-1.1609653.

foreign minister Heiko Maas called her "a real influencer": Heiko Mass, speech at Eric M. Warburg Award ceremony, December 8, 2018, auswaertiges-amt.de/en/newsroom/news/maas-warburg-award-freeland/2169798.

CHAPTER EIGHTEEN

Other photos and a video of Trudeau: "What We Know about Justin Trudeau's Blackface Photos—And What Happens Next," CBC News, September 20, 2019, cbc.ca/news/politics/canada-votes-2019-trudeau-blackface-brownface-cbc-explains-1.5290664.

On February 7, 2019, the *Globe and Mail* reported: Robert Fife, Steven Chase, and Sean Fine, "PMO Pressed Wilson-Raybould to Abandon Prosecution of

SNC-Lavalin; Trudeau Denies His Office 'Directed' Her," *Globe and Mail*, February 7, 2019.

Wilson-Raybould said she'd experienced "veiled threats" and "a consistent and sustained effort": Kathleen Harris, "Wilson-Raybould Says She Faced Pressure, 'Veiled Threats' on SNC-Lavalin; Scheer Calls on PM to Resign," CBC News, February 27, 2019, cbc.ca/news/politics/wilson-raybould-testifies-justice-committee-1.5035219.

while she believed Wilson-Raybould had spoken "her truth": Chrystia Freeland, "Chrystia Freeland on CBC *Ottawa Morning*," interview with Robyn Bresnahan, CBC Ottawa, February 28, 2019, soundcloud.com/cbcottawa1/chrystia-freeland-on-cbc-ottawa-morning.

Robyn Urback called it "obsequious blather": Robyn Urback, "If Jane Philpott Doesn't Have Confidence in Justin Trudeau, Why Should Anyone Else?," CBC News, March 5, 2019, cbc.ca/news/opinion/philpott-resignation-1.5042965.

"I really appreciate that, and my kids really appreciate it": Amanda Connolly, "Freeland 'Very Sad' about Philpott Resignation over SNC-Lavalin Affair, Defends Trudeau as 'Feminist,'" Global News, March 5, 2019, globalnews.ca/news/5023907/chrystia-freeland-jody-wilson-raybould-snc-lavalin/.

a "grateful daughter of Alberta": Chrystia Freeland, "New Deputy Prime Minister Chrystia Freeland," interview with Catherine Cullen, *The House with Catherine Cullen*, CBC, November 23, 2019, cbc.ca/listen/live-radio/1-64-the-house/clip/15747987-interview-new-deputy-prime-minister-chrystia-freeland.

"There are only 37 million Canadians": Rachel Aiello, "'I Did Not Take on This Job to Be a Spokesmodel': Freeland on Deputy," CTV News, November 21, 2019, ctvnews.ca/politics/i-did-not-take-on-this-job-to-be-a-spokesmodel-freeland-on-deputy-pm-role-1.4696269.

Donald Mazankowski: as the "chief operating officer": Brian Platt, "'He Was a Giant': Don Mazankowski, Former Deputy PM in Mulroney Government, Dies at 85," *National Post*, October 28, 2020, nationalpost.com/news/politics/he-was-a-giant-don-mazankowski-former-deputy-pm-in-mulroney-government-passes-away-at-85.

Chrystia's mandate letter: "Deputy Prime Minister and Minister of Intergovernmental Affairs Mandate Letter," Office of the Prime Minister, December 13, 2019, pm.gc.ca/en/mandate-letters/2019/12/13/archived-deputy-prime-minister-and-minister-intergovernmental-affairs.

"The prime minister and I felt like we came up with a successful way": Chris Hall, "Chrystia Freeland Faced Off with Trump and China—but Is She Ready for Jason Kenney?," CBC News, November 23, 2019, cbc.ca/news/politics/chrystia-freeland-western-alienation-national-unity-trudeau-1.5370341.

The number of cases soon climbed: Michael Levenson, "Scale of China's Wuhan Shutdown Is Believed to Be without Precedent," *New York Times*, January 22, 2020.

"We cannot say this loudly enough": "WHO Director-General's Opening Remarks at the Media Briefing on COVID-19," March 11, 2020, who.int/director-general/speeches/detail/who-director-general-s-opening-remarks-at-the-media-briefing-on-covid-19---11-march-2020.

"This is a whole-of-government": Joan Bryden, "Freeland Chairs Cabinet Committee on 'Whole-of-Country' Response to Coronavirus," Canadian Press, March 4, 2020, toronto.citynews.ca/2020/03/04/freeland-chairs-cabinet-committee-on-whole-of-country-response-to-coronavirus/.

worked harder, maybe, than she ever had in her life: Chrystia Freeland, "This City Live: Chrystia Freeland in Conversation with Sarah Fulford," interview with Sarah Fulford, *Toronto Life*, July 7, 2020, torontolife.com/events/this-city-live-chrystia-freeland-in-conversation-with-sarah-fulford/.

"I think I have the messiest house in Canada": Chrystia Freeland, "No Women Left Behind | The Exchange: Conversations for a Better Future with Chrystia Freeland," interview with Kristalina Georgieva, International Monetary Fund, April 30, 2021, youtube.com/watch?v=2ZrAAbi2fHo.

she hearkened back to the lesson: Chrystia Freeland, "Chrystia Freeland Is Trying to Supercharge Canada's Growth," interview with Stephanie Flanders, Bloomberg News, May 28, 2021, bnnbloomberg.ca/chrystia-freeland-is-trying-to-supercharge-canada-s-growth-1.1609653.

an interview with Sharon Hodgson: Chrystia Freeland, "Character, Collaboration and Canada: A Conversation with Deputy Prime Minister Chrystia Freeland," interview with Sarah Hodgson, Ivey's Ian O. Ihnatowycz Institute for Leadership, September 29, 2020, ivey.uwo.ca/leadership/news/2020/09/character-collaboration-and-canada-a-conversation-with-deputy-prime-minister-chrystia-freeland/.

two of Finance Minister Bill Morneau's immediate family members also had involvement with WE: Jesse Brown, "Finance Minister Bill Morneau Also Tied to WE Charity," Canadaland, July 10, 2020, canadaland.com/finance-minister-bill-morneau-also-tied-to-we-charity/.

he had lost the "moral authority": Ryan Patrick Jones, "Conservatives Call for Morneau's Resignation as Finance Minister Says He Repaid $41K in WE Trip Expenses," CBC News, July 22, 2020, cbc.ca/news/politics/finance-committee-morneau-we-charity-1.5658627.

Morneau said it was the right time for a new finance minister: "Bill Morneau Resigns as Canada's Finance Minister, MP," Global News, August 17, 2020, youtube.com/watch?v=cwL24RbN13I.

Chrystia recognized that it was "unfortunately" still true: "Janet Yellen, Introduced by the Hon. Chrystia Freeland," Atlantic Council, September 28, 2023, youtube.com/watch?v=Fi6VWJ4-LwE.

"I am conscious of the fact that I am Canada's first woman finance minister": "PM Trudeau on Prorogation of Parliament, Chrystia Freeland's Move to Finance," CPAC, August 18, 2020, youtube.com/watch?v=W78nX4x5I3I.

"I'm on vacation but can't stop watching the train wreck": John Ivison (@IvisonJ), Twitter, August 19, 2020, x.com/IvisonJ/status/1296081767884099585.

"if we're seeing the beginning of the beknighting of Chrystia Freeland": "Freeland Replaces Morneau as Trudeau's Finance Minister," CBC News Special, August 18, 2020, youtube.com/watch?v=NxI1Wr68LAw.

The Liberals had promised to create a national child-care program: Steve Paikin, "Child Care Tiff a Case Study in Liberal-NDP Animosity," TVO.org, September 11, 2015, tvo.org/article/child-care-tiff-a-case-study-in-liberal-ndp-animosity.

The federal government, the budget said, would share the costs: budget.canada .ca/2021/report-rapport/p2-en.html.

"If they had any intention of doing it": Janice Dickson, "Federal Budget 2021: Ottawa Proposes Establishing National Child-Care Program," *Globe and Mail*, April 19, 2021.

"I was just so tired, and I was worried I wasn't doing a good job": Freeland, "No Women Left Behind."

"I would suggest Rome was not built overnight": Daniel Leblanc and Laurence Martin, "Less than Half of Daycare Spaces Promised by Ottawa Have Been Created Ahead of 2026 Deadline," CBC News, March 13, 2024, cbc.ca/news/ politics/child-care-ten-dollars-day-trudeau-daycare-1.7141421.

the snark that Chrystia had warned about in her 2014 *Politico* essay: Chrystia Freeland, "How I Gave Up on Snark to Become a Canadian Politician," *Politico Magazine*, January 14, 2014, politico.com/magazine/story/2014/01/chrystia-freeland-politician-journalist-102053/.

the election cost hundreds of millions of dollars: John Paul Tasker, "Canadians Have Re-elected a Liberal Minority Government," CBC News, September 20, 2021, cbc.ca/news/politics/federal-general-election-results-2021-1.6182364.

In an October 2021 column, the *Globe and Mail*'s Gary Mason wrote: Gary Mason, "Politics Has Become a Thankless, Dangerous Job," *Globe and Mail*, October 19, 2021.

In a clip that went viral, the man could be heard yelling: Mark Villani, "Politicians Denounce Video of Alberta Man Verbally Harassing Deputy Prime Minister Chrystia Freeland," CTV News Calgary, August 27, 2022, calgary.ctvnews.ca/ politicians-denounce-video-of-alberta-man-verbally-harassing-deputy-prime-minister-chrystia-freeland-1.6045106.

after telling Mercedes Stephenson: "Finance Minister Cuts Disney+ Subscription amid High Living Costs," Global News, November 6, 2022, globalnews.ca/ video/9254960/finance-minister-cuts-disney-subscription-amid-high-living-costs.

coming off as "smug," "elitist," "clueless," and "entitled": Sarah Ritchie, "Freeland's Disney+ Comment Made Her a Villain, Records Show," Canadian Press, April 19, 2023, cbc.ca/news/politics/freeland-disney-plus-1.6815024.

Canada's economy would "come roaring back": Anne-Sylvaine Chassany, "The 'Minister of Everything' Pins Her Hopes on a Consumer-Led Rebound from COVID-19 Setbacks," *Financial Times*, May 12, 2021.

CONCLUSION

"When Vladimir Putin ordered his tanks across the Ukrainian border": "Deputy PM Chrystia Freeland Speaks at Brookings Institution Event in Washington, DC," CPAC, October 11, 2022, youtube.com/watch?v=vdW-Rm_Eq4E.

As journalist Paul Wells wrote in his Substack newsletter: Paul Wells, "Who's Talking When Freeland Is Talking?," Paul Wells Substack, October 12, 2022, paulwells.substack.com/p/whos-talking-when-freeland-is-talking.

October 30, 2023, speech to the Economic Club of Canada in Toronto: "Foreign Affairs Minister Mélanie Joly Delivers Speech amid Global Conflicts," CPAC, October 30, 2023, youtube.com/watch?v=LtNsEYTAC2s.

consistently polling ahead of the Liberals: David Coletto, "Abacus Data Poll: Big Conservative Lead Stabilizes as Evaluations of Trudeau Government Performance Drop," Abacus Data, March 10, 2024, abacusdata.ca/conservatives-lead-by-18-evaluations-drop-trudeau-government-abacus-data/.

Following the 2021 election: Aaron Wherry, "Are Canadians Still Willing to Give Justin Trudeau a Second Look?," CBC News, January 27, 2024, cbc.ca/news/politics/trudeau-liberal-leadership-wherry-analysis-1.7096456.

Index

CATHERINE TSALIKIS is a writer and journalist based in Toronto, covering foreign policy, politics, and gender equality. After completing her undergraduate and graduate degrees at the University of Toronto and the London School of Economics and Political Science, she worked as an editorial assistant for *The World Today* magazine, published by Chatham House, and as a politics producer for London's Sky News. Most recently, she was the senior editor for OpenCanada.org, an award-winning international affairs site.